JAN 1 2 2010
Airdrie

D0093060

"THANKS FOR THE BUSINESS"

K. C. Irving, Arthur Irving, and the Story of Irving Oil

DONALD J. SAVOIE

NIMBUS
PUBLISHING
— NIMBUS.CA —

Copyright © 2020, Donald J. Savoie

All rights reserved. No part of this book may be reproduced, stored in a retrieval system or transmitted in any form or by any means without the prior written permission from the publisher, or, in the case of photocopying or other reprographic copying, permission from Access Copyright, 1 Yonge Street, Suite 1900, Toronto, Ontario M5E 1E5.

Nimbus Publishing Limited
3660 Strawberry Hill St, Halifax, NS, B3K 5A9
(902) 455-4286 nimbus.ca

Printed and bound in Canada

NB1522

Editor: Barry Norris
Editor for the press: Angela Mombourquette
Design: John VanderWoude, JVDW Designs Inc.

Photos courtesy of the Arthur Irving family.

Library and Archives Canada Cataloguing in Publication

Title: "Thanks for the business" : K.C. Irving, Arthur Irving, and the story of Irving Oil / Donald J. Savoie.
Names: Savoie, Donald J., 1947- author.
Identifiers: Canadiana (print) 20200200879 | Canadiana (ebook) 20200200895
    ISBN 9781771088909
(hardcover) | ISBN 9781771088916 (HTML)
Subjects: LCSH: Irving, K. C. (Kenneth Colin), 1899-1992. | LCSH: Irving, Arthur.
    LCSH: Businesspeople—New Brunswick—Biography. | LCSH: Irving Oil Limited—History.
Classification: LCC HC112.5.I78 P58 2020 | DDC 338.092/27151—dc23

Nimbus Publishing acknowledges the financial support for its publishing activities from the Government of Canada, the Canada Council for the Arts, and from the Province of Nova Scotia. We are pleased to work in partnership with the Province of Nova Scotia to develop and promote our creative industries for the benefit of all Nova Scotians.

To Sandra Irving, a lady of substance
with a generous heart

CONTENTS

PREFACE

THIS BOOK IS THE STORY OF IRVING OIL, ITS FOUNDER, K.C. Irving, and, in particular, Arthur Irving, who, with the participation of his two brothers, especially in the earlier years, grew the firm to what it is today. Arthur Irving learned everything about business from his father, Canada's most successful entrepreneur of the previous century. I note that K.C. Irving, like me, was from a small New Brunswick coastal community, Bouctouche. I recall as a young boy driving by the Irving service station in Bouctouche, the first built in what would become a global business. The Irving Oil story is one of remarkable success, at least in part because of where it was born and from where it grew. This journey has always fascinated me, and it is the central theme of this book.

Readers who are familiar with my work on economic development know that my economic heroes are entrepreneurs. It is the entrepreneurs who propel economies forward. My admiration is greatest for the talented entrepreneurs from my region, Atlantic Canada. They have to pull against gravity if they wish to build a business empire that extends to other parts of Canada and the world. I owe it to them to write their story, as I already have for

Harrison McCain and as I do now for Arthur Irving.

I want to paint as accurate a picture of Arthur Irving and Irving Oil as I possibly can. I want to warn readers, however, that they might well detect a bias. Not only is Arthur a friend; it is also impossible for many Atlantic Canadians not to take great pride in what K.C. and Arthur Irving built. This is especially true for Acadians like me from the Bouctouche area, where K.C. Irving was born and started out in business.

When I told Arthur I was thinking about writing a book about him, his father, and Irving Oil, I detected no enthusiasm on his part. It might come as a surprise to those who do not know him that Arthur is a very modest man. He is unpretentious, and he does not like pretentious people. But being an Irving in New Brunswick is not without challenges. Starting with the family patriarch, K.C. Irving, the Irvings like to go about their work quietly and draw as little attention to themselves as possible. My sense is that Arthur does not see the need for anyone to tell the Irving story in a book. He likely would point to Canada's largest refinery, the multitude of Irving service stations that dot the landscape of Atlantic Canada, Quebec, New England, and now Ireland, the thousands of employees at Irving Oil, and his substantial contributions to a multitude of community projects as all that anyone needs to know. I nonetheless decided to write his story because it holds important lessons for aspiring entrepreneurs, for our business schools, for public policy, and particularly for my region. In a CBC interview, Arthur Irving explained the importance of business success to his employees, his province, and his region: "We are good to nobody if we are not successful."

I have often heard Arthur Irving say, "Thanks for the business." He has said this to me on many occasions and to many others whenever they tell him that they stopped for gas at one of his service stations. "Thanks for the business" is also an appropriate title for this book. Arthur places a great deal of emphasis on the individual, on the customer, and on the employee. Business, he reports, is never given; it has to be earned, one customer at a time. This is one of many lessons he learned from his father.

I recall stopping for gas several years ago in a small northern New Brunswick community when Arthur's wife, Sandra Irving, called to discuss an initiative for the Royal Society of Canada. I told her it was ironic that she should call while I was pumping gas at an Irving service station in Saint-Quentin. Within seconds, Arthur was on the phone: "Hi, Donald, thanks for the business. I know the manager, a real good guy. Please say hello to him. Could you let me know if the restroom is in good shape and clean?" The restroom was clean, and the manager was indeed a good guy. Arthur has a single-minded purpose, a trait common to all highly successful entrepreneurs. Like his father, he pays very close attention to details, about which I say much more in the pages that follow.

Many people helped with the book. I want to single out Sandra Irving, a very special friend. She has, over the years, strongly urged me to write a book about her husband and his contributions to the business community and our region. Despite his lack of enthusiasm for a book about either his contributions or Irving Oil, I had numerous discussions with Arthur Irving about both. He answered every question I put to him. I never felt that he wanted to steer the discussion in a certain direction. I did not ask any questions about his family or his relationships with members of the other Irving families. That was my decision, not his. I did not want to lose the focus of the book. This is about business: the development and growth of Irving Oil and its contributions to my region. I also benefited greatly from interviews I undertook with business associates and friends of Arthur Irving. I owe all of them a thank you; they are identified in the

Appendix. I also want to say a special thanks to friends in Bouctouche who were able to track down the photo on this book's cover of the first-ever Irving service station built there in the mid-1920s.

Word that I was working on this book got around, and I received calls from publishers asking if I would consider publishing with them. I decided to go with Nimbus Publishing. Nimbus has seen impressive growth in recent years, and it has firmly established itself as a highly credible publisher. There is another reason: two dynamic entrepreneurs from my region—Terrilee Bulger and Heather Bryan—have guided Nimbus's growth. There is an important message here. The book is about Arthur Irving, a Maritimer and one of Canada's leading businessmen, written by a Maritimer, and published by a firm under the leadership of two energetic entrepreneurs from the Maritime region. We did it all from here.

Several friends and colleagues read parts or all of the manuscript of this book, and made important suggestions. I owe special thanks to Wade MacLauchlan, who carefully read the manuscript and made numerous suggestions to improve it. Samuel LeBlanc, a colleague at the Université de Moncton, also read the manuscript and suggested a number of revisions.

I once again owe a special thank you to Linda for putting up with my insatiable appetite for work, while Ginette Benoit and Céline Basque put up with my less-than-clear handwriting to produce the manuscript. I would also like to say thanks to Angela Mombourquette and Barry Norris for their help in making some sentences read better and to Noeline Bridge for producing the excellent index.

Donald J. Savoie
Université de Moncton

INTRODUCTION

THIS IS NOT THE FIRST AND WILL NOT BE THE LAST BOOK written about New Brunswick's Irvings. We now have a number of books and countless articles on the Irvings, on their impact on the media, on the life and times of K.C. Irving, on how generations of the Irvings have contributed to the business world, and on family conflicts.[1] We also have CBC and National Film Board of Canada documentaries on the Irvings and their businesses. This, even though the Irvings, to this day, are widely known for keeping things close to their chest. As one keen observer of New Brunswick wrote, "You can love them or you can hate them, but you have to respect them....You cannot help but be fascinated by them."[2]

I have a different take. This book is not a biography of Arthur Irving. I feel ill-equipped to write a biography, given that it is not my field of research. I do, however, borrow from biographies written about the Irvings, notably *K.C.: The Biography of K.C. Irving* by Douglas How and Ralph Costello. This book is also not an attempt to settle old scores on behalf of anyone. Readers interested in such things should go elsewhere. Rather, I report on a remarkable business success story launched by K.C. Irving and developed to its potential by Arthur Irving. I wanted to know how K.C. Irving launched his oil and gas business and how Arthur was able to expand it to the point that it now operates Canada's largest refinery, with a growing presence in both the United States and Europe.

Writing this book took me back to my childhood. I grew up in a small hamlet a few kilometres from Bouctouche, which was a major metropolitan centre to a seven-year-old. I recall my father stopping for gas at the Irving service station in Bouctouche. This was the very first Irving station, built in 1924. I also recall going inside the J.D. Irving General Store in Bouctouche, which, to a young boy from Saint-Maurice, was the size of the West Edmonton Mall. I remember well clerks sending and receiving cash in little bottle-like containers that flew overhead at great speed through tubes. My mother told me that the tubes went somewhere in the basement, where someone was waiting to count the money. This youngster was very impressed. I asked my mother if we could go to the basement to see where the tubes ended up and find out who was counting the money and what they did with it. The answer was a firm no. I saw K.C. Irving in Bouctouche on a few occasions, particularly in the summer months, as he pulled up for gas at the Irving station. I remember him as a tall, distinguished-looking gentleman with an easy smile.

My father and brother were demanding, hard-working, and successful entrepreneurs. My father had a great deal of respect for K.C. Irving, telling us that he was a tough and smart businessman, and often reminding us that he was from Bouctouche. Entrepreneurs know that, to succeed in business, they have to be both tough and smart. My brother once sold a building in Moncton to K.C. Irving. He was proud of his dealings with that man, telling me he learned important lessons from him on how to negotiate a business deal.

I have become a good friend of Arthur Irving, his wife, Sandra, and their daughter, Sarah. We have had numerous chats over a fifteen-year period. We have gone on holidays together, and I have gone shooting with Arthur. The reader can be assured that the grouse were always safe with me. Indeed, I had the feeling that, when they saw us, they all flew toward me knowing that they would be a great deal safer than if they flew toward Arthur.

I decided to write this book because the Irving story is a tremendous success story that needs to be told—a story that had a humble beginning. The image of the old Irving service station strategically located at a crossroads as one entered Bouctouche has stuck with me through the years. From that modest store, K.C. and Arthur Irving grew a multi-billion-dollar business that is home to Canada's largest refinery, owns a refinery in Ireland, and has stores throughout Atlantic Canada, Quebec, New England, and Ireland. I wanted to understand this story better in order to share it with Atlantic Canadians, to show that business success is possible in our region, and to provide business students and aspiring entrepreneurs the ingredients of that success.

What about my friendship with Arthur Irving? I decided to tell the reader up front about it. I also admit that, like the great majority of people with close ties to Bouctouche, I have applauded the Irvings' contributions over the years. In Bouctouche, at least, K.C. Irving will always be known as its most famous native son.

Harvey Sawler, in his book on the Irvings, reported an interview he had with me. He wrote:

If you want to get Savoie all riled up, just mention someone dumping on the Irvings for being all-consuming, all-dominating, omnipresent business monsters who stifle and snuff out entrepreneurs. "That's absolute crap," says Savoie. This attitude, which he calls "an alibi for failure," is used by nay-sayers against the Irvings and other people...as an alibi for any number of their own failures, for any number of reasons: not working hard enough; being under-capitalized; not negotiating effectively; being short on ambition, aptitude, or vision; failing to take care of their customers.[3]

I said this to Sawler some fourteen years ago, and my view has not changed.

Atlantic Canadians, particularly Bouctouche Acadians, of which I am a proud member of the community, have close ties to K.C. Irving. He was never known as a bigot or as anti-French, which, sixty years ago, was the one important trait that mattered to us. Ties between K.C. Irving and Acadians were very strong, and they remain strong with his sons. K.C. explained why:

With the exception of my father and perhaps George Weeks and one or two others, everything that I learned was taught to me by the French people....I remember a saying that if you treat a dog well in hard times, he remembers it in prosperous times, and in that way a dog is different than a lot of people who don't remember in the same way. So I guess there is a bit of dog in me, and I have never forgotten what the French people did and have done for me.[4]

Until the 1960s, and in some cases much later, certain large New Brunswick firms had a policy of not hiring Acadians. It was widely known, for example, that one large Moncton-based firm that runs auto dealerships and furniture stores in the province would not hire many Acadians or, for that matter, Roman Catholics. Things changed, however, when a new CEO took over the firm in 1994.

K.C., meanwhile, was known for hiring Acadians and giving them the same opportunities as English-speaking New Brunswickers. At the time, this held enormous significance for Acadians. This is not to suggest, however, that he would lower Irving standards for Acadians. One Bouctouche acquaintance contacted K.C. Irving for a job. He said: "Now, K.C., don't tell me that you do not have much work. It does not take much to keep me busy."[5] He was not hired.

K.C. Irving and his descendants, especially J.K. Irving and his family, have also given a great deal to Bouctouche. One of their businesses, Kent Homes, has provided stable employment in the community since 1958. The Irvings have also built a marina, an arboretum, a sports centre–town hall complex, a monument, a farmers' market—and an eco-centre that includes a two-kilometre-long structure selected by the World Travel and Tourism Council as the "only Canadian finalist" in 2008 for the top destination award.[6] Today, Bouctouche is a proud, self-confident, and thriving community, and K.C. Irving had a great deal to do with it.

There was a time when K.C. Irving and Acadians went through a rough period, when he publicly declared his strong opposition to Premier Louis J. Robichaud's decision to overhaul New Brunswick's tax policies in implementing his Equal Opportunity program. But things got back to normal after the program was fully implemented and after Robichaud left active politics. I know this because I know both sides of the story.

Louis J. Robichaud and I became close friends. I organized a conference in his honour in Bouctouche in 1999. Shortly before Robichaud passed away, he asked me to organize his funeral. I did, and I invited one of K.C. Irving's sons to be an honorary pallbearer. I can report that Robichaud's widow and his three children fully supported my decision. I can also report that Louis J. Robichaud told me that he always had a deep respect for K.C. Irving's business acumen.

In July 2019, I was interviewed by a CBC journalist about a proposed airport in western Cape Breton near the Cabot Links and Cabot Cliffs golf courses. I supported the proposed airport, making the case that it would promote tourism, that the role of the private sector is to create economic opportunities, and that the role of the public sector is to support economic development through infrastructure and other measures.

The journalist, quite correctly, asked if I was a paid consultant for Cabot Links or Cabot Cliffs. I responded: "I am not now, never have been a paid consultant for this firm, and never will be." I added: "I am a golfer and went to golf there on two occasions. I paid my green fees, the hotel, and all meals. If I were offered remuneration, a free stay at the hotel, or free green fees, I would refuse." The journalist said: "Well, that is pretty clear."

I have never been a paid consultant for Irving Oil or any of the Irving businesses. I have never been offered remuneration for work carried out for Irving Oil or other Irving firms. I was never offered any honorarium by Arthur Irving or Irving Oil to work on this book nor did they ever offer to pay any expenses while I was working on it. Had I been offered such funding, I would have declined. I do note, however, that I have been on many trips with them. I also note that they have made very generous contributions to my university, starting with K.C. Irving in the 1960s, and most recently to my university's latest fundraising campaign. I hasten to add, however, that none of this funding will go to support any of my work or research at the university.

I faced a similar problem several years ago when I wrote *Harrison McCain: Single-Minded Purpose*, which was shortlisted for the 2014 National Business Book Award. In the preface of that book, I stated up front that Harrison McCain was a good friend and that I had no interest in writing about the McCain family feud. I did not receive funding in any form from the McCain family for writing the book. I also noted that the McCain family has contributed to my university's fundraising efforts, as it has for other universities in Atlantic Canada. Readers understood that my purpose in writing about Harrison McCain was to offer a highly successful business and economic development story that was born in my region and grew to become one of the world's leading businesses in the frozen food market. I also wish to underline the point that New Brunswick is a small province with a population of only three-quarters of a million. Many New Brunswickers know one another, and we are a tightly knit population. It is also easy to connect with anyone who rises above the parapet in New Brunswick in business, politics, government, or academe.

K.C., ARTHUR, AND IRVING OIL

THERE ARE MANY IRVING BUSINESSES AND MANY IRVING STORIES. This book is about K.C. Irving, Arthur Irving, and Irving Oil, with the focus on the latter two. It seeks to shed light on economic development in Atlantic Canada, on the challenges of growing a business in the region, and on how business decisions are made. I also, through the story of K.C., Arthur, and Irving Oil, want to contribute to answering the age-old question: are entrepreneurs born or made? A growing body of literature is exploring this question, and we are making progress, but we still do not have a definitive answer. I doubt that anyone will ever arrive at one. The best we can do is draw lessons from entrepreneurs. I maintain that K.C. Irving is the most successful entrepreneur in Canadian history, and his and Arthur's success at Irving Oil should give us fresh insight into the work of entrepreneurs and how they flourish.

Many students of business now argue that entrepreneurs are both born and made. Greg Davies, a leading executive at Barclays Bank, argues that there "are definitely elements of entrepreneurship that can be taught." But, he adds, "there is a surprising amount of entrepreneurial success that can be attributed to genetics or personality development in early childhood."[7] On the face of it, Arthur Irving's success in the business world appears to be a combination of both genetics and lessons learned from his father, his grandfather, and his great-grandfather.

K.C. built his business in Saint John, New Brunswick. Building a business empire in Canada's industrial heartland is one thing. Building it in Atlantic Canada is another. One has to pull against gravity to compete against the large firms from away and national economic policies that favour the more populated regions. K.C. launched Irving Oil in 1924, so he had to guide it through the Great Depression in the firm's early years. He thus put to the test and beat the old saying that, when launching a business, "timing is everything."[8]

K.C. Irving said, time and again, that making money was not his main motivation. Other highly successful entrepreneurs, such as Sam Walton and Harrison McCain, have said the same thing. K.C. liked to build things, to "see wheels turn," to make things work, and to create economic activities in his beloved Atlantic Canada.

In interviews, including the few he gave early in his business career, he repeatedly pointed to national policies to explain the Maritimes' economic difficulties. In one interview in 1964, for example, he said: "Over the years the federal government—regardless of party—has been responsible for policies which have resulted in New Brunswick being a forgotten section of Canada."[9] I have published articles and books making the same point. I have never heard anyone question my motives. The same, however, is not true for the Irvings. I point this out because K.C. Irving and his three sons have created thousands and thousands of jobs in the Maritime provinces and established head offices in our region. In contrast, I have created no more than six jobs in my region through research grants and contracts.

History matters in all things, and economic development is no exception. This story begins in Dumfries, Scotland. It is not possible to write about Arthur Irving or Irving Oil without looking to history, going back to when George Irving arrived in eastern New Brunswick in the 1820s. The Irvings have moved around a lot, but they and their head offices have always remained in New Brunswick, even when it might well have made more economic sense to move elsewhere. They went from Mill Branch, to Beersville, to Coal Branch, to Bouctouche, to Saint John, all in New Brunswick. Arthur Irving's entrepreneurial spirit and business acumen, meanwhile, can be traced back to his father, K.C., his grandfather J.D. Irving, and his great-grandfather Herbert Irving. In brief, Arthur Irving's business abilities run deep in his DNA.

It is also not possible to write about Arthur Irving without first writing about his father. The two were very close. In November 1991 Arthur Irving was asked to represent his father, who was being fêted for his lifetime contribution to the economic development of Atlantic Canada. K.C. was unable to attend the ceremony to receive the Distinguished Service Award from the Atlantic Canada Plus Association. Arthur Irving is never one to give a carefully prepared formal speech. He prefers a staccato, no-nonsense style, while often shifting gears in mid-sentence to make a point. He spoke from the heart, with no notes, as he always does. He spoke about what it was like to be K.C.'s son and to work with K.C. He spoke with passion, explaining that there "was excitement every day. Every day there was something new" when working with his father. He explained that his father was "a fighter, a competitor, a winner. Every day was a new game. The score was three to two. We were two and the other guy was three. We had about ten seconds to play—and we had to win. He got a big charge out of being successful." He ended his talk by making a deeply felt statement: "He's been a great father, a great friend."[10] The apple does not fall far from the tree. Arthur Irving likes to compete, he likes to win, and he thrives on seeing something new every day.

Irving Oil has all the ingredients for a case study on a business that had a modest beginning in a remote community, in a slow-growth region, that grew into a global business. We will track the evolution of Irving Oil from its first service station in Bouctouche, to building and expanding an oil refinery, making it the biggest in Canada, to the purchase of a refinery and two hundred gas stations in Ireland. Arthur Irving played, and continues to play, a pivotal role at key moments in the growth of Irving Oil.

There is a distinct Irving approach to growing and managing businesses, or what some observers have labelled the "Irving School of Business."[11] One observer insists that the Irving School of Business offers more than could possibly be learned in any semester at a top business school. Why attend a business school at all when "you have your own, with an unbeatable curriculum, right at home?"[12] We need to gain an appreciation of the Irving curriculum and its main requirements. My hope is that students of business and aspiring entrepreneurs can have access to some of the curriculum by reading this book.

Arthur Irving, like his father, has a deeply felt commitment to his community, his region, and Canada. He has given a great deal back to his community, much more than is generally known. He is an Irving, and starting with K.C. Irving, the Irvings have always tended to hide their light under a bushel. He also has a special zest for life and a remarkable energy level. I met with him in February 2019 and saw that he had injured his foot. I asked what happened. He said he broke it while skiing. Knowing that he was eighty-eight, I said, "Well, that's it for skiing for you." His response: "Yeah, for this year."

Everyone I consulted for this book spoke about Arthur's exceptional energy. I can vouch for that. I went to Boston with Arthur on July 18, 2019. We were to leave Saint John at 7:30 A.M. to enable him to attend to some business and a series of meetings in Boston. The plan was also to catch a Red Sox afternoon game at Fenway Park, but he had to be in Richibucto, New Brunswick, by 6:00 P.M. that day. He rescheduled the morning departure because he wanted to attend a funeral in Saint John for an Irving Oil employee. We arrived in Boston at 11:30 A.M. We went to Fenway Park, but, as is always the case on Red Sox game days, traffic was very heavy. He said, "Let's walk." We walked nearly one kilometre. We saw the Red Sox play the Toronto Blue Jays for six innings, then we were rushed to the plane, and arrived in Moncton on schedule at 5:30 that evening. We were very quickly moved to a helicopter, and off we went to Richibucto, arriving at 6:00 P.M. for a ceremony where Irving Oil turned over land to the Kent County community to build a municipal park. He spoke at the event, and we stayed until the end at 8:00 P.M. When we got to the helicopter, he said, "Hey, we are not far from Beersville, let's go see the stone put in place to mark where the first Irving who came to North America built his home." One person in the group spoke for the others, and said, "No, Arthur, I am too tired." He responded: "Well then, let's go see the Bonar Law House—the only British prime minister born outside of the UK." Again, the individual said, "No, I am much too tired." Arthur said, "Okay, but let's fly along the coast rather than in a straight line so that we can see communities dotting the coastline," including Bouctouche. I got an email early the next morning to say that Arthur was off to the Gaspé Peninsula, where he had business to attend to. I remind the reader that Arthur Irving turned eighty-nine on July 14, 2019. His zest for life extends to everything he does, and business is certainly no exception.

Irving Oil will be celebrating its centenary in 2024. It has prospered through the Great Depression, the war years, an OPEC oil embargo, a few oil crises, the Great Recession, and the market challenges brought on by the COVID-19 pandemic. There is more rough water ahead, and this book will seek to identify the challenges the oil and gas sector faces.

The desire to hide its light under a bushel does not make it easy for those wishing to study the business practices of an Irving enterprise. K.C. Irving saw no merit in showing his cards before they were played, or even after. But this is not unique to the Irvings. Privately held businesses keep things close to their chests. More to the point, privately held businesses tend to do their business in private, while publicly held businesses have no choice but to offer a degree of transparency. A journalist once began an interview with Harrison McCain with: "I am here to talk about your business." His response: "My business is none of your business." In brief, there is no need for privately held family firms, large or small, to open up about their business practices, how decisions are made, or about their success or lack of it.

J.D. Irving accepted a lifetime achievement award on behalf of his late grandfather in Halifax in 2008. In accepting the award, he spoke about the advice K.C. Irving would have given him before walking to the podium. "He would reach over and quietly pat you on the arm and say, 'Jimmy, don't say too much.' That is the way it was."[13]

The reader might well ask, why do I want to write a book about Arthur Irving and Irving Oil? To be sure, my friendship with Arthur and Sandra is an important consideration. The fact that K.C. Irving was from my hometown, that he did so much for Bouctouche, and that he won the respect of many local businesses and inspired local entrepreneurs to go into business are also important factors.

There is another important reason. I have spent a good part of my career promoting economic development in my region. It will be recalled that, at the request of Prime Minister Brian Mulroney, I wrote the report that led to the establishment of the Atlantic Canada Opportunities Agency (ACOA). I have also contributed to the regional economic development literature, more often than not from an Atlantic Canada perspective.

As already noted, I recognize that the private sector, notably local entrepreneurs, must drive economic development in my region. I cannot think of better role models to launch and grow a business than K.C. and Arthur Irving. If this book can motivate aspiring entrepreneurs from my region, offer lessons learned to the local business community, and demonstrate that it is possible to start with a small service station on a street corner in a small, remote community in New Brunswick and grow the firm into a highly successful global business, then my central purpose in writing this book will have been well served. I have a feeling that both K.C. and Arthur Irving would agree, as would other Irvings. My hope is that more and more Maritimers will want to celebrate business success and local entrepreneurs, if only because our economic future is tied at the hip to the success of our local business leaders, entrepreneurs, and aspiring entrepreneurs. In brief, entrepreneurs will be the ones to take the lead in promoting economic development in my region.

I also want to remind Atlantic Canadians that neither K.C. nor Arthur Irving ever saw the need to go down the road to generate a series of remarkable economic success stories. They remained true to their New Brunswick roots, unlike K.C.'s contemporaries from the region who also generated remarkable economic success. Max Aitken (Lord Beaverbrook) made his millions first in Montreal and then in London, England. James Dunn also left to take up residence in Montreal and London to generate his millions. Izaak Killam, for his part, looked to Montreal and Toronto for his economic success. Not K.C. and not Arthur Irving. They stayed with New Brunswick through thick and thin. This, more than anything, explains why I decided to dedicate my book *Looking for Bootstraps: Economic Development in the Maritimes*, published in 2017, to K.C. Irving.

It is hardly possible to overstate the importance of head offices to the local economy, a point that I will return to time and again in this book. Leaving aside Irving Oil, J.D. Irving, Cooke Aquaculture, and a handful of others, New Brunswick has precious few head offices of large global firms. Does it matter? Yes, and for many reasons. Head offices employ highly skilled and well-paid professionals. They also turn to highly qualified professional consultant services in virtually every facet of management. Key strategic decisions about investments and operations are struck in head offices. The head offices decide which lawyers, financial services, auditors, and IT specialists to retain. Key head-office staff are not only well educated, they are also high-energy, high-achieving individuals who are often willing to help their communities.[14] Head offices invariably look to local charities when making philanthropic contributions. There are also head-office biases. It is the head office, for example, that decides where to locate the firm's research and development (R&D) efforts, which, much more often than not, will be in the same city. It is the head office that decides which regional operations to support and which ones to cut back or let die. The head office does not die, unless the business dies. It is also important to note that regional operations tend to favour the status quo, with head offices often the only ones to drive meaningful change. Indeed, generally, only senior head-office personnel have the mandate to define and pursue change.

All too often, rather than applaud those who want to stand tall and succeed, many resent and criticize their achievements—envy is a powerful emotion. This "tall poppy syndrome" is particularly evident in have-less regions such as the Maritimes. To be sure, it is not limited to the Maritime provinces or to Canada. But it is visible in both, and there is research to support the case.[15] Rather than look in the mirror for their lack of success, it becomes a great deal easier for some businesses and even individuals to point the finger at highly successful business people and blame them. If K.C., Arthur Irving, and Irving Oil had not built and substantially expanded the Saint John refinery and set up many service stations and points of service, one can easily speculate that there would not be an oil refinery in Saint John and that the Irving name would appear on no service stations in the Maritimes.

I note on several occasions in this book that the Irvings are wellknown for avoiding publicity and for not boasting about their economic success. They never bought into the biblical saying, "Let your light so shine before men, that they may see your good work." Many New Brunswickers, however, do see the Irving contributions to their province. As earlier mentioned, I went to Richibucto with Arthur, Sandra, and Sarah in July 2019 to unveil a new park for the community. Irving Oil had donated the land, which sits a few metres from where George Irving first set foot in the New World with his wife and two children nearly two hundred years before.

I saw an Acadian in his seventies standing tall and proud with his back straight as a plank. He might once have been a fisherman or a construction worker. He stood six feet tall, had a weather-beaten face, piercing brown eyes, and large, well-worn hands that had performed more than their share of manual labour. He walked up to Arthur, extended his hand, and in a thick Acadian accent said, "Mr. Irving, I want to thank you for what you and your father did for New Brunswick." That was it. The gentleman said what he had to say, turned around, and was on his way. He saw no need to say anything more. I saw in him a level of genuine sincerity that I rarely see today. In leaving the park, I thought that this gentleman's voice needed to be heard beyond Richibucto. After Arthur Irving spoke, he was given a standing ovation. It made the point, once again, that Acadians and the Irvings, going back to K.C. Irving and his father, J.D., have a strong mutual respect for one another.

I want to see my fellow Atlantic Canadians celebrate success, particularly economic success. When our local businesses win, when they establish their head offices in our region, when they identify economic opportunities that no one else sees, and when they are successful in pursuing these opportunities, we all win in Atlantic Canada. Accordingly, there is a double meaning to this book's title, *"Thanks for the Business."* As noted, Arthur Irving always says this whenever anyone tells him that they stopped at one of his service stations for gas. But there is another reason I chose this title. As my career as a student of government, public administration, and economic development is coming to a close, I have learned a number of insights through my research.

First, Canada's national policies have played havoc with economic development in Atlantic Canada—of that, I am certain. Atlantic Canadians have come to terms with the reality that "national policies" are code words for the economic interests of Ontario and Quebec. Both K.C. and Arthur Irving have made this very point on a number of occasions, as have many other Atlantic and Western Canadians. Ottawa's political power is concentrated in vote-rich Ontario and Quebec, and its bureaucratic influence can be found in the Ottawa-Gatineau region. In the case of Atlantic Canada, the federal government has sought to deal with its inability to accommodate regional economic circumstances in shaping its policies by sending guilt money our way. We have seen a veritable alphabet of regional programs—ARDA, FRED, DREE, DRIE, ACOA, the list goes on—and a host of federal transfer payments to our provincial governments. Without putting too fine a point on it, Ottawa has created a dependency problem in Atlantic Canada.[16]

Second, if Atlantic Canada is to develop to its potential, the business community will have to show the way. Government policies can establish an agenda for economic development through taxation policies, matching the skills and competences the workforce is offering and the ones employers actually need, breaking down barriers to interprovincial trade, and accepting that what works in one region will not always work in another.

I have learned that it is the business community, with its bias for action, that will—as it has in the past—move our region forward. I have also learned that government bureaucracies have the ability to give the appearance of change while standing still. Businesses, meanwhile, must learn to compete, to enlarge their market share, and to ensure revenues outpace spending, or die. Government bureaucracies do not die, and go out of their way to avoid risks. Successful businesses learn to manage risks or quickly fall behind. They are lean, and move human resources around to accommodate changing circumstances. Government bureaucracies, in contrast, typically add staff to meet new demands.

I have recently seen important economic growth in some parts of Atlantic Canada. In all instances, it was local entrepreneurs who led the way: K.C., J.K., Jack, and Arthur Irving, John Bragg, Harrison and Wallace McCain, Normand Caissie, Jean-Claude

Savoie, David Sobey, John Risley, Glenn Cooke, Robyn Tingley, Regis Duffy, Jim Casey, and many others. Atlantic Canadians should celebrate their economic success because it speaks directly to Atlantic Canada's economic success. And so, to them, to future generations of entrepreneurs from my region, and to Arthur Irving: "Thanks for the business."

HOW THE STORY UNFOLDS

I AM FORTUNATE TO HAVE HAD NUMEROUS CONVERSATIONS with Arthur Irving about economic development and business over the past fifteen years or so. I recall many of these chats, and in recent months I decided to take notes. I draw on these conversations and on others with family members, Irving Oil executives, community leaders, and front-line employees. A list of those interviewed is provided in the Appendix.

I also note that, notwithstanding their reluctance to speak publicly about their businesses and their contributions to communities, universities, and hospitals, there is a great deal of material on the Irvings currently available to researchers. I consulted the various books published about them, as well as numerous articles and archival material.

My focus, leaving aside how Irving Oil was born and the role K.C. Irving played in its development, is on the past fifteen years at Irving Oil and the role Arthur Irving played in those years. Those are the years when I got to know Arthur Irving and had many discussions with him. More to the point, I did not know Arthur Irving, his family, or Irving Oil other than by reputation before 2005; as a result, I do not cover that period nearly as well as I do the period since 2005.

This book traces the Irvings back to their roots in Scotland. One can see some evidence of entrepreneurial talent in the first Irving to arrive to eastern New Brunswick. It would have taken courage and an entrepreneurial bent for George Irving to gather his family and embark on the long journey from Scotland to New Brunswick in 1822. It was, however, the second generation of the Irving family in New Brunswick that first demonstrated the strong entrepreneurial spirit that continues to this day.

Canada's History Society has identified ten business titans who helped shape Canada's economic development. They include John Molson, Hart Massey, Sir John Craig Eaton, Harvey Reginald MacMillan, and K.C. Irving. The Society labels K.C. Irving "The Empire Builder"—and empire builder he was—and goes on: "Unlike many Canadian entrepreneurs, K.C. Irving stayed at home."[17] It is important to go back to the beginning to see how Irving Oil was born and the challenges K.C. Irving met in growing the business from a small service station in a remote rural New Brunswick community to what it is today.

Arthur Irving makes the case that "the apple does not fall far from the tree." As we will see, he is like his father in many ways, from paying attention to the details of the day, to showing civility to others no matter their station in society, to being unpretentious and having a very strong work ethic.

Like his father, Arthur also takes great delight in explaining how things work and "how wheels turn." He once explained to me with great enthusiasm how he was able to pump water at his Red Pine camp without electricity, gasoline, or energy input other than water flowing from a higher point to a lower point. It is called a "ram pump," and was invented in England 250 years ago. He relished explaining not only how, but also why it works. Though I am not mechanically adroit, I took it all in. I was more impressed, however, by Arthur's enthusiasm in explaining the workings of the ram pump than in knowing how it actually works.[18]

Like K.C. Irving, Arthur is not one to boast. He told the *National Post*: "We are not interested in showing off what we have or we don't have. We just do what we have to do and it's been a lot of fun and it still is."[19] Much like his father, Arthur is deeply committed to his region and has energy to burn. The economic health of Atlantic Canada is often top of mind and very often comes up in our discussions.

All large businesses begin somewhere, the great majority of them modestly. Steve Jobs and Steve Wozniak, for example, launched Apple in a garage. Jeff Bezos, too, started his business, Amazon, in a garage, as did William Hewlett and David Packard. Phil Knight did not even have a garage to launch Nike; he did it from the trunk of his car. Irving Oil is not much different. It all began with a simple gas tank located in front of a general store in a small, remote Canadian community. The company has not stopped growing from that moment. Arthur Irving joined the firm in 1951, and became chief executive officer in 1972, working by his father's side to grow the business.

I chart the growth of Irving Oil from its first service station in Bouctouche, to its move to Saint John and the construction of Canada's largest oil refinery, to the opening of new markets throughout Atlantic Canada, Quebec, and New England, and now to Europe, establishing a trading office in London, blending gasoline in Amsterdam, and buying a refinery and distribution network in Ireland.

The road to the Irvings' success has had more than a few bumps along the way. It might come as a surprise to many readers, but K.C. Irving encountered some very challenging moments, particularly during the 1930s. I relate these challenges and discuss how they were met.

I also look at the aforementioned "Irving School of Business," the curriculum of which remains in place at Irving Oil, and the influence this has had on a number of high-profile, successful entrepreneurs, including Harrison and Wallace McCain.

I explore the role Arthur Irving played in shaping Irving Oil's growth. Few people know Arthur or, for that matter, any of the Irvings, well. When I told a colleague I was writing a book about Irving Oil and Arthur Irving, his response was revealing: "I know that you are from Bouctouche, but you know that there has been a lot of negative stuff written about the Irvings. Are you sure that you want to get into this debate?" I replied: "Yes, of course, I am sure." My assistant, Céline Basque, summed up the situation well when I started working on this book: "No need for you to write anything negative about the Irvings. It has already been done." She has a point.[20]

I asked former premier Frank McKenna for his views on some of the anti-Irving feelings found in our province. His response resonates with me. McKenna, as he always does, went to the heart of the issue: "The great majority of New Brunswickers have a high opinion and respect for what the Irvings have done and continue to do. We are talking about a small but a highly vocal minority that does not represent, by any measure, the views of New Brunswickers." McKenna should know. He was one of New Brunswick's most successful premiers. One thing is beyond dispute: no other premier did more for New Brunswick's economic development than McKenna. I return to this point in the concluding chapter.

I decided to write this book because I believe that, more than ever, our region needs to celebrate economic and business success, particularly in the goods-producing sector. K.C. and his sons, more than anyone else, showed us that economic success in this sector and in our region is possible. In short, the time has come to focus on the business side of the Irvings, and on how K.C. and Arthur Irving grew Irving Oil.

Notes

1 See, for example, Douglas How and Ralph Costello, *K.C.: The Biography of K.C. Irving* (Toronto: Key Porter, 1993). See also Jacques Poitras, *Irving vs. Irving: Canada's Feuding Billionaires and the Stories They Won't Tell* (Toronto: Viking Canada, 2014).

2 Francis P. McGuire, "Foreword," in Harvey Sawler, *Twenty-First-Century Irvings* (Halifax: Nimbus, 2007), vi.

3 Quoted in ibid., "Introduction," xiv–xv.

4 Quoted in How and Costello, *K.C.*, 281–2.

5 J.K. Irving to author, Saint-Joseph, NB, July 3, 2009.

6 "Historical Bouctouche wins a tourism boost," *Globe and Mail*, February 7, 2008, online at theglobeandmail.com/news/national/historic-bouctouche-wins-a-tourism-boost/article667277/.

7 Greg Davies, quoted in Freddie Dawson, "Are Entrepreneurs Born or Made?" *Forbes*, December 25, 2014, online at forbes.com/sites/freddiedawson/2014/12/25/are-entrepreneurs-born-or-made/#1aafa6047e4b.

8 John Oechsle, "When Launching a Business, Timing Is Everything," *Forbes*, December 5, 2014, online at forbes.com/sites/groupthink/2014/12/05/when-launching-a-business-timing-is-everything/#608a7e635820.

9 K.C. Irving, quoted in Ralph Allen, "The Unknown Giant K.C. IRVING," *Maclean's*, April 18, 1964.

10 Quoted in How and Costello, *K.C.*, 381–2.

11 See, for example, Sawler, *Twenty-First-Century Irvings*, chap. 8.

12 Ibid., 70.

13 Quoted in Dean Jobb, "Rich 100: Inside Irving," *Canadian Business*, December 22, 2008, online at canadianbusiness.com/lifestyle/rich-100-inside-irving/.

14 See, for example, Michael Bloom and Michael Grant, "Valuing Headquarters (HQs): Analysis of the Role, Value and Benefit of HQs in Global Value Chains" (Ottawa: Conference Board of Canada, 2011).

15 See, for example, Sarah Dobson, "Many 'tall poppies' cut down at work," *Canadian HR Reporter*, October 1, 2018, online at hrreporter.com/article/38033-many-tall-poppies-cut-down-at-work/.

16 I am hardly the only one to make this point; see, for example, Thomas Courchene, *Equalization Payments: Past, Present and Future* (Toronto: Ontario Economic Council, 1984).

17 Joseph E. Martin, "Titans: From brewers, to rail barons, to oil-and-gas giants, these tycoons changed Canada," *Canada's History*, September 13, 2017, online at canadashistory.ca/explore/business-industry/titans.

18 The ram pump was first conceived by John Whitehurst in England in 1772.

19 Claudia Cattaneo, "Playing the piper," *National Post*, n.d., online at business.financialpost.com/playing-the-piper-in-an-exclusive-interview-arthur-irving-the-spotlight-shy-head-of-irving-oil-makes-the-case-for-energy-east-a-project-he-believes-isnt-just-good-for-his-company-but.

20 See, among others, David MacDonald, "The Wrong Way to Make Millions," *Maclean's*, August 15, 1953, online at archive.macleans.ca/article/1953/8/15/the-wrong-way-to-make-millions; Bruce Livesey, "Are the Irvings Canada's biggest corporate welfare bums?" *Canada's National Observer*, March 30, 2017, online at nationalobserver.com/2017/03/30/news/are-irvings-canadas-biggest-corporate-welfare-bums; and Russell Hunt, *K.C. Irving: The Art of the Industrialist* (Toronto: McClelland and Stewart, 1973).

CHAPTER 1

FROM SCOTLAND TO BOUCTOUCHE

GEORGE IRVING LEFT DUMFRIES, SCOTLAND, FOR THE New World in 1822. Dumfries was a relatively prosperous community in the early 1800s. It saw its population grow from five thousand in the early 1790s to thirteen thousand by 1821 due in large measure to rapid growth in the linen industry, particularly the manufacture of table linen.[1] The community was also politically stable, having enacted in 1811 both a police act and a rate-raising improvement commission. To be sure, other Scottish communities, particularly in the Highlands, were experiencing far more economic hardships than Dumfries. Many residents in the Highlands were forced to move to find work and feed their families. Residents of Dumfries were not nearly as desperate, but some felt the need to seek new economic opportunities elsewhere. George Irving was one of them.

Dumfriesshire is a county steeped in Scottish history. Robert the Bruce, in his quest to become king of the Scots, arranged for a meeting with his arch-enemy Red Comyn at a church in Dumfries. History does not tell us what happened inside, but we know that Robert the Bruce came out of the church alive and Comyn did not.[2] Bonnie Prince Charlie, the "Young Pretender" and grandson of James II of England, briefly made Dumfries his headquarters in his failed struggle to regain the British crown for the House of Stuart.[3] Adam Smith, the father of modern economics, was born in Kirkcaldy, less than two hundred kilometres from Dumfriesshire. Robert Burns, the poet and famous author of "Auld Lang Syne," made Dumfries his home; his house still stands. The Bank of Scotland, one of the oldest commercial banks in the world, opened its first successful branch in Dumfries in 1774.

George Irving, then, left a fairly prosperous and stable community for North America. It could not have been easy for him to leave a such a place for the colonies and the unknown, away from friends and extended family. He and his wife, Jane (Stitt), joined a torrent of other Scots leaving for England, North America, Australia, and New Zealand in the 1820s and 1830s. Scotland lost between 10 and 47 percent of its natural population increase every decade in the 1800s. The economic depression that followed the end of the Napoleonic Wars was felt everywhere in Scotland and, though relatively well off, Dumfries was no exception. The search was on for economic opportunities in the New World. Immigrants from Dumfriesshire, like those from the Lowlands, were mostly small farmers, craftsmen, and labourers.[4]

George and Jane Irving had very little money, which influenced their choice of destination. Fares to Britain's loyal Maritime colonies in New Brunswick and Nova Scotia were cheaper than those to places such as the United States and Australia. These colonies were also easily accessible to Scottish immigrants, who had already moved there in large numbers. New Brunswick, in particular, had a flourishing timber trade with Britain that provided room for passengers on empty sailing vessels going west and landing in ports dotting the colony's shorelines in search of timber. Pamphlets circulated throughout Britain encouraging immigration to the North American colonies. One such pamphlet described New Brunswick as "most remarkably healthy, and congenial to the natives of Great Britain" and its soil as "a rich vegetable mold on the surface, varying in depth; highly fertile, and suited for all purposes of cultivation."[5] The British government also actively encouraged Scots to migrate to the North American colonies to ease high unemployment at home and make the colonies more economically self-sufficient and better able to defend themselves against the Americans.

George and Jane Irving were devout, God-fearing Presbyterians. John Calvin and John Knox had shaped the Presbyterian Church by giving an intellectual, unemotional, and austere approach to its teachings.[6] The Calvin-Knox Presbyterian Church promoted a strong work ethic, discipline, and frugality, which, the argument went, gave rise to, or at least strengthened, capitalism.[7] Calvin insisted that poverty was not a virtue, and capitalists did not become rich on the backs of workers. In short, Presbyterian teachings argued that both hard work and material success were moral goods.

Canadian-born Harvard economist John Kenneth Galbraith argued in *The Scotch* that some want money for the power it gives, others for what it can buy, but that the Scots want "it for its own sake."[8] Presbyterians applauded business success, in sharp contrast to Roman Catholics, who were often told in Sunday sermons that "it is easier for a camel to go through the eye of a needle, than for a rich man to enter into the kingdom of God." I recall hearing this very point made in Sunday sermons at our local church, only a few kilometres away from St. John's Presbyterian Church in Bouctouche.

George and Jane Irving and their two children disembarked in Richibucto, on the Northumberland Strait. Richibucto, then the third-largest port in New Brunswick, was booming by exporting timber to Britain.[9] The town was already known to some Scots as "an important, old-established shipbuilding, sawmilling and top-timber shipping centre," and Scots had already settled in the area.[10] Life in the colonies, however, was very difficult, and hardly resembled the pamphlets' promises. Because much of the port area had already been granted to earlier settlers, George Irving was forced inland, about forty kilometres upriver from where he and his family had landed, to see the Crown land he had been granted. He was likely disappointed.

Mill Branch remains an isolated community on the northern edge of Kent County, New Brunswick. It never had, and still does not offer, much economic potential. The land around, much of it barely arable and of limited potential as a profit-producing forest, probably looks as it did when George and Jane Irving first arrived. The community is still sparsely populated, with only about twenty houses strung along a seven-kilometre road. There is a hundred-year-old church that has remained true to the Presbyterian religion, and across the road is the cemetery where both George and Jane Irving, and many of their descendants, are buried.

George had written to New Brunswick colonial officials asking for one hundred acres of Crown land, a request that an archivist with the provincial archives describes as common from "a typical bunch of Scottish settlers."[11] He paid two shillings and sixpence per acre, amounting to $1,440 in 2019 Canadian dollars. On the back of the property assessment, a government official wrote "poor squatter."[12] Like many newly arrived colonials, the Irvings had to struggle simply to survive. Like other Scots arriving in the New World, however, George Irving had a strong work ethic, and knew how to cope with a harsh climate.[13]

George and Jane Irving found pioneer life particularly demanding in Mill Branch. They arrived on their one hundred acres empty-handed, with two children in tow, and had eight more children as they went about carving out a life in their new home. George was able to secure only a modest amount to pay his first instalment for the survey and registration of the acreage in Mill Branch. Nine years would pass before he could come up with the funds to make the final payment to secure title to the land.[14] In the meantime, he was able to clear the land and build a house and barn near the Richibucto River. He was also able to provide for their ten children—no small accomplishment, to be sure, in New Brunswick of the 1820s and 1830s. One of his children, Arthur Irving's great-grandfather, would later build another house a few hundred metres away from the river.

THE FIRST IRVING ENTREPRENEUR

GEORGE'S ELDEST SON, HERBERT IRVING, WOULD GIVE LIFE TO the Irving entrepreneurial spirit. He saved enough money to secure his first 60-acre land grant at age twenty-five in Coal Branch, not far from Mill Branch. He farmed on this land, and then quickly expanded his enterprise by acquiring another 110 acres nearby, and a few years later another 375 acres in nearby Chockpish. He imported prized bulls, was the first in the area to embrace innovative practices in farming, grew a variety of apples, employed fertilizers, and even had hired hands to help him grow his business.[15] He became one of the region's most successful farmers.

His farm produced butter, cheese, oats, potatoes, pork, and the list goes on. He won cash prizes at agricultural fairs and exhibitions. He was also appointed Surveyor of Roads and Justice of the Peace. By 1860, he had accumulated a net worth of $3,440, a substantial amount in his day. This enabled him to become the local banker for many in Kent County. Banks, at the time, were located in faraway Moncton and Saint John, and were unable or unwilling to loan money to local residents. Local lenders then needed no government permission to make loans, and Herbert Irving loaned money in the form of mortgages to Kent County residents with names such as Mills, Melanson, McKie, Belliveau, and Collette. He also bought and sold properties in Richibucto, Acadieville, Harcourt, and later all over Kent County. He expanded his lines of business in October 1883 when he purchased a steam-powered sawmill located on the Bouctouche waterfront. He built one of the nicest homes in the area, and was able to send some of his seven children to college. In short, he was a well-respected community leader, even holding a mortgage on the local Presbyterian church.

Herbert Irving left the sawmill and the family homestead, along with his debts, promissory notes, and securities, to his son, J.D. Irving, having laid the groundwork for future generations of Irvings to succeed in business. The community-minded Herbert forgave the mortgage to the Presbyterian church, left funds to assist the poor of the parish, and other money to support the local Sunday school.[16]

J.D. IRVING

J.D. IRVING WAS A MAN-ABOUT-TOWN IN BOUCTOUCHE. RATHER than waste his father's inheritance, he expanded it by growing substantially the businesses he inherited and creating new ones. He quickly became the town's leading businessman and a high-profile community leader, which made him well known throughout Kent County. He successfully operated a sawmill, a gristmill, a cold storage, a lumber business, and three farms, and also ran a general store in Bouctouche. The general store was located in the heart of the community, where local residents went to buy all that was needed from food to clothes and also to hear the latest town gossip. With the help of his son Kenneth, he also became the local distributor for Imperial Oil, and sold gas to local automobile owners.

J.D. Irving was one of the first in Bouctouche to buy an automobile, which strengthened further his visibility in the community. The car, a Pierce-Arrow, could go up to twenty miles per hour, and was a status symbol owned by early Hollywood stars and US President William Howard Taft. But it had another advantage, one that was important for J.D. Irving. It was a rugged car, able to go where other cars could not. It was particularly well-suited to rural areas, with their rough or largely non-existent roads.[17]

J.D. Irving was also a highly successful farmer. Like his father, he was innovative, introducing several new techniques to farming. The *Maritime Farmer* in its 1912 edition labelled him "a model to be emulated." He, like his father, won several prizes at agricultural fairs. And, again like his father, he was a philanthropist. In the immediate aftermath of the great 1917 Halifax explosion, for example, he put together windows and window panes, and assembled a team of his men to deliver them to Halifax, at no financial gain to himself.

His sawmill employed seventy-five men. When woodland came up for sale in Kent County, he would buy it when the price was right. When he saw an economic opportunity, he pursued it, whether in farming or forestry. He owned tugboats, built a warehouse on piles extending over the riverbank in Bouctouche, and continued to buy land. The outline of the history of the J.D. Irving firm on its website proudly reports that J.D. Irving "was an innovator and a dedicated investor in new methods, equipment to improve productivity and service—a tradition that we carry on today," and that his son K.C. was a "dynamic builder of enterprises."[18]

J.D. Irving attended the local Presbyterian church, a short walk from his house. He became a pillar of the church, which became known as "the Irving Church" or, as some Acadians called it, "*l'église des Arvins.*" J.D. Irving kept a close watch on his church and was always ready to give it a helping hand. His grandson, Arthur Irving, remembers well his grandfather's house and the nearby church. As was the custom of the day, J.D. let his wife raise the children. He had a son and daughter with his first wife, who died young, and two daughters and a son, Kenneth, with his second wife, Mary Elizabeth Gifford.

J.D. Irving had a passion for hard work and for business. He carried his Presbyterian ethos proudly. K.C. Irving had this to say about his father: "He knew what hard work was. He knew how much a man should do and he knew how to fix a piece of machinery. And if he didn't know, he would learn very quickly. I suppose I am a bit like him in many respects. I always liked machinery and that sort of thing. I like to see wheels turn."[19] K.C. and Arthur inherited the same passions: hard work and business. I asked Arthur about his passion for both. His response: "I cannot imagine life without a passion."

J.D. Irving became a widely respected business leader. He learned to converse in French to communicate with his francophone employees and customers. He kept a very close watch on all his businesses and proved to be a tough negotiator, particularly when it came to wages. He also became a respected community leader. He was very active in politics, becoming the leading Liberal in Bouctouche, the party of Sir Wilfrid Laurier in Ottawa and

Walter E. Foster and Peter J. Veniot in New Brunswick.[20] His home often became the place where local Liberals met to map out their political strategies and decide who should run under the Liberal banner in the local constituencies. He became the local power broker for the Liberal Party in the area. When J.D. Irving passed away in 1933, he left a net worth of $88,307, a considerable amount in Depression-wracked Canada.[21]

There is a link between J.D. Irving and my family. A relative, Dosithé (Dos) Savoie, was fatherless at a very young age and unschooled. J.D. took him under his wing, gave him a job, and raised him "as good as his own." Dos recalled when J.D. told him to take one of his horses for a run and "give it a few miles" and to take his favourite girl.[22] He also learned the ways of business from J.D. Irving. Dos Savoie was often talked about at my home, and he became a successful businessman with a Moncton street named after him. He successfully operated a large farm near Moncton, and harvested and sold pulp to Canadian and European buyers. He and K.C. Irving remained lifelong friends. Arthur remembers Dos well—in particular, his big booming voice telling workers where to park pulpwood when loading ships in the Bouctouche Harbour.

K.C. IRVING

J.D. IRVING KEPT A CLOSE EYE ON HIS SON KENNETH, commonly known even then as K.C. At a very young age, K.C. displayed a strong entrepreneurial talent. He searched for ways to make money by working in the family store, by selling produce from his garden, and even by selling the lead that sealed up tea boxes going to the local junk dealer.[23] By the age of ten, he had saved enough money to buy a used Ford for $8. When his father found out, he told Kenneth in no uncertain terms that he had to sell it. After tough negotiations, Kenneth sold the car for $11, turning a quick 38 percent profit.[24]

K.C. was like his father in his work ethic, his desire to see the wheels turn, and his willingness to know how to fix a piece of machinery. Though it is not clear whether his father knew about it, K.C. took his father's car apart and rebuilt it when he was only eight years old, demonstrating at an early age his strong mechanical aptitude.[25]

K.C.'s mother, Mary Elizabeth Gifford, also had a profound influence on him. She drilled into K.C. that, "if you are going to do something, do it right." K.C. would repeat this time and time again, until the saying became a family creed. I also heard it many times from Arthur Irving. K.C. said his mother told him "never to touch liquor and I'd never want to, and I never did." She was also set against smoking, and ingrained in her son that "to waste anything was a sin." K.C. had a very strong relationship with his mother, explaining that "she demanded and gave respect, and she didn't mind what others thought. She was a tremendous help to me."[26]

K.C. showed early on that business would be his vocation. His cousin Leigh Stevenson reports that, when K.C. was six years old, he hit on a money-making idea. With the help of a friend or two, he would offer to clean out cellars and basements in return for keeping whatever they could salvage for sale, such as old bottles. K.C. also helped to thresh grain, worked on the farm, sold cucumbers and carrots for three or four cents, and sold newspapers. At a very young age, he learned from his mother the need to be frugal.[27]

At the outbreak of the First World War, Kenneth decided that he wanted to serve in the military. Though underage—he was only sixteen—he went to Moncton to enlist in the army. His father was set against it, and sent him off to university at Dalhousie. Once in Halifax, however, Kenneth enrolled in the Officers' Training Corps, and tried once again to enlist with a local regiment. Once again, his father put a stop to that. This time, he sent Kenneth to Acadia University, far from Halifax and military regiments.

Kenneth, never one to give up, was able to enlist in the Royal Flying Corps in the spring of 1918. His parents finally accepted that they could no longer hold him back. He was quickly sent off to England for pilot training. With the help of his cousin Leigh Stevenson, he learned how to fly a two-seat Sopwith Camel training plane. He enjoyed the military, the discipline, and the opportunities to learn navigation and how airplane engines worked. The war ended, though, before he could complete his pilot training and see any military action. Leigh Stevenson and K.C. Irving remained lifelong friends.

K.C. returned to Bouctouche with zero interest in returning to university. While in Britain, he met soldiers from faraway places, which whetted his appetite to see the world. Shortly after his return to Bouctouche, he set off for Australia and New Zealand via Vancouver. He reached Vancouver, stopping along the way for short-term work opportunities. He never made it to Australia: after a few false starts, Kenneth hopped on a train for the return trip to Bouctouche.

TURNING THINGS OVER TO K.C.

TWENTY-TWO-YEAR-OLD K.C. WASTED NO TIME PONDERING HIS future on his return from Vancouver. It was not in his nature simply to put in idle time, and in any case one can only assume that his father would not have tolerated it. There was plenty of work waiting for K.C. at the mill, at the farm, and in the general store. He rolled up his sleeves, and decided to help in the store, which was soon up against the new, large Eaton's department store in Moncton. Eaton's also had a mail-order catalogue that proved devastating to small-town stores. It was a classic case of Joseph Schumpeter's theory of creative destruction, whereby innovation establishes new products and processes that replace outdated ones.[28]

Many in Bouctouche, including K.C.'s half-brother, felt that the family's general store could never compete against the Eaton's catalogue. K.C. disagreed, and introduced new products and new sales techniques to go head-to-head with the big Toronto-based emporium. He had a hole dug to install a 250-gallon tank in front of the store that would enable the Irvings to sell gasoline to the growing number of car owners, something Eaton's and its catalogue could not do. K.C. explained to his father that he decided to do this because he wanted to make "darned sure" they would not be "going out of business."[29]

K.C. had many reasons to ensure the general store's survival. Family pride, for one thing. He saw his future in business, and losing the family store would not be the way to start. But he had another important reason. Harriet MacNarin, an energetic and strong-willed young woman, had moved to Bouctouche from Galloway, a small community twenty kilometres north of Bouctouche, to work at the J.D. Irving general store. K.C. would later hire her to keep his books; later still, he would marry her.

In addition to gasoline, K.C. began to sell Fords, Canada's most popular brand of automobile by far in the 1920s. He first sold for the Ford dealer in Richibucto, the small seaside community that had welcomed his great-grandfather some one hundred years earlier. K.C. proved particularly adroit at selling cars, so much so that the Richibucto dealer persuaded Ford to turn the southern half of Kent County over to K.C.

Although the automobile retail sector was then taking off, sales were slow to make headway in New Brunswick, particularly in rural areas where the roads were little more than beaten-down logging roads. K.C.'s father was not convinced that one could be successful selling cars around Bouctouche. He did not think that farmers could afford to buy cars, even the cheap Model T. Nevertheless, K.C. was determined to make it work. He explained how: "If you thought a farmer was serious, the first thing was to get him to say he wanted a car. Then he'd say he didn't have any money. You'd ask him when he was going to get some or how much he did have. Then you had to work it out. You made a lot of suggestions. You took in on trade all sorts of things—horses, carriages, harnesses, cattle. Then you had to sell them, too. Moving around that way, you got a good idea of how you could dispose of things. I even took in a load of groceries."[30] Selling cars in Bouctouche was markedly different from selling cars in a big city. One had to adapt to local circumstances to succeed, and K.C. did just that.

K.C., like other Ford dealers, required capital to set up a showroom and garage. But K.C. had an advantage: he was able to set up operations from his father's general store.[31] His success, however, soon raised the ire of other Ford dealers in southern New Brunswick. The Moncton dealer, whom K.C. Irving was outhustling in his own backyard, told Ford it had to move K.C. out or find ways to limit his sales in the Bouctouche and southern Kent County area. Ford offered K.C. the Halifax or Saint John territory. K.C. selected Saint John.

K.C. also ran into the same difficulties when he decided to get into the gasoline and oil business. He saw that the cars he sold required both, and it would be better that they buy both from him. He turned to Imperial Oil, the dominant gas and oil company in the region, asking to be its agent in the Bouctouche area. The company initially agreed.

K.C. soon proved as successful selling oil and gas as he was selling cars. A jack of all trades, he was also a handy mechanic, able to take apart a car and rebuild it. He expanded his oil and gas business by installing a 350-gallon tank on the back of his truck to enable him to service clients in remote areas. He even accepted horse-drawn buggies as trade-ins, which helped him sell more Ford Model Ts. He knew that by selling more cars he would also be selling more gasoline. Before long, K.C. dominated by a wide margin both car and gasoline and oil sales in Kent County.[32]

Complaints, however, soon poured in from nearby agents who insisted they would be better off dealing directly with Imperial Oil or other firms than having to deal with K.C. Irving. Unlike Ford, Imperial Oil simply terminated its association with him, deciding that it could do better by bypassing K.C. and selling directly to customers. It would now have a full-time representative on site in Kent County, rather than a part-time agent. Imperial Oil also decided to send a message to K.C. in his own backyard by announcing it would install a ten-thousand-gallon gasoline tank in Bouctouche. The view, even in Bouctouche, was that K.C. would not be able to compete against Imperial Oil, given its size and its domination of the oil and gas market. The betting was that K.C. would soon fold.[33]

K.C., however, was not about to throw in the towel, but resolved to go head-to-head with Imperial Oil. He risked his limited capital by buying a railway tank car full of gasoline from a firm in Tulsa, Oklahoma. He also built a rudimentary storage tank near Bouctouche to store the gasoline. The decision to buy the tank car of gasoline was based on sheer business instincts. To be sure, it was high risk, but K.C. believed he could beat Imperial Oil by offering a better level of service to customers on his home turf. K.C. turned to his father for financial support, which he received, and to a prominent local business leader, Tom Nowlan. Nowlan lived in a large red-brick house that still stands on the outskirts of Bouctouche. He had done well in business, particularly as a rum-runner in this era of Prohibition. Nowlan, together with J.D. Irving, decided to invest $10,000, then a substantial sum of money, in K.C.'s oil and gas business.

The story heard around Bouctouche—one I heard many times from my father and others—claims that Tom Nowlan got cold feet and went to K.C.'s father, wanting out of the business. I was told that Nowlan said to J.D. Irving, "I don't think that K.C. has the makings of a solid businessman," and asked to be bought out. I remember well my father saying that it had to be the worst business decision in history. If it's true, one can appreciate what an incredibly bad business decision it was. I have no idea if the story is true, and neither does Arthur Irving. It might well be old Bouctouche lore, with the locals wishing to ascribe to K.C. greater business acumen than other business leaders. What is known for certain is that Tom Nowlan did sell his shares to K.C. and J.D.[34] True or not, K.C. and Tom Nowlan remained good friends long after Nowlan sold his shares. Arthur Irving recalls visiting Tom Nowlan with his father after Nowlan had moved away to Riverview, New Brunswick.

At age twenty-five, K.C. Irving built his first garage on family land kitty-corner from his father's general store. He hired an Acadian, Ephrem Cormier, to construct the building, but he also worked on-site pounding nails. He also continued to sell Fords, gas, and oil, and repair automobiles at the new location. He was hands-on, always present on-site, a practice that would stay with him as he built his various businesses.

Arthur Irving told me it was not unusual for someone to knock on K.C.'s door in the middle of the night looking for gas. K.C. got up every time, no questions asked, to serve the customer. Some of these customers were rum-runners, carrying liquor from the French-owned islands of Saint-Pierre et Miquelon to the US northeast coast from Boston to Atlantic City. Saint-Pierre et Miquelon, with its deepwater port and relatively easy access to Cape Breton and Prince Edward Island, had a clear geographical advantage for rum-runners. Saint-Pierre et Miquelon also operated under French law, making it legal to produce, transport, store, and drink alcohol. L'Hôtel Robert became a temporary home to many gangsters, including Al Capone.[35] Bouctouche was a convenient stop for gas in the middle of the night as the rum-runners made their run from Cape Breton or Prince Edward Island to the United States. Rum-running provided well-paying employment opportunities. At the time, Maritimers could fish for $35 a month or they could work smuggling alcohol for American operators who paid $100 for every successful trip.[36]

Saint-Pierre et Miquelon distillery wholesalers were operating at full capacity during the Prohibition era, shipping three hundred thousand cases of liquor every month.[37] Arthur Irving reports that his father provided the same level of service to his customers, rum-runners and all, from his first day in business in Bouctouche. The customer was always king, no matter his or her status in society. That, he concluded, was the way to win against the big firms from away. It was also a lesson that K.C. ingrained in his sons. Nearly one hundred years after K.C. Irving launched his oil and gas business, Lisa Keenan, in presenting Arthur Irving for the Rotary Club's Paul Harris Fellowship, underlined the point that Irving Oil serves "large and small customers every day, the same."[38]

SELLING PRIMROSE GAS

I WELL RECALL THE FIRST IRVING SERVICE STATION. TO A young boy from a small hamlet where, apart from my father's construction company, the only businesses were a bootlegger and a small corner store in the living room of a modest house, K.C. Irving's garage seemed to stand out as a large commercial enterprise. Old photos of the garage, however, reveal a single-storey building with two glass-topped gasoline pumps in front and a repair bay. A large window opened to a makeshift office where the cash register was located.

K.C. initially sold gas under the Primrose banner. There are two versions explaining the origin of the brand. One is that K.C. borrowed the name from his father's gristmill, which was turning out high-qualify flour under the Primrose name. The other is that Imperial Oil had a brand called Premier, while another large firm, Canadian Oil, had the White Rose brand, which K.C. combined to make Primrose. Arthur Irving tells me that K.C. did indeed borrow the name from the gristmill.

The garage was not limited to oil and gas; it also gave K.C. an ideal location to sell Fords and to showcase a big Ford eagle insignia. The garage was a busy place, with people, mostly men, hovering around to buy gas and exchange gossip. K.C. occasionally would join in the discussions. One evening, a local who'd had too much to drink began taunting K.C. He was bullying the wrong guy. K.C. had a reputation at school of being quick with his fists and often unwilling to back away from a scrap whenever challenged. K.C. would have made easy work of the "half drunk," but he laughed off the taunts. Willie Duplessis recalls telling K.C. that he "shouldn't have to take that." K.C. told him: "If I give some back there's no way I'll be able to sell him a car."[39]

K.C. Irving pursued business and sales opportunities with single-minded purpose. He let nothing get in the way. He also became a role model for the few Acadians around Bouctouche in the 1950s willing to give entrepreneurship a go. I recall seeing him on weekends at his service station in the summer months wearing a straw hat and keeping an eye on the business. One young Acadian from Saint-Antoine, a community near Bouctouche, got a job at the service station selling gas. He had set his heart on becoming an entrepreneur, something not often seen among young Acadians at the time. One day K.C. came to buy gas, and the young man saw an opportunity to impress him and ask for advice on how to become a successful businessman. He decided to give K.C. the complete service and then some. He carefully poured the gas, washed not just the windshield but all the car windows, cleaned the headlights, and even wiped the front and back bumpers with a cloth. He was careful to do all of this with great care. All the while, K.C. stood by, arms crossed, watching this young man giving it his all and not saying a word, but waiting patiently until the work was done. The aspiring entrepreneur then went to K.C. to collect the money, and said, "My goal is to be a businessman. Any advice?" K.C. calmly responded: "You will need to work a lot faster if you ever want to be successful." I am happy to report that the aspiring entrepreneur did learn to work faster, and he became a highly successful businessman producing and selling construction materials.

In 1957, my father decided to break from Acadian tradition and start his own business. Although the Roman Catholic Church was hardly the only factor, the dominant role it played in Acadian society until the late 1960s did inhibit Acadians from going into business. In Kent County, the parish priest was king and master of the parish, commanding tremendous respect and power. The Church ran many things, from education to health care and even, to some extent, the economy. It permeated most activities, commercial or otherwise, and had an enormous hold on all of us. When they came of age, Acadian males were expected to get a job in the construction industry, the fishery, or the forestry. Those who were fortunate enough to further their education were expected to become priests, lawyers, or medical doctors. Business was left to the English. I do not know if it was because K.C. Irving was from Bouctouche or because he was the leading businessman of his day, but my father always held a great deal of respect for his business talents. One can never be certain, but I believe that K.C. Irving inspired more than a few Maritimers to start a business. One thing is certain: K.C. Irving gave new life to Bouctouche and, in time, created hundreds of private-sector jobs in the community.

K.C. Irving never forgot his Bouctouche roots. He often said that Bouctouche was the one place where he truly felt at home. The town's main street, which dominates the community, is called Irving Boulevard. K.C. often returned to Bouctouche to visit old friends, until the end. He never forgot those who did him a good turn. Arthur Irving told me that, on a few occasions, K.C. would drop in to see Zoël Dallaire, who lived near McIntosh Hill, a short distance from Bouctouche. I remember Zoël, a hermit who lived by himself in a small, dilapidated two-room house next to the hill. It was difficult for me to understand why K.C. would drop by to see him. Arthur explained: "K.C. got stuck in a winter snow storm, and Zoël came to his rescue."

K.C. also rarely came to Bouctouche without seeing Monsignor Désiré Allain, Bouctouche's parish priest and dominant political figure in the 1950s. Monsignor Allain oversaw the construction of the new church, Saint-Jean-Baptiste, which was completed in 1955. K.C. Irving helped, donating bells for the bell tower, one of which bears the names of his three sons, J.K., Arthur, and John (Jack). K.C.

Irving's first major donation, though, was a $500,000 gift to five-year-old Université de Moncton, the first large donation received by my university. He knew well and respected Father Clément Cormier, the priest who founded the university. Arthur Irving tells me that he accompanied his father when he met Father Cormier to present the cheque for the university's first fundraising campaign.

K.C. kept in contact with Kent County entrepreneurs long after he moved away from Bouctouche. He heard that a leading businessman from the area, E.P. Melanson, who ran a large lobster processing plant in Cocagne, a few kilometres south of Bouctouche, was running into problems. At its peak, during lobster season, Melanson's plant employed more than five hundred people. K.C. called to offer a word of encouragement and to urge Melanson to battle back as best he could. Melanson explained his main challenge: "I have these guys from Ottawa calling me about income tax. What the Christ is that?"[40]

FORD FORCES K.C.'S HAND

K.C. IRVING'S DAYS IN BOUCTOUCHE WERE COMING TO AN END. Ironically, it was his business success—not the lack of it—that made it impossible for him to stay. Imperial Oil had dumped him, and Ford, as we have seen, dealt with complaints from its Moncton agent by offering him a new sales territory in Saint John. K.C. took up residence there in 1925.

Saint John, New Brunswick, was hardly a booming urban centre at the time. John DeMont explains that,

by the mid-1920s Saint John's future looked anything but great; the munitions factories and shipyards had closed just as the war veterans filed home in search of jobs. The city's machine shops and foundries sat silent. The port was losing business to Toronto and Montreal. When North America plunged into a new recession, more companies closed down in Saint John and the soup lines lengthened. Canadians everywhere were abandoning the rural areas for cities.[41]

Few, however, were heading for Saint John, while many Saint Johners were going down the road in search of work. The city was hardly a promising community in which to grow a business.

Still, K.C. Irving left small-town Bouctouche, where he was comfortable, well known, and well liked. Douglas How and Ralph Costello write that "[t]he Irvings were *the* family in town and J.D. Irving was its leading citizen," and that he was "recognized as the Liberal party in town."[42] J.D.'s house was always a beehive of activity, with a constant stream of visitors, businessmen, politicians, and aspiring politicians calling to talk about business or politics. The dining room table sat fourteen, and it was full house at many lunches and dinners. K.C. took it all in.

J.D. Irving worked well with Acadians, a trait that he passed on to his son. K.C. admired his father and his abundant common sense. As noted earlier, his mother, Mary Elizabeth Gifford, also had a profound influence on him. She moved to Bouctouche to keep house for J.D. Irving after his first wife died. She later worked in the general store. K.C.'s biographers write that she was a serious woman, and from her K.C. got "his seriousness, his tenacity, his determination and perseverance."[43]

LOOKING BACK

BOUCTOUCHE HAD AN INDELIBLE INFLUENCE ON K.C. IRVING. Leigh Stevenson recalled that, whenever he and K.C. got together, "we'd start talking about our favourite subject—Bouctouche."

K.C. would often say, "In Bouctouche, you learned which end of a wheelbarrow to take hold of."[44]

Taking charge of his father's store, K.C. learned that he could take on the big firms from away and win. While others were prepared to throw in the towel when Eaton's opened a large general store in Moncton and began to circulate a mail-order catalogue, K.C. introduced new merchandise, modernized operations, sold gas, and underlined the importance of providing first-class service to customers to compete with Eaton's. The general store continued to prosper well into the 1960s.

It was in Bouctouche that K.C. Irving started his business selling Ford cars and Imperial Oil products. He succeeded too well, forcing both Ford and Imperial Oil to move him out of Bouctouche. By the time he moved, however, K.C. had built his own garage there and another in nearby Shediac, and had been able to put in place the elements to become a highly successful independent agent in the region's oil and gas retail sector.

Bouctouche also taught K.C. Irving how to get along with people from various ethnic backgrounds—Acadians, Scots, Irish, English, and Mi'kmaq—who made it, and still make it, their home. Bigots were not easily tolerated in Bouctouche. With a population of no more than six hundred at the time, people had to get along to make the community work. In fact, Bouctouche was in sharp contrast to other New Brunswick communities when it came to ethnic and religious tolerance. In the 1920s, some communities were home to the Ku Klux Klan. By 1926, for example, the province had seventeen "Klaverns" of Klan organizations, whose members feared that the purity of the "Anglo-Saxon race" was at risk because of immigrants and the Roman Catholic Church.[45] Starting with J.D. Irving, the Irvings "formed a high respect for the Roman Catholic priests and what they did to keep the village on a straight and narrow path"; they also "liked Acadians,"[46] which remains true to this day for Arthur Irving and his brother J.K. Irving.

Bouctouche also taught K.C. Irving that one should never get "too big for his britches." K.C. saw no difference in talking to a CEO in Toronto and a fisherman in Bouctouche, and neither does Arthur. Indeed, I often think that Arthur Irving much prefers talking to the fishermen. Gérard Maillet recalls K.C. Irving walking around the Kent Homes plant in Bouctouche, stopping to talk to front-line workers. He reports that "K.C. really enjoyed talking to us, you could tell. Oh, he liked Bouctouche, that's for sure." Maillet adds that K.C. did his best to say more than a few words in French, something that was rarely seen from anglophones at the time, but something that was highly appreciated.[47]

It was also in Bouctouche that K.C. Irving learned that the "customer is king." He became convinced that the best way to beat the big firms from away was to focus on the customer by providing quality service. It is a lesson that lives on through Arthur Irving.

K.C. had little knowledge of Saint John before he moved there. He had visited the city once before with his father. He would now make it his home and the head office for his businesses. He would soon learn that Saint John was different from Bouctouche in both important and unimportant ways. It was a city—at the time, the biggest in New Brunswick—and home to much larger firms than Bouctouche had to offer, such as Crosby's Molasses and Red Ball Brewery. But Saint John did not offer the same warm and friendly atmosphere that Bouctouche did. K.C. was from the backwoods of Kent County, from a small community that made little impression on other New Brunswick communities, least of all Saint John. K.C. would have to earn the respect of the local business community the old-fashioned way. He had to work for it.

Notes

1   Bob Harris, "Cultural Change in Provincial Scottish Towns c. 1700-1820," *Historical Journal* 54, no. 1 (2011): 105–41.
2   "Five churches of Scotland with dark and bloody pasts," *Scotsman*, April 29, 2016, online at scotsman.com/news-2-15012/five-churches-of-scotland-with-dark-and-bloody-pasts-1-4115249.
3   Frank McLynn, *Bonnie Prince Charlie: Charles Edward Stuart* (London: Random House, 2003).
4   John Gray Centre, "A Brief History of Emigration and Immigration in Scotland," *Library Museum Archive Archaeology*, n.d., online at johngraycentre.org/about/archives/brief-history-emigration-immigration-scotland-research-guide-2/.
5   New Brunswick and Nova Scotia Land Company, *Practical information respecting New Brunswick, including details relative to its soil, climate, productions, and agriculture, published for the use of persons intending to settle upon the lands of the Company* (London: Arthur Taylor), 1834, 3–4.
6   James Stevenson McEwen, "John Knox," *Encyclopedia Britannica*, May 3, 2019, online at britannica.com/biography/John-Knox.
7   Max Weber, in his widely read *The Protestant Ethic and the Spirit of Capitalism*, makes this point, although it has been challenged by others, including Joseph Schumpeter.
8   John Kenneth Galbraith, *The Scotch* (Toronto: McClelland and Stewart, 1964), 27.
9   "Richibucto: A Rich and Vibrant History," n.d., online at richibucto.org/history?id=history.
10 "Timber Colony," *Royal Gazette*, October 6, 1841, 33.
11 Shane Fowler, "Early Irving in province deemed a 'poor squatter' in historic documents," CBC, June 11, 2019, online at cbc.ca/news/canada/new-brunswick/george-irving-poor-squatter-new-brunswick-archives-1.5169310.
12 Ibid.
13 "Experience of Scots abroad 1830s–1939," BBC, n.d., online at bbc.co.uk/bitesize/guides/z9pbkqt/revision/1.
14 Harvey Sawler, *Twenty-First-Century Irvings* (Halifax: Nimbus, 2007), 3.
15 Ibid., 4.
16 Ibid., 6–7.

17 See, for example, Nick Georgano, *Cars: Early and Vintage, 1886–1930* (London: Grange-Universal, 1985).

18 Irving, "About Us—Our History," n.d., online at jdirving.com/jd-irving-about-us-history.aspx.

19 Quoted in Jacques Poitras, *Irving vs. Irving: Canada's Feuding Billionaires and the Stories They Won't Tell* (Toronto: Viking Canada, 2014), 8.

20 See, for example, Hugh G. Thorburn, *Politics in New Brunswick* (Toronto: University of Toronto Press, 1961).

21 Ibid., 8.

22 Douglas How and Ralph Costello, *K.C.: The Biography of K.C. Irving* (Toronto: Key Porter, 1993), 11.

23 John DeMont, *Citizens Irving: K.C. Irving and His Legacy* (Toronto: McClelland and Stewart, 1992), 15–16.

24 Ibid., 16.

25 Susanna McLeod, "K.C. Irving's ride to the top," *Kingston Whig Standard*, January 17, 2017, online at thewhig.com/2017/01/17/kc-irvings-ride-to-the-top/wcm/9924d73d-17dc-9745-5374-57f32ce907d3.

26 How and Costello, *K.C.*, 14.

27 Ibid., 15–16.

28 See, among many others, Joseph A. Schumpeter, *Capitalism, Socialism and Democracy* (London: Allen and Unwin, 1976).

29 How and Costello, *K.C.*, 24.

30 K.C. Irving, quoted in ibid., 28.

31 DeMont, *Citizens Irving*, 20.

32 Ibid, 21.

33 Ibid.

34 Ibid., 21–2.

35 J.P. Andrieux, *Rumrunners: The Smugglers from St. Pierre et Miquelon and the Burin Peninsula from Prohibition to Present Day* (St. John's: Flanker Press, 2009).

36 See, for example, C.M. Davis, "Prohibition in New Brunswick, 1917–1927" (MA thesis, University of New Brunswick, 1978).

37 B.J. Grant, *When Rum Was King: The Story of the Prohibition Era in New Brunswick* (Fredericton: Fiddlehead, 1984).

38 Remarks by Lisa Keenan, 2019 Rotary Club of Saint John Gala, May 24, 2019. I was present at the Gala and took notes.

39 Quoted in DeMont, *Citizens Irving*, 22.

40 Donald J. Savoie, *Looking for Bootstraps: Economic Development in the Maritimes* (Halifax: Nimbus, 2017), 25.
41 Quoted in DeMont, *Citizens Irving*, 25-6.
42 How and Costello, *K.C.*, 11–13.
43 Ibid., 14.
44 Ibid., 15.
45 Simon Delattre, "Quand le Ku Klux Klan sévissait au Nouveau-Brunswick," *L'Acadie Nouvelle*, September 29, 2018.
46 How and Costello, *K.C.*, 13.
47 Author's interview with Gérard Maillet, former Kent Homes employee, Moncton, May 30, 2019.

CHAPTER 2

FROM BOUCTOUCHE TO SAINT JOHN

K. C. Irving headed off to Saint John in his Model T to do what he did in Bouctouche: sell Fords and gasoline. But Saint John did not offer Bouctouche's friendly confines. In Bouctouche, K.C. was the son of the community's leading citizen and had, at a young age, established a reputation as a successful entrepreneur. In Saint John, he was an unknown, a country bumpkin from the backwoods of New Brunswick. Although he knew how to sell Fords and gas, in many ways he had to start all over again. Still, he felt the need to let the city know that he had arrived to start a business. He bought an ad in the local paper, in capital letters, that declared: "Our policy is better and more satisfactory service, to be honest in our relations with our customers."[1]

Saint John was not an easy place to break into and make a name in business. Proud of its Loyalist roots, the city, large by New

Brunswick standards, was far more impersonal than Bouctouche. It is no exaggeration to say that K.C. Irving was viewed as an upstart from nowhere. Howard P. Robinson, New Brunswick's leading businessman in his day, is reported to have said he would "chase that fellow Irving back to Bouctouche."[2] Robinson dominated the business community in Saint John, much like K.C.'s father dominated Bouctouche. He lived at 197 Mount Pleasant Avenue, on top of the hill overlooking the city. Robinson controlled the telephone company, the local power company, and the local newspaper. When he spoke, the Saint John business community listened. He was the role model for the local business community and aspiring entrepreneurs.

K.C., asking around how one could connect with the city's business and community elites, was told to join the Riverside Country Club, a private golf club in Rothesay. He did, and rented a locker in which to store his new-bought golf clubs. He never once took them out, and they burned with the clubhouse in 1966. It wasn't golf that interested him but the business world and work.

The local business community did not know quite what to make of this young entrepreneur from Bouctouche. First things first, however: he needed to establish a strong relationship, including a line of credit, with a local bank. It did not matter to the manager of the bank, however, that K.C. had already established a successful track record in business in Bouctouche and had always paid his debts. The bank manager said K.C.'s father would have to guarantee all loans and the line of credit.

By chance, K.C. ran into A.J. MacQuarrie, the manager of the local Bank of Nova Scotia and an old acquaintance who had visited his father in Bouctouche on several occasions. MacQuarrie asked, "How could you do it, Kenneth—how could you come to Saint John and not do business with me?"[3] K.C. told him he was prepared to give MacQuarrie his business provided he could secure a line of credit without his father's having to co-sign for it. The next morning, K.C. met with banker Horace Enman, got his line of credit, and became a customer of the Bank of Nova Scotia. The widely respected Enman later would become its head.[4]

With the Bank of Nova Scotia on his side, K.C. set out in search of business opportunities in the automobile and oil and gas sectors. He was quick off the mark selling cars, taking over a Ford dealership at 300 Union Street that had been operated by a local businessman who wanted out. The dealership had two gas pumps in front, moreover, which suited K.C. just fine. He quickly outperformed expectations with Ford, even though he had trouble getting stock when Ford shifted from the Model T to the new Model A. He solved that problem by buying from rival dealers representing other brands. Ford liked K.C.'s track record, and offered him other territories as well as the Maritimes franchise for its tractors.[5]

It was not long before the local competition took notice of K.C.'s Ford dealership. One advertised that it was outselling everyone in Saint John, that no other dealer did much business in the city, and made some negative comments about K.C.'s dealership. K.C. was out of the province on a business trip, but Bill Moore, who worked for K.C. at the dealership, reacted. He bought an ad in the local newspaper quoting the dealership's unit sales of new cars for the past year and the competitor's lower unit sales, and at the bottom he added, "and the dogs barked but the caravan rolled on."[6] Upon his return, K.C. told Moore he had made a mistake, explaining that he had woken up the competition and they would now have to work much harder. K.C. added that it was never good business to brag, a philosophy that constitutes an important component of the curriculum of the Irving School of Business. The ad, however, became a legend around Saint John, and it has long been held that it was K.C. who came up with the idea.[7] It was not.

K.C. quickly understood that, if there was money to be made, it would be in the gas and oil business. He readied himself to compete not just in Saint John, but also in other New Brunswick communities and eventually throughout the Maritime provinces. But competition in that business was tough in the 1920s. A growing number of independent operators were importing products cheaply from the United States. Major oil companies were also moving into the region, with their own agents selling their in-house products. To succeed, K.C. would have to go head-to-head with both independents like him and the big companies. Of the majors, one stood out in the Maritimes: the dominating firm of Imperial Oil, owned by Standard Oil of New Jersey, the same Imperial Oil that had dumped him a few years earlier. Convinced that it would do better without him, Imperial Oil revoked K.C.'s agency and established its own agents throughout the region to sell directly to clients.

K.C. had his work cut out for him. The large firms among the competition were endowed with both capital and strong representation on the ground, and a number of small independent operators were bought out. But K.C. Irving stood firm. By the mid-1920s, he not only had the backing of the Bank of Nova Scotia; he owned four Ford dealerships in New Brunswick, each equipped with tanks to sell gas. In October 1927, K.C. went before the Saint John Common Council for permission to establish three 500-gallon gasoline pumps on Rothesay Avenue, and was constantly searching new sites. He also had a growing infrastructure to sell oil and gas. Within a few years of arriving in Saint John, he had established service stations in several communities in southern New Brunswick, and was moving into the northern part of the province.

K.C. dropped the Primrose brand to go with Irving Oil, and in 1929 incorporated the firm Irving Oil Company.

K.C. retained the hands-on, down-to-earth approach he had learned in Bouctouche. If he saw a lineup at one of his service stations, he did not hesitate to man the pumps. When his staff needed help to dig holes or install tanks, he put on his overalls, rolled up his sleeves, and started digging. Putting in long hours came naturally to him.

He saw merit in attracting high-profile individuals as partners. He signed up Charles "Charlie" Gorman, for example, who won the 1926 world speed skating championship, to operate one of his service stations in Saint John. It proved to be a successful move. Gorman went on to operate three service stations in the city.

By the late 1920s, K.C. was firing his oil and gas business on all cylinders, and had begun to extend Irving Oil beyond New Brunswick. In 1931, he decided to build the five-storey Golden Ball Building in Saint John, even though the Great Depression was starting to bite. He had ambitious plans for this multipurpose building. It was to be a showroom to sell Ford automobiles, a place for him and his staff to work, and it would have service bays to repair cars and pumps to sell gas.

He could, and did, make decisions on the fly, albeit backed by experience. And unlike agents representing large firms, he did not have to check with several management layers at a head office out of the province. He was the head office, and he was quick to decide when he saw an opportunity. The competition, meanwhile, looked on, convinced he was moving too fast and would not make it. How could he, they asked, establish new service stations and build a multi-storey office building at a time when the Depression was ravaging the economy? An executive with the McColl-Frontenac Oil firm predicted that K.C. Irving would "be gone in two years."[8]

He and others, like Imperial Oil, would badly underestimate K.C.'s business sharpness and resolve. It was not the first time, nor would it be the last, that the competition would do so.

LOOKING TO OIL AND GAS

K.C. IRVING MADE A KEY STRATEGIC BUSINESS DECISION WITHIN a few years after arriving in Saint John. He would look to Irving Oil rather than to his Ford dealerships for future growth. He saw only modest growth selling cars, although his competitors viewed him as the top car salesman in the region. Mike Lawson, the local General Motors dealer, said that K.C. Irving "was the best car salesman he ever knew."[9] No matter. K.C. saw he could do better in oil and gas. He drew up an ambitious plan to sell oil and gas throughout the Maritimes and Quebec, and never stopped building service stations and acquiring existing businesses. His decision to team up with champion skater Charlie Gorman proved highly successful, and he kept an eye out for other high-profile athletes to run his Irving service stations. He signed up well-known Moncton hockey players Gordon "Doggie" and Clarence "Skeet" Kuhn, who were soon selling Irving gas in Moncton and Truro, Nova Scotia.

K.C. did things differently from his competitors. He understood the importance of branding, and decided to build a network of identical Irving Oil service stations throughout the Maritime provinces. He personally searched out the most promising sites. Arthur Irving recalls getting a call from his father late on a Friday evening to say that he'd just spotted a potential site for a new service station in Calais, Maine. He asked Arthur to pick up his brother Jack and come take a look. They did, and liked what they saw. An Irving station still stands on the site.

To build his first service station in Halifax, K.C. turned to Samuel Roy, an Acadian from Bouctouche. Roy was an architect, but explained that "no one was ever really an architect for K.C. Irving."[10] K.C. had his own ideas about how his service stations should be built, and he kept a close watch on all facets of building them. Roy had a close working relationship with K.C. his whole career, even owning shares in Irving Oil at one point. K.C. later bought the shares, but Roy did well on the sale. K.C. Irving, as is well known, never wanted to go public with Irving Oil or any of his businesses. He explained: "When you go public, you have certain rules you have to go by. Those may not make it the most convenient way of accomplishing what you set out to do. You can take a calculated risk if you only have to account to yourself."[11] More is said about this later in the book.

K.C. built his service stations one at a time and always kept a close eye on costs. That first service station in Halifax was made of brick, but those that followed were built of wood. He established an in-house capacity to build service stations, which gave him yet another comparative advantage over large firms from away. When a Halifax dealer told K.C. that he could not afford to install gas tanks because he had already spent a lot of money expanding his business, K.C. went to meet him in overalls, with a pipefitter in tow, to help put in tanks.

Responding to ever-increasing demand, K.C. never stopped securing new outlets to sell Irving gas. He installed tanks, often helping to dig the holes, all over the Maritimes. He moved into Amherst and Yarmouth, among other Nova Scotia communities. He went to Prince Edward Island, taking a chance on dealers that the larger firms would not consider. This, too, proved to be successful. He bought two small firms on the Island and began to sell oil and gas in these locations. He later moved onto the Magdalen Islands, securing new locations.

He tried to move into Newfoundland, but it did not work out, at least initially. The local authorities, confronting a serious economic crisis, had to borrow money from Imperial Oil. The government, in turn, gave Imperial Oil an exclusive right to sell oil and gas on the island. The government had looked to K.C. to borrow funds, but Arthur reports that K.C., at the time, did not have the financial resources to loan the kind of money Newfoundland was looking for. But Imperial Oil did, and it struck a hard deal. It would loan the government funds on the condition that it would have full control of the oil and gas sector on the island. The government agreed, and asked K.C. to remove his tanks and equipment as quickly as possible. This proved to be an important setback for the fledgling business.

As in other things, however, K.C. never gave up on Newfoundland. He would go on to become a friend of Premier Joey Smallwood, and saw the construction of the Trans-Canada Highway as the signal to expand his business into the province. Smallwood saw that Irving Oil was a "local" business, while Imperial Oil was from away. He not only opened Newfoundland to Irving Oil; he also facilitated sales of land to K.C. for service stations on the island. K.C. hired a young lawyer and promoter, J.C. Van Horne, to scout out sites in the province. He also hired a young, aggressive developer named Harrison McCain to help grow the business. Within ten years, the Irving diamond sat on top of service stations from Corner Brook to Stephenville to St. John's, and several points in between, going head-to-head against Imperial Oil's one-time monopoly on the island. Irving made up for lost time by outhustling Imperial Oil on the island at every turn and by allowing employees on the ground to make decisions after having to consult only him.

K.C. did the same in Quebec. He put together an aggressive expansion plan designed for Trois-Rivières going north and east, leaving Montreal to the big firms. At one point he was opening a service station in the province every three weeks. He also bought small firms, such as Les Pétroles de Québec, and absorbed them into Irving Oil. Again, he had a firm hand on the move to Quebec, personally inspecting all new construction. He made certain that new service stations would be built near the parish church and post office because these locations generated more traffic.[12]

K.C. Irving also looked to sell oil and gas to governments. He sent one of his most senior executives, Jim Flemming, a well-known and widely respected Saint John businessman, to see Premier J.B.M. Baxter at his home. K.C. soon learned, however, that his father's ties to the Liberal Party would come back to haunt Irving Oil. The conversation between the premier and Flemming went like this: "Irving...Irving...K.C. Irving?"

"Yes, sir," said his visitor. "Mr. K.C. Irving of Saint John."

"K.C. Irving...Mr. K.C. Irving....Why, isn't he the son of J.D. Irving of Bouctouche?"

"Yes, I believe so."

"Why," said Baxter, "J.D. Irving's the Liberal who fought us for years. No, there'll be no business for Mr. Irving. No, no business whatsoever!"[13]

K.C. Irving might not have been a fervent Liberal before that meeting, but he was after, at least for a while. He decided to give the Liberal Party a helping hand in the next provincial election. As in other things, he did not go for half measures. He decided to go all-in for Allison Dysart, a Bouctouche lawyer and a friend of the family, and raised funds in New Brunswick, Montreal, and Toronto. Dysart's Liberals easily defeated the Baxter government in the 1935 election, winning forty-three of the province's forty-eight seats. In time, however, K.C. would attenuate his efforts for the Liberals, realizing that it was good business to contribute funds to both major political parties.

K.C. Irving always looked after the details of the day, whether they dealt with construction issues, marketing, or staff. He broke new ground in marketing.[14] He insisted that his service stations look the same, no matter their location. He was the first in Atlantic Canada to have separate men's and women's washrooms in service stations, and he proudly displayed the same Irving diamond on all his stores. He understood the importance of marketing and visibility to promote sales. Although he owned four Ford dealerships, he decided, albeit out of character, to buy a fully loaded sixteen-cylinder Cadillac. He drove it around the Maritimes, and attracted onlookers wherever he went. His competitor and GM dealer Mike Lawson said: "He got more advertising out of that car! It got people talking about him." As the year was 1931, K.C. Irving sent out another message in buying the car and constructing his Golden Ball Building: optimism in the face of Depression.[15]

COPING WITH THE GREAT DEPRESSION

THE *CANADIAN ENCYCLOPEDIA* SUMS UP THE IMPACT OF THE Great Depression on Canada:

> The Great Depression of the early 1930s was a worldwide social and economic shock. Few countries were affected as severely as Canada. Millions of Canadians were left unemployed, hungry and often homeless. The decade became known as the Dirty Thirties due to a crippling drought in the Prairies, as well as Canada's dependence on raw material and farm exports....The Depression was the result of widespread drops in world commodity prices and sudden declines in economic demand and credit. These factors lead to rapid declines in global trade and rising unemployment.[16]

To be sure, the Prairies had it rough, but so did New Brunswick. The lumber and fishery industries were hard hit. Lumber mills closed throughout the province, and by 1932 some eight thousand New Brunswickers were out of work. Many migrated to Quebec, Ontario, and New England looking for jobs.[17] Images of the Dirty Thirties stayed with many Canadians for a long time—the Dust Bowl in the Prairies, long soup lines, and the "Bennett buggy," an automobile without an engine turned into a horse-drawn carriage.[18] The New Brunswick government did not have the financial resources or the administrative capacity to launch programs to deal with such an economic crisis, while the Dominion government, initially at least, stood on the sidelines because it did not have a constitutional basis to intervene. Relief costs drove some county councils into bankruptcy. The province's private sector struggled to survive, coping as best it could with collapsing demand and falling prices. Bankers started to call in loans.

Ernest Forbes, the widely read New Brunswick historian, writes that the province saw the "virtual collapse" of its manufacturing sector during the 1920s and 1930s. The sector was hard hit by the Depression and by national policies and tariffs that "created and maintained a manufacturing sector in central Canada."[19] Many companies in New Brunswick went out of business or into bankruptcy in the 1930s. This was the case for a number of small, independent oil and gas agents in the province. K.C. Irving was not one of them.

I recall telling Arthur Irving that I was worried about the economic future of our region. His response: "You should never be worried, you should be concerned." As I was thinking about the difference, I said, "That must be something your father said." "Yes," he replied. I took it to mean that if you are worried, you do not think you can do much about it, but if you are concerned, you see the problem and you want to do something about it.

K.C. Irving might have been worried about the Great Depression, but he did not show it. To be sure, there were challenges. Horace Enman, the Bank of Nova Scotia executive who had agreed to give K.C. a line of credit, called in a loan K.C. had with the bank that amounted to close to $2 million.[20] This, at a time when K.C.'s lumber business was going through a very difficult period. He could not sell all of the lumber he cut. However, instead of selling it at a loss, like his competitors, he waited for the market to turn. It eventually did, but the wait must have been disconcerting for K.C. Still, he repaid the loan.

He also never let up in his oil and gas business. He kept buying land, at times as low as $50 a lot, kept installing tanks, and kept opening service stations. This, while small owner-operated outlets in the oil and gas business were going broke. Irving saw that people were keeping their cars longer, which meant that they needed repairs and, given their age, were harder on gas. His business instincts told him that if he could weather the economic storm ravaging the Canadian economy, he would eventually come out of it stronger. K.C. also saw new opportunities emerge because there were fewer competitors.

The Dirty Thirties did not slow K.C. down—quite the opposite. He explained: "You had to use your head and your ingenuity. You couldn't sit around sucking your thumbs. You could be twice as busy as you had been because you had to be out looking for business."[21] He was constantly on the road. K.C. was once asked why he worked all the time. He said that he had tried everything else, but that he was not able to find anything he liked as much. He outworked both his employees and his competitors. Arthur Irving told me that his father had no sense of time and had incredible energy. He could outlast people thirty years younger. Harrison McCain once observed that K.C. Irving had "great energy, wonderful energy. Never got tired."[22] Arthur is much like his father: he sees no merit in slowing down, and he never does.

K.C. instilled in his employees a central purpose in their work: provide top service to customers. He was convinced that the best way to survive during the Depression and to beat the competition was to provide a higher level of service than anyone else. He never let up drilling this message into his staff. He often operated on the margin during those times, but he never threw in the towel.

His accountant, Hilus Webb, believed at the time that K.C. "was going to be big or he was going to go bust." Webb added that "mostly we were selling service and we had to make sure we gave it." While Irving Oil employees made every effort to provide the best possible level of service, K.C. also kept looking for new sites on which to build service stations and expand his oil and gas business. He had a knack for coming up with catchy slogans to define his Irving brand, including "More miles, more smiles."[23] He always sought to live by the commitment he made to potential customers in a purchased ad when he first arrived in Saint John that his businesses would always provide a better level of service than the competition.

K.C. also did everything to cut costs in his businesses as the most promising way to cope with the Depression. He negotiated hard on land purchases. He negotiated hard when building service stations, making sure Irving Oil came in on or under budget. He cut salaries by 10 percent, but then often made it up through Christmas bonuses. He defied predictions. He not only survived the Great Depression, he successfully expanded some of his businesses. By 1934 he owned thirty service stations, had the capacity to store five million gallons of gasoline, and sold products in many non-Irving outlets. In the same year, Irving Oil had revenues of $570,410 and turned a $174,538 profit.[24] By 1936 he was selling gas at one hundred stations and employed 212 people in Saint John and nearly 500 elsewhere.[25] He had gone head-to-head in the Maritimes with large capital-rich firms with their own sources of oil and gas, and he was not defeated—indeed, he prospered.

PLENTY OF IDEAS

K.C. WAS NEVER SHORT OF BUSINESS IDEAS, AND HE HAD AN instinctive ability to connect the dots between them. He might not have invented vertical integration, but he certainly mastered it. Many successful large businesses pursue vertical integration, and K.C. was able to build a large and successful business empire by employing that strategy. K.C. sold cars, and he saw the advantages of selling oil and gas and developing a capacity to repair and service them. To do so, he had to build service stations. Therefore, he decided to get into real estate and the construction business. He then quickly saw the need to have a hardware store. Since he was selling gas and home heating oil, which required transportation, he also decided to go into the trucking business and pursue ship-building. Wanting to grow his oil and gas sales, he saw an opportunity in owning a bus company, because buses need both to operate. As he was selling more and more oil and gas, he realized that he could benefit from having a refinery. He followed the same logic in the forestry sector.[26]

Academics and schools of business have debated the merits of vertical integration. Some observers argue that "adequate vertical integration" is or can be important to a firm's survival. Others insist, however, that vertical integration, particularly excessive integration, can explain corporate failure.[27] They point to problems confronting US automobile manufacturers in the 1980s, and make the case that vertical integration led them to lose market share to Japanese and German manufacturers.

The advantages of vertical integration are clear: it reduces buying or selling costs, it ensures a regular and reliable supply of materials, and it promotes innovation because senior managers are direct participants in all aspects of the business. There is also a downside: vertical integration eats up a lot of capital, not all facets of the business might be competitive, it discourages specialization, and it inhibits flexibility.[28] In seeking to establish when best to pursue vertical integration, McKinsey & Company too makes the case that vertical integration is costly to implement, can inhibit a firm's ability to get close to the customer, and can distort the market's ability to establish supply and demand, which might make the firm's products more costly.[29] The McKinsey & Company study, however, also identifies advantages to vertical integration.

As is often the case with management ideas, vertical integration has been in and out of fashion over the years. Over one hundred years ago, Ford owned rubber plantations, coal and iron mines, and railways. Today, auto manufacturers outsource well over 50 percent of the parts for their products. Some sectors increasingly see merit in vertical integration, albeit now calling it the "full stack" business model. Amazon has its own fleet of trucks and airplanes. Starbucks sells its own coffee through company-owned stores, and Delta Airlines owns a refinery to source aviation fuel.[30]

What about K.C. Irving? He embraced vertical integration for two reasons: cost and the realization that suppliers from away held too much power over his operations. To be sure, K.C.'s early years were trying for him. His father died in the middle of the Depression, and K.C. had to take over the operations in Bouctouche at a time when his own were stretched to the limit. In addition, he had to find the funds to buy out his siblings, who also owned shares in J.D.'s businesses. While he borrowed heavily from banks, many in the oil and gas business were predicting that K.C. would not survive or would eventually be bought out by a large firm like Imperial Oil. In brief, K.C.'s decision to embrace vertical integration was more one of necessity than of a carefully thought management theory or strategy. K.C. saw an opportunity, for example, to get into the passenger bus business, since roads were of better quality and many New Brunswickers could not afford an automobile. The problem: he could not afford to buy buses built in central Canada or in the United States. The solution: he decided to cut Ford bodies into two, add space to put in seats, and then sit them on top of imported British Leyland chassis. He now had buses to compete for passenger traffic. To others, this was a classic example of vertical integration because buses needed oil and gas to operate. To K.C., it was simply a case of finding an affordable way to get into this line of business.

To be sure, buying from suppliers from away was more expensive, and it was not always easy to get products when operating from Saint John. There were few local suppliers, so, whenever possible, it was best to create your own supplies. Initially, at least, the need to cut costs while launching and operating businesses with limited access to financial resources pushed K.C. to create new companies to supply his existing ones. Having decided not to go public, he could only look to his own capital and the banks or other financial institutions to secure the necessary financial resources. In short, vertical integration became for him the best way to do business because the local business community often could not produce the products and services he needed to operate or expand. The result was that, by 1942, K.C. had established businesses in several sectors, including oil and gas, construction, real estate, forestry, transportation, hardware retail, commercial equipment, and in producing a variety of wood products.

TAKING ON THE BIG BOYS

K.C. IRVING WAS NEVER ONE TO BACK AWAY FROM A FIGHT when challenged, whether in grade school in Bouctouche or throughout his business career. He also never bought into the old saying, "you can't fight City Hall." K.C. had a long battle with Halifax entrepreneur Fred Manning and the Saint John Common Council over who would have the right to operate buses in the city. The city's bus franchise in the early 1930s was owned by the New Brunswick Power Company, which, in turn, was owned by Federal Light & Traction Company, a New York–based firm. The firm decided to unload its Saint John assets, which included a street railway, a gas distributing network, and power plants.

Manning was a wealthy entrepreneur with much deeper pockets than K.C. Irving's at the time. In short, Manning was what K.C. Irving would later become: the region's leading businessman. K.C., like Manning, wanted the street railway and bus routes. Manning, however, was able to convince the Council to go with his proposal. The city would buy the power company, and in return he would secure a forty-year franchise to operate buses on Saint John streets. Manning retained the services of Saint John lawyer W.A. Ross, who, by happy coincidence, also doubled as secretary to the Saint John Common Council. Given the influence Ross was able to exercise over the Council, no one was surprised when the city decided to go with Manning's proposal. Manning was then able to deal with the New York firm and buy some of its assets, which helped him set up his bus operations.

K.C. Irving, however, would not give up. He turned to the courts and lobbied members of the Council and the provincial government. It became a long, drawn-out affair for both sides, but K.C. stayed the course. After twelve years, Fred Manning gave up the fight, and K.C. Irving was finally given a thirteen-year franchise to operate buses in Saint John. The battle required a great quantity of resources and a great deal of tenacity on the part of K.C. to take on a wealthier and better-connected Manning. The message was heard throughout the Maritime provinces that K.C. was in for the long term and that he did not back down, even from the likes of Fred Manning.[31]

In the depths of the Great Depression, Canadian National Railways (CNR) raised freight rates, which proved particularly difficult for the thinly populated Maritime region. K.C. made his views known to the government-owned Crown corporation that it was the worst time to hike rates, particularly in the Maritimes. CNR dismissed his concerns. To make matters worse, CNR decided not to raise rates for Imperial Oil, insisting that one should not compare Irving Oil to Imperial Oil, in part because Imperial had a refinery and Irving did not. K.C. Irving kept making his case, but CNR kept saying no, at one point telling him that, given that his businesses were in the Maritime provinces, he could always turn to coastal waters to transport his products by boat.

K.C. did just that. He went to Scotland to shop for a tanker. He bought one, the *Elkhound*, able to carry 95,000 gallons of fuel. He also added trucks and built new terminals at key locations. A few years later, CNR told K.C. that he had to get rid of his tanker and that, if he did not, it would cut freight rates to the point that his competitors would have an unfair advantage over him. K.C. stood firm. CNR responded by cutting freight rates between 28 and 45 per-cent to force K.C.'s hand. Again K.C. did not back down, Instead, he bought a second tanker and more trucks. He was now in the transportation business, with oil tankers, trucks, and buses.[32]

He also went head-to-head with giant Imperial Oil. The firm did not know what to do with K.C. Irving. It will be recalled that

K.C. sold oil and gas for Imperial Oil when he first broke into the business. Imperial Oil pushed him aside, deciding to have its own agents on the ground, even housing one in Bouctouche. No matter. K.C. continued to buy oil and gas from Imperial Oil's Halifax refinery to serve his customers. When K.C. decided to expand in all parts of the Maritimes and into Quebec, Imperial Oil threatened to cut off supply in order to keep him from growing the business outside of New Brunswick.[33] Again, K.C. would not back away, as we will see later.

K.C. Irving was one of the few independent operators to survive the Great Depression. The bulk of the independents and even many of the larger operators, such as McColl-Frontenac, went out of business. K.C. not only survived, he expanded in several other sectors. For example, he increased by a wide margin the scope of the forestry business he inherited from his father. In the late 1930s, the owners of Saint John–based Canada Veneers came to him for help. They were slowly moving toward bankruptcy. Their bank was looking at calling in a loan, and the company also had difficulty accessing quality wood—not a good combination. K.C. agreed to guarantee a bank loan, and he was able to secure better-quality logs.

K.C. took full ownership of Canada Veneers in 1938, at what proved to be a very fortuitous moment. Harrison McCain often made the point that a successful business person who does not admit that he or she was lucky at some point is lying.[34] K.C. had luck on his side when he took control of Canada Veneers. Demand for laminated wood products shot up sharply with the Second World War. In England, De Havilland developed a new airplane, the Mosquito, most of which was built with plywood rather than metal. Nicknamed the "Wooden Wonder," the plane was fast and very flexible, able to manoeuvre as a tactical bomber, a high-altitude night bomber, a fighter bomber, and a maritime strike aircraft. It first saw action in January 1943.[35] To manufacture the Mosquito, the British government made a call to purchase all the plywood that could be produced.

K.C. responded. He saw the opportunity for what it was. He decided to get directly involved in managing the plant. He oversaw the plant's transformation from 180 employees producing 200,000 square feet a week to over 500 employees producing over 4 million square feet. The plant was in operation night and day, and K.C. was at the plant at all hours, pushing for more efficiencies.[36] He enjoyed every minute, saying at one point that he "could do that sort of thing all night and never get sleepy."[37]

K.C. Irving also turned to Bouctouche to produce landing craft to carry allied forces to beaches in Europe. There, too, workers went at it night and day.[38] Arthur Irving recalls visiting the site with his father and seeing busy workers building landing craft at all hours. Given the restrictions at home on private automobiles, K.C.'s bus business also saw strong growth, as did his oil and gas business: by the end of the war, K.C. owned about one-third of that business in the region.[39]

There were also bumps in the road for K.C. during the war years. The heavy hand of government in regulating business for the war effort held more than a few challenges. Before the war, K.C. sold pulp to Germans as well as pit props for coal mines. These were leaving Bouctouche on a fairly regular basis, but because Bouctouche Harbour was not deep enough to accommodate large German ships, the pulp and pit props would be loaded onto barges and taken out to meet the German cargo ships anchored in deeper water. One German cargo ship was fully loaded when Canada declared war on Germany in September 1939. The ship immediately pulled away, leaving K.C. unpaid. Dr. Kraemer, the German agent buying the pit props, contacted K.C. a few weeks later asking to meet him in Portland, Maine, where he paid the invoice in full.[40] The United States had yet to declare war on Germany.

Some observers have argued that New Brunswick entrepreneurs, notably K.C. Irving, benefited from the war and made "big" fortunes generated by profits flowing from the war effort.[41] To be sure, K.C. Irving did very well because of the war effort, particularly with the purchase of Canada Veneers. It is important, however, to put things in perspective. The British government was looking for a specific product to build its Mosquito planes, and Canada Veneers provided the answer. The capacity already existed in Saint John, ready to swing into action when the war effort came calling.

Contrast this with Ottawa's directed war effort. It was a case of *deux poids, deux mesures*. When the private sector could not deliver what the war effort required, Ottawa created the capacity by establishing government-owned Crown corporations. Thirty-two Crown corporations were created, all of them in Ontario and Quebec. Crown corporations represented a significant new source of investment, with the potential to generate a great deal of new economic activity. Indeed, they would provide the basis for future development in the manufacturing sector in the postwar years.[42] For example, wartime Crown corporations gave rise to aircraft manufacturers, synthetic rubber producers, and an advanced technology company called Research Enterprises Limited.

Although many of the Crown corporations established during the war were later disbanded, some continued, including Polysar and Canadian Arsenals Limited. Crown corporations served the war effort very well, but they also served in the long run to considerably strengthen Central Canada's manufacturing sector and to make many wealthy investors. And that is not all. The Department of Munitions and Supply made extensive new investments in Canadian industries, but by 1944 only about 3.7

percent of these had been made in the Maritimes, mainly for aircraft and naval repair. In fact, even the bulk of the shipbuilding for the war was carried out elsewhere. Historians now recognize that "C.D. Howe and his bureaucrats favoured the concentration of manufacturing in central Canada,"[43] even though locating certain activities in the Maritime provinces made more economic sense because of geography and the presence of entrepreneurial talent and industrial bases in Saint John and Halifax.[44] This was one time geography should have favoured the Maritime provinces; it was Central Canada, not Halifax or Saint John, that was far from the war theatre.

Ottawa established the war capacity in Central Canada even when military considerations suggested otherwise. After a visit to Canada in 1940, the British Admiralty Technical Mission concluded that "political issues weigh heavily" in military decisions. It underlined the problems with building ships in yards cut off from the Atlantic Ocean for five months, and questioned the need for vessels to make the long trip down the St. Lawrence. American military advisors also came to the same conclusion. The first ten ships built for Britain barely escaped getting trapped in the St. Lawrence in the winter freeze-up, and "required substantial work in the Maritimes before they could risk an Atlantic crossing."[45] The British tried as best they could to convince Ottawa to make Halifax the logical naval headquarters for their Canadian convoys and as the repair centre for the larger vessels. They were not successful.[46] In its first activities report tabled on April 30, 1941, the Department of Munitions and Supply made clear its bias for Central Canada. The Canadian and British governments had committed $484 million to the war effort. Prince Edward Island and New Brunswick received nothing, while Nova Scotia received only $8.7 million, with $3 million of it actually allocated to a Montreal firm to build a floating dry dock for Halifax.[47] I note that the federal government even decided to build Mosquito airplanes in Downsview, Ontario, with K.C. Irving's plywood.

I have often wondered what K.C. Irving would have accomplished had he been born in Southern Ontario or launched his businesses there. To be sure, he would have been helped by gravity in the form of national policies and Ottawa's procurement policies, rather than having to pull constantly against gravity.

LOOKING BACK

K.C. IRVING HAD ENTREPRENEURIAL TALENT *HORS PAIR*, WAS tenacious, was never cowed by bigger and richer competitors, and had an uncanny ability to seize the moment. He outworked everybody and, as Arthur Irving once told me, he was always on top of his game. K.C.'s story is truly one of remarkable success. In the end, Howard P. Robinson, the New Brunswick business tycoon of his day, did not "chase that fellow Irving back to Bouctouche." That fellow from Bouctouche actually bought Robinson's house at 197 Mount Pleasant Avenue, overlooking Saint John. It is where Arthur Irving now lives.

K.C. stood firm against the Great Depression, creating new businesses and expanding existing ones while many small and medium businesses in his sector went out of business. He improvised whenever he had to. Unable to purchase buses, he took the saw to some of his Fords, cut them in two, added seats, and welded them back together, and he was in the bus business. He embraced vertical integration, initially at least, because it was the only way to grow his businesses out of Saint John. Rather than turn to management or economic theories, K.C. trusted his own business instincts. He never backed down when confronting a challenge, an economic crisis, or, as we have seen, when battling bigger foes, such as CNR, Imperial Oil, or Fred Manning.

K.C. did his part in contributing to the war effort, but he was a small player, with virtually all the benefits of the effort going to businesses in Ontario and Quebec. K.C. responded to demands because he had the capacity to do so. In many other cases, the federal government established the capacity to respond to the demands, thus creating new businesses.

In the immediate aftermath of the Second World War, K.C. Irving had an infrastructure in place to grow his businesses, an enviable track record in business, and the financial resources to pursue new economic opportunities or simply lay back and live a life of luxury. K.C., however, was never one to rest on his laurels, as the next chapter demonstrates.

Notes

1 Douglas How and Ralph Costello, *K.C.: The Biography of K.C. Irving* (Toronto: Key Porter, 1993), 34.
2 Ibid., 37.
3 Ibid., 35.
4 Ibid., 36.
5 Ibid.
6 Quoted in Donald J. Savoie, *Harrison McCain: Single-Minded Purpose* (Montreal; Kingston: McGill-Queen's University Press, 2013), 216.
7 Arthur Irving set the record straight in an interview with the author, August 10, 2019.
8 Quoted in Savoie, *Harrison McCain*, 43.
9 Mike Lawson quoted in ibid., 45.
10 Quoted in How and Costello, *K.C.*, 43.
11 Quoted in Russell Hunt and Robert Campbell, *K.C. Irving: The Art of the Industrialist* (Toronto: McClelland and Stewart, 1973), 44.
12 How and Costello, *K.C.*, 139.
13 Quoted in ibid., 53.
14 See John A. Jakle, "The American Gasoline Station, 1920 to 1970," *Journal of American Culture* 1, no. 3 (1978): 520–42.
15 Ibid., 40–1.
16 James Struthers, "Great Depression in Canada," *Canadian Encyclopedia*, July 11, 2013, online at thecanadianencyclopedia.ca/en/article/great-depression.
17 New Brunswick, "New Brunswick Experiences the Depression," in *Pioneers, Ploughs, and Politics: New Brunswick Planned Settlements*, Provincial Archives of New Brunswick, n.d., online at archives.gnb.ca/Exhibits/PlannedSettlements/TextViewer. aspx?culture=en-CA&t=Allardville&p=5of19.
18 Michiel Horn, "The Great Depression of the 1930s in Canada," Historical Booklet 39 (Ottawa: Canadian Historical Association, 1984), 3.
19 Ernest R. Forbes, "New Brunswick," *Canadian Encyclopedia*, April 3, 2008, online at thecanadianencyclopedia.ca/en/article/new-brunswick.
20 John DeMont, *Citizens Irving: K.C. Irving and His Legacy* (Toronto: McClelland and Stewart, 1992), 37.
21 Quoted in How and Costello, *K.C.*, 41.

22 Quoted from an interview Harrison McCain gave to James Downey, February 19, 2001, 12.
23 How and Costello, *K.C.*, 40, 42.
24 DeMont, *Citizens Irving*, 39.
25 How and Costello, *K.C.*, 43.
26 See, for example, Hunt and Campbell, *K.C. Irving*, 45.
27 See, for example, Robert D. Buzzell, "Is Vertical Integration Profitable?" *Harvard Business Review*, January 1983.
28 David J. Teece, "Vertical Integration in the U.S. Oil Industry," in *Vertical Integration in the Oil Industry*, ed. Edward J. Mitchell (Washington, DC: American Enterprise Institute, 1976), 105.
29 John Stuckey and David White, "When and When not to Vertically Integrate," *McKinsey Quarterly*, August 1993, online at mckinsey.com/business-functions/strategy-and-corporate-finance/our-insights/when-and-when-not-to-vertically-integrate.
30 Ken Favaro, "Vertical Integration 2.0: An Old Strategy Makes a Comeback," *Strategy + Business*, May 6, 2015, online at strategy-business.com/blog/Vertical-Integration-2-0-An-Old-Strategy-Makes-a-Comeback?gko=7a868.
31 DeMont, *Citizens Irving*, 42–3.
32 See, for example, How and Costello, *K.C.*, 46–9.
33 Jacques Poitras, *Irving vs. Irving: Canada's Feuding Billionaires and the Stories They Won't Tell* (Toronto: Viking Canada, 2014), 16.
34 Harrison McCain made this comment to me on several occasions.
35 Edward Bishop, *The Wooden Wonder: The Story of the De Havilland Mosquito* (London: Max Parrish, 1959).
36 DeMont, *Citizens Irving*, 45.
37 Quoted in How and Costello, *K.C.*, 62.
38 Hunt and Campbell, *K.C. Irving*, 100–3.
39 "Irving Oil financial results," *Financial Post*, June 19, 1948.
40 Arthur Irving told me this story on several occasions.
41 See, for example, DeMont, *Citizens Irving*, 43.
42 Donald J. Savoie, *The Politics of Public Spending in Canada* (Toronto: University of Toronto Press, 1990), 242–3.

43 Carman Miller, "The 1940s: War and Rehabilitation," in *The Atlantic Provinces in Confederation*, ed. E.R. Forbes and D.A. Muise (Toronto: University of Toronto Press, 1993), 325. C.D. Howe was a powerful minister known as "the Minister of Everything" who served in the Mackenzie King and St-Laurent governments.

44 See, for example, Donald J. Savoie, *Visiting Grandchildren: Economic Development in the Maritimes* (Toronto: University of Toronto Press, 2006).

45 Ernest R. Forbes, ed., *Challenging the Regional Stereotype: Essays on the 20th Century Maritimes* (Fredericton: Acadiensis Press, 1989), 180.

46 Ibid., 181.

47 Ibid., 178.

CHAPTER 3

SAINT JOHN TO STAY: "BECAUSE I LIVE THERE"

K. C. IRVING ONLY KNEW ONE DIRECTION AND ONE speed: fast forward. Given his success with Canada Veneers, he now had the financial resources not only to grow his forestry and oil and gas businesses, but also to launch new ones. It was never his practice to spend on luxury homes or yachts. He decided, from his very first days in business, to reinvest profits into his businesses. Growing his businesses was what motivated him. He often said that the problem with many business owners is that they want to sit back and enjoy success rather than keep growing.[1] That would never be K.C.'s approach.

The Second World War put a damper on some parts of K.C.'s businesses. The oil and gas sector was heavily regulated, which forced K.C. to tread water in growing that side of his business. The military essentially took over the Golden Ball Building to store and maintain equipment. K.C. put his energy into areas where he was free or even encouraged to expand because of the war effort, such as Canada Veneers. He always had highly tuned business instincts—knowing when to grab an opportunity and when to drop a business that had run its course. By the end of the war, for example, he saw that it was no longer economical to build buses, and got out of that business before it was too late.[2]

K.C. also saw at the end of the war that the future was bright for the oil and gas sector, and he decided to pour new resources into that. He asked his cousin and long-time friend Leigh Stevenson to go into the business with him. By then, both cousins had become highly successful, albeit in different fields—K.C. in several businesses and Stevenson in the air force, serving as vice-marshal in charge of Western Air Command and, later, as senior Canadian officer on the staff of Lord Mountbatten, Allied Commander in South East Asia. Stevenson, however, saw that it was not wise to mix family and friendship with business, and declined K.C.'s very generous offer, making the point that his friendship with K.C. was more important than pursuing a business opportunity, however promising. The friendship between the two remained very strong until Leigh Stevenson passed away in 1989.[3]

K.C. was quick to spot talent, as he had with Leigh Stevenson, and he did not hesitate to pay handsomely and then give the person the space to help grow his or her businesses. He also expected in return that senior staff would deliver results. It is worth revisiting how Harrison McCain joined K.C. Irving's oil and gas business. It speaks directly to K.C.'s approach to growing his businesses. He met Harrison McCain with a simple message: he needed "sales help and sales supervisors," insisting that there was a "huge future in the oil business for me and for everybody." He then asked Harrison how much money he was making. Harrison admits that he "stretched the truth," adding expenses and bonuses to his salary. K.C. Irving replied that he would "add substantially" to it if Harrison would take the job.[4] McCain signed on with Irving, where he would learn a great deal about how to run a business. He also demonstrated his ability to negotiate a good deal. Harrison told K.C. Irving: "Give me 10,000 bucks and a big car and I am your man." That was a hefty salary for a young man just two years out of university in 1951 in New Brunswick. Having a big car, in turn, was important to Harrison as a sure sign of success. Though it was an extremely generous salary, it quickly proved to be a very wise investment for K.C. Irving. Harrison McCain became one of Irving Oil's leading salesmen. He came to admire K.C.'s business acumen, his management abilities, and his businesses' public image. According to Jim Coutts, one of Harrison's close friends, K.C. Irving "was the man Harrison most admired."[5]

K.C. Irving knew better than anyone how to push the envelope, how to get his senior managers to deliver that extra effort, and how to outperform even their own high expectations. Harrison claimed that K.C. Irving was not happy if you delivered 95 percent of your objectives—he wanted the 100 percent. One case that Harrison worked on makes this point. He had worked for a long time to secure a contract to supply a large power station with Irving fuel. After eighteen months, he was successful. Delighted, he called K.C. to share the good news. K.C.'s response? He asked Harrison if he had been able to add lubricating grease to the deal.[6] The grease represented only some 4 percent of the deal. The message was not lost on Harrison: 100 percent of the business is better than 96 percent, and a successful business owner always looks into the details of any business deal or business activities.

Harrison McCain once told me that K.C. Irving was a gentleman, a demanding boss who had an uncanny ability to see how things would play out five or ten years down the road, and who understood that if you do not go after the business, someone else always will. Harrison said that K.C. raised plenty of eyebrows when he bought Saint John Sulphite, a small, struggling mill in poor financial health. Few in New Brunswick believed that anyone could turn things around and make a business success out of Saint John Sulphite. To many, it was a case of throwing good money after a bad idea. At the same time, however, K.C. also bought substantial woodland from the province. K.C. was ahead of the pack, and saw the potential in forestry when no one else did. Harrison once said to me, "Call it luck, strategic thinking, or taking a risk. Whatever you call it, you have to know when to pull the trigger, and Irving knew that better than anyone."

Harrison also admired how K.C. Irving managed his public image, because it, along with his reputation, was crucial to his business success. Harrison maintained that, because K.C. Irving rarely gave interviews, people simply believed he had little interest in projecting a public image. Harrison insisted that nothing could be further from the truth. K.C. Irving knew better than anyone the importance of public image in business and how to manage it. Irving cultivated the image of a tough, demanding, shrewd, austere, tireless, sober, no-nonsense businessman, never to be outgunned. "Christ," Harrison explained, "when K.C. Irving walked in to negotiate a business deal, the competition was ready to give up and say I can't compete with this guy. The competitor would lose before the competition began because everyone knew that you could never beat K.C. Irving." Otto Miller, chairman of Standard Oil Company of California (Socal), who knew a thing or two about how to negotiate hard, said: "To negotiate with K.C. Irving is quite an undertaking."[7]

Harrison also admired K.C.'s management style, which he said was based on "suggestion." It is worth quoting him at length on this point:

One, he had a style, he had a style all his own. I've never seen the like of it in all my life. I must have heard him, but I can't recall an example of him ever giving me a direct order, "Harrison, here's what I want you to do on Thursday. Go down and see Jack and do this, this, this and this." Maybe it happened, probably happened, but I can't recall it. Mr. Irving ran the business with his top people by suggestion. His style. He'd make a suggestion that if we had such-and-such an account, that would fit in just exactly what our expenses and our business plans in buying this area, and that would be the cornerstone for a new location. And if we got that, that would convince me that we should go ahead and spend the money and get the damn thing done. If we could just find somebody that could just talk the fellows into swinging that damn deal around. And what that meant was, get your ass out there and get that account.[8]

Harrison also described K.C. as "kind and good fun. We used to have great fun." He added, "He used to sing, you know. We used to be riding in his car late at night, 10 or 11 o'clock at night, going to some goddamn place to see a service station site and, jeez, he'd start singing. He was a fine fellow."[9] Arthur Irving also told me that business trips with his father, while demanding, were also enjoyable—long hours but fun when they unwound at the end of the day.

K.C. Irving's hiring of Harrison McCain and his willingness to give him all the room he needed to help grow the business spoke to K.C.'s approach to management. K.C. saw himself at the centre of his businesses, leading by example. He was the "conductor" or the "maestro."[10] K.C. would always outwork and put in longer hours than anyone who worked for him. Arthur Irving has adopted the same approach to management. Like his father, Arthur pursues business goals with a single-minded purpose, he is competitive, he is demanding and tireless, he has an extremely high level of energy, he expects results, and, also like his father, he is deeply committed to the Maritimes, as we will see later.

K.C., the maestro, led the charge in expanding Irving Oil into more communities in New Brunswick, elsewhere in the Maritimes, and in Quebec in the postwar era. He also decided to initiate a move into the United States, starting with Maine. K.C. saw growth for Irving Oil to the east (Prince Edward Island and Newfoundland), to the west (eastern Quebec), and to the south (Nova Scotia and Maine, and beyond to the rest of New England). K.C. also appreciated the importance of building a solid, well-respected brand and a public relations capacity at head office. He personally made sure that his service stations looked the same and that they all proudly displayed the Irving diamond. He had many catchy phrases to promote his business, and, as we have seen, he recognized the advantages of working with high-profile athletes to promote Irving Oil. He also teamed up with well-known Maritime-born country and western legend Hank Snow.

Snow was born in absolute poverty in a small hamlet in Nova Scotia. His parents divorced when he was eight years old, and he was forced to move in with his paternal grandparents. His grandfather subjected him to both psychological abuse and harsh physical beatings. He often ran away. He eventually found his way back to live with his mother and stepfather. Things did not improve much for him at home. He took on occasional work, including unloading coal ships in Lunenburg, raking scallops, and serving as a cabin boy on a fishing schooner. He saved the necessary $5.95 to buy a guitar from the Eaton's catalogue. He toured the Maritime provinces, playing anywhere he could, at times for a meal, a beer or two, and a bed for the night. I recall my father telling me that Hank

Snow sang and played guitar at one of the local Bouctouche boot-leggers.[11] Snow was a heavy drinker, and he could not always afford a place to sleep at night. On a number of occasions, he found night comfort at an Irving service station.

Hank Snow and K.C. Irving became friends, and the friendship continued with Arthur Irving. K.C. followed his career, proud that a Maritimer struck it big in Nashville. K.C. had Hank Snow open a number of his service stations, including at Aulds Cove, Nova Scotia, in 1985. He sang there on opening day while Irving Oil hot-air balloons floated over the service station.[12] In Nashville, Snow recorded numerous number one hits, including his "I've Been Everywhere," and became one of the best-known country and western stars of the day. In 1954, Snow talked the Grand Ole Opry into inviting a young Elvis Presley to appear onstage. Snow asked Presley to open his act, and he introduced him to Colonel Tom Parker.[13] Snow was later inducted in the Country Music Hall of Fame and the Canadian Music Hall of Fame. Hank Snow never forgot his Maritime roots. Notwithstanding the hard poverty he had to contend with in Nova Scotia, he kept close ties with his home province. He recorded his *My Nova Scotia Home* album in 1968.

Arthur Irving attended the official opening of the Hank Snow Home Town Museum in Liverpool, Nova Scotia, in 1997, as a special guest. Snow was not able to attend because of ill health, but he and Arthur had a conversation for all to hear on the public address system. The museum is lodged in the old Liverpool train station where Snow often found a place to rest for the night. Friends until he died, Snow gave Arthur one of his guitars. Many years later, Arthur gave the guitar to an Irving Oil customer from Bouctouche who not only played guitar, but also was passionate about Hank Snow. I hear from mutual friends that he is very proud of his Hank Snow guitar, and it is unlikely that he will ever part with it.

K.C. Irving also befriended other high-profile Maritimers. He was a keen supporter of Yvon Durelle, the fighting fisherman from Baie-Sainte-Anne, on New Brunswick's north shore. Durelle was an Irving customer, buying Irving products for his fishing boat. Every Maritimer, certainly every Acadian of my generation, remembers the December 10, 1958, match when Durelle fought Archie Moore for the world light heavyweight title at the old Montreal Forum. I was eleven years old, and I was allowed to stay up and watch the fight, which sports columnist Greg Smith—and others—labelled "the standard by which great fights are measured."[14]

One year earlier, I had gone to the old Moncton Stadium with my father to see Yvon Durelle knock out Gordon Wallace, a fighter from Ontario, in the second round to win the British Empire light heavyweight crown. This was no small accomplishment for the "fighting fisherman" from Baie-Sainte-Anne. I also recall everyone in my home village jumping for joy the next day.

On that December 1958 night in Montreal, Yvon Durelle leaped into the ring with Archie Moore with a big heart and strong arms, but little pre-fight training. Mike Dunn, another sports columnist, wrote that "Durelle did most of his 'training' on the job, hauling lobster traps from the frigid waters near Baie-Sainte-Anne." The question was whether he was in good enough shape to last fifteen rounds in the ring against the crafty and well-trained Moore. The thinking was that Durelle needed to get to Moore early, and he did. Early in the first round, Durelle knocked Moore to the canvas three times, and it appeared to everyone that the fight was over. But a controversial "long count" followed one of the times Moore hit the canvas, and he came back to win the fight in eleven rounds. After the fight, Moore had this to say about Durelle: "he hit me harder than I'd ever been hit in my life."[15]

Arthur Irving and his father were at the fight in ringside seats. Douglas How and Ralph Costello have this account of what happened: as K.C. was watching the fight, he heard someone say something derogatory about Durelle. Perhaps, K.C. said, the man would care to go outside and settle it man-to-man. The invitation was declined. Again, one should not view K.C.'s civility as a lack of grit.[16] Arthur told me that he and his father went to Durelle's dressing room afterward to congratulate him for waging a good fight against one of the best boxers of his era. He recalled that Yvon Durelle was in tears. K.C. offered him words of encouragement for the next time and a flight home on his plane.

HARD LESSONS LEARNED

K.C. LEARNED A FEW HARD LESSONS IN GROWING HIS BUSInesses. He saw that the "big boys," whether Imperial Oil or CNR, could play havoc. It will be recalled that he dealt with the challenges by going head-to-head with them, importing refined oil products from other sources in the case of Imperial Oil, and looking to boats and trucks to transport his products in the case of the CNR. The hard lessons would serve him well as he developed a well-honed capacity for the give-and-take of the business world, always with a preference in future for the "give" rather than the "take" or for being on the offensive.

As early as 1945, K.C. began exploring the idea of building a refinery, an idea he had been pondering since he first went into the oil and gas business. Initially, he envisaged a small refinery, only 7,500 barrels a day to supply his service stations. He quickly recognized, however, that he did not have the knowledge to build or operate a refinery or, at the time, the necessary financial resources to go solo on building one, however modest. In short, he required a partner with the necessary capacity and financial resources. The logical choice at the time was Imperial Oil, but the idea never got off the ground for a variety of reasons, mostly having to do with Imperial Oil's wishing to dominate the market while Irving Oil wanted to secure a greater share of the business. However, K.C. was not about to give up.[17] He kept building his oil and gas business one dealer at a time, expanding outward from his New Brunswick base. K.C., his close business associates, and his sons Arthur and Jack Irving were constantly on the lookout for new sites. They pursued opportunities at every turn, community by community, province by province. They would grow the oil and gas business by building new service stations and securing new customers for oil-fuelled home furnaces.

As already noted, K.C. grew his businesses by reinvesting prof-its in them. Arthur Irving does the same today. In addition, K.C. never hesitated to borrow from banks. He said: "I always borrowed a lot of money; I don't really know of a bad bank."[18] Growing his oil and gas business meant a greater appetite for his products, and a greater appetite for products also meant a greater need for sources of supply. By the 1950s he was selling as much oil and gas in the Maritimes as giant Imperial Oil. K.C. knew that eventually he would need a refinery to supply his thousands of outlets. When executives at Imperial Oil threatened to cut off supply at the same time as K.C. started to move into Quebec, he went over their heads to their parent company, Standard Oil of New Jersey (now Exxon). Standard Oil had no problem supplying K.C. with the products he required, but also had no interest in helping K.C. build his refinery so that he could compete against them in eastern Canada or else-where. K.C. would have to look for another suitor.

In the mid-1950s, K.C. initiated discussions with another large multinational, British Petroleum (BP), which sent a number of its officials to visit Saint John to negotiate with him. Subsequently, K.C. went to Montreal to finalize the agreement. Things went well until the very last minute, when negotiations at the Ritz-Carlton Hotel broke down. K.C. explained that they had reached an agreement: "We had the price of crude set. We had the grade set. We had it all worked out."[19] K.C. had a change of mind, however, when he read the agreement BP had drafted for his signature. BP included a clause that gave it the option to acquire Irving Oil when K.C. retired or passed away. BP also wanted to see the refinery built elsewhere than Saint John. BP officials argued that it did not make business, market, or economic sense to build a refinery there, away from both large markets and sources of supply. K.C. made it clear that he would not sign the proposed agreement and was ready to walk away from it. K.C. told BP officials that the two demands were never discussed at earlier meetings, and so it was best to end the negotiations then and there. One BP official asked K.C. to keep the negotiations going and at least look at other possible sites, including Halifax, for the refinery. Puzzled at K.C.'s intransigence, a senior BP official asked him, "Why do you insist on a Saint John site?" His reply: "Because I live there."[20] K.C. stood firm and walked away from the negotiations.

It did not take long, however, for another suitor to come knocking on K.C.'s door: Standard Oil of California, which later became Chevron. In the 1950s, it had a surplus of oil from its wells in the Middle East, and saw a clear economic advantage in building a refinery on Canada's east coast. Arthur does not know how Standard Oil of California became aware that K.C.'s negotiations with BP had broken down, but it clearly saw important advantages in joining forces with Irving Oil. In particular, a new refinery would be able to absorb some of the company's surplus crude from the Middle East. Standard Oil of California saw Irving Oil as complementary to its own business interests; it had no intention of building an infrastructure of retail outlets in Atlantic Canada.

K.C. negotiated essentially the same deal he had almost struck with BP, but he would be free to build the refinery in Saint John and there was no requirement to sell Irving Oil at any point. Standard Oil of California would own 51 percent of the new company called Irving Refining Ltd., while Irving Oil would own 51 percent of the marketing business. The agreement would change over time so that Irving Oil achieved majority ownership. Standard Oil of California would oversee the building of the refinery and provide crude oil and research and management advice, while essentially leaving control of the partnership to K.C. Irving.

At the time Irving Oil was building the refinery, Ottawa announced it wanted to give Alberta oil producers exclusive access to the Canadian market, including east of Montreal.[21] K.C. Irving came out four square against the idea, insisting that Ottawa should not play havoc with the free market and force producers to purchase crude oil at prices higher than what the import market made available. Ottawa also met stiff opposition to the idea in Quebec. The federal government, in the end, decided that the Ottawa River would constitute the boundary for Alberta oil, leaving producers east of the river to purchase crude oil from the international market. K.C would thus be able to continue making inroads into the Quebec market, but the move would inhibit his entry into the Ontario market.[22]

K.C. Irving built his refinery on a large strip of land that he had quietly bought over the years. He kept a very close eye throughout the construction process, from start to finish, paying attention to detail. He had several of his own businesses working on the construction, from Ocean Steel, to Commercial Equipment, to Thorne's Hardware. K.C., whenever possible, also sought to flow business from building the refinery to local firms. A sign was put up on the construction site listing all the firms working on the refinery. Thirty firms were listed, of which K.C. Irving owned seven. It was a huge industrial accomplishment that impressed everyone associated with the oil and gas business, including senior Standard Oil executives.[23] The cost of building the refinery, however, was higher than he had projected, amounting to $50 million.

K.C. Irving officially opened the refinery on July 20, 1960. The opening was widely reported in the media, from New Brunswick dailies to the *New York Times*. There is a photo of opening day with K.C. beaming with pride, standing tall next to his wife and his three sons. The refinery was built to process nearly forty thousand barrels a day and to accommodate future expansion plans. K.C. explained that he had struck "about the best deal I could have made. We've had our difficulties but overall Standard proved to be an excellent partner."[24]

K.C. now had his refinery. Imperial Oil could no longer threaten to cut off supply as it had when he expanded Irving Oil deep into Quebec and New England. Was Saint John the most logical place to build a refinery from a business or economic perspective? At the time, the answer was no, and BP had it right. It would have made more sense to locate it closer to major markets. It is fair to say that, if it were not for K.C. Irving, there would be no refinery in Saint John, New Brunswick. K.C. was the only one who saw Saint John as a logical site for an oil refinery. We know today, however, that Saint John holds advantages that other sites, including Halifax, do not—such as a year-round deepwater port able to accommodate supertankers.

GROWING THE OIL AND GAS BUSINESS

K.C. HAD HIS REFINERY AND A GROWING INFRASTRUCTURE OF retail outlets to sell an expanding array of products. Whenever an opportunity surfaced, he was always at the ready to pounce.

The refinery undertaking led K.C. and his sons to build Canaport, on the Bay of Fundy. The facility proved to be a very wise investment. It enables supertankers from around the world to deliver large quantities of crude to the Saint John refinery year-round. It is important to underline the point that, until about ten years ago, the three sons were participants in all of the Irving businesses. J.K. and Jack had a say in the oil and gas business and Arthur had a say in the forestry and all other Irving businesses.

The refinery now had the capacity and the products for Irving Oil to relaunch an invasion of Newfoundland and to push farther into New England. K.C. and Arthur assembled an aggressive sales team to make certain that the expansion into new markets would stick. How and Costello outline the Irving approach to expansion into Newfoundland in their biography of K.C. Irving.[25] It is worth revisiting the approach in some detail, which speaks to how K.C. and Arthur grew Irving Oil's retail capacity. It also speaks, more generally, to the Irving approach to building the oil and gas retail business.

K.C. Irving hired manager Earl Emeneau, from Lunenburg County, Nova Scotia, to lead the charge. Emeneau spent ten years in Newfoundland building service stations and looking after Irving Oil interests on the island. He hired crews, paying them the going wage, and he reports that K.C. never said a word—"he'd leave it to me." Emeneau's crews built service stations and storage tanks from Corner Brook to Harbour Grace and in several communities in between. With K.C.'s full support, he went head-to-head with Imperial Oil, winning more often than losing choice locations. He worked closely with Arthur Irving, who was never more than a telephone call away whenever a quick decision had to be made, as well as with Charlie Van Horne ("a damned nice fella"), and Harrison McCain ("a live wire"). Emeneau also always had a strong and direct working relationship with K.C. Irving. He described K.C. as "a man you could reason with, a very reasonable man. And no matter how dirty your hand was he'd take it."[26]

Arthur Irving hustled new business in Newfoundland with fishers, fish plant owners, and pulp mills. He pushed and pulled every lever to secure new business, look after existing customers, and outperform the competition. He was as much a live wire as Harrison McCain, and he did not limit his activities to Newfoundland, but pursued new clients in all areas where Irving Oil had a presence.

RUNNING THE REFINERY

K.C., WITH ARTHUR IRVING BY HIS SIDE AND WITH MANAGEment help from Standard Oil of California-Chevron, ran the refinery as smoothly as could be expected. There were only a few hiccups. They built six large storage tanks, the right number to have six letters—I-R-V-I-N-G—highly visible on the sides of the tanks. The six letters remain eye-catching to Saint Johners and visitors to this day.

They now had a ready supply of products for their fast-growing number of service stations. The refinery quickly proved to be a wise investment. In two short years, Irving Oil sales jumped from 6.9 million barrels of gasoline, heating fuel, and other products in 1959 to 12.5 million by 1961.[27] They also had both sides of the business—the goods-producing side and the infrastructure to sell the goods—and were geared to go full speed ahead.

But there was a problem, one with which all refineries in eastern Canada were struggling. Irving Oil was importing crude oil from the Middle East, paying higher-than-world-market rates. The oil giants had decided to harmonize prices so that their Canadian subsidiaries would pay more for crude oil, thus overcharging Canadian consumers. Though it was not a subsidiary of Standard Oil of California, Irving Oil was one in all but name because it had signed a crude supply contract as part of the understanding to build the refinery. By the early 1960s, Irving Oil was overpaying about $1.12 per barrel of crude.

In September 1962, K.C. drafted a letter to the chairman of Standard Oil of California outlining the problem. It speaks to K.C.'s to-the-point style, laying down both the problem in clear terms and the groundwork for a solution. It is worth quoting from the letter at length:

> When we entered into our original contracts we agreed that the prices charged the Oil Company by the Refinery and the Refinery by your company should be computed by a formula based on competitive world prices. In drawing up the contracts your people felt that some misunderstanding might develop if these expressions were used so they suggested that the pricing formulas be based on posted prices. At that time posted prices were true selling prices....Unfortunately, this condition no longer exists. Posted prices are now artificially maintained at the same time that sales are being regularly made at a percentage of these so called posted prices....By using a price formula based on these artificial standards, Irving Oil has been overcharged approximately $13,776,000 in the past eighteen months. We are now placed in the position where the harder we work to develop sales for the oil company and refinery, the greater our loss....We are at

a point where my personal obligations to not only Irving Oil and Irving Refining but to my family make it necessary that I press immediately for a realistic pricing formula instead of an artificial standard which no longer represents true pricing conditions.... If the present trend continues we will bankrupt Irving Oil and Irving Refining and I estimate the personal loss of my family to be close to $15,000/day.[28]

Standard Oil of California did not want to see its partner go out of business, and looked for ways to cut the cost of the crude it was selling to Irving Oil. In addition, by 1969 K.C. would have the upper hand, since the original contract gave him the right to renegotiate prices at that time. The senior vice-president and chief financial officer at Standard Oil of California sat across the table from K.C. and Arthur Irving to negotiate a new arrangement. The senior Standard Oil officials were known to be tough negotiators, but they had met their match. K.C. made it clear at the outset that he wanted a cut of Standard Oil's profits on both the sale of crude and the cost of transporting it from Saudi Arabia to Saint John. There was considerable profit to be made on both. K.C. knew this, while Standard Oil officials were well aware that Irving Oil could walk away and turn to other sources of supply.

It was because of these talks that Otto Miller, the chair of Standard Oil, said: "To negotiate with Mr. Irving is quite an under-taking."[29] Miller, the youngest man to be named a general manager of manufacturing at Standard Oil, was himself no shrinking vio-let when it came to negotiations.[30] Miller wanted a solution that would work for both his firm and Irving Oil. The problem, in a nutshell, was that he did not want to sell crude oil to a Canadian refinery below world market levels. He also did not want profits from the production of crude and transportation to be subject to

Canadian taxes because, he insisted, Canada had nothing to do with either. K.C., meanwhile, was adamant that Irving Oil had a legitimate claim to a share of both the production and transportation profits. If profits were good for one side of the partnership, they should also be good for the other side.

Standard Oil of California came up with a solution. It called on Irving Oil to establish a non-Canadian subsidiary that would purchase crude at a price established in the Persian Gulf plus transportation costs, thus delivering crude at the market price to Irving Oil in Saint John. The offshore subsidiary would flow profits to Irving Oil in the form of dividends. K.C. and his sons carefully went over the details of the proposal before signing on. The deal was done on July 28, 1971, when Irving Oil secured half the shares of Bomag International, a company incorporated in Bermuda. The deal saw Bomag purchase crude at approximately $2.00 a barrel and then sell it to Irving Oil around $3.00 a barrel. As a result, Irving Oil's profits grew handsomely. I note that Bomag later became Irvcal, all the while leaving the process intact.

Irving Oil and Standard Oil of California were hardly alone in setting up an offshore trading company. More to the point, this was no side deal available only to Irving Oil. Standard Oil and Irving Oil did what other large oil firms had done. In addition, both Canadian and US tax authorities were well aware of the workings of the oil firms with their offshore trading companies. Revenue Canada did challenge the arrangement, making the case that Irving Oil was using it to avoid paying its taxes fully. It argued that Irvcal existed to inflate prices and to create inflated profits in order to avoid paying part of its income tax. Irving Oil, for its part, insisted it was a legitimate arm's-length business, that the price paid for crude was competitive and enabled Irving Oil to compete on world markets. The Federal Court ruled that the government had erred when it taxed Irving Oil $142 million. Revenue Canada appealed the decision, but, in a unanimous 3-0 decision, the Federal Court of Appeal ruled in favour of Irving Oil, saying that Irvcal's supply chain was not a sham, that there was no undue or artificial reduction of income, and that Irving Oil did not pay an inflated price to reduce tax but always paid for crude in a fair market value range.[31]

KEEP ON GROWING

K.C. AND HIS THREE SONS DID AS THEY ALWAYS DO WHEN PROFits jump: they reinvested in their businesses to ensure continued growth. No sooner had they signed a new agreement with their Standard Oil partner than they decided to invest large sums in the Saint John refinery and in building new Irving retail outlets.

It will be recalled that the 1970s saw the cost of crude oil go up sharply and then down just as sharply and quickly. The end of certainty in crude oil pricing had arrived. Investors and large oil firms moved very cautiously in the sector. But not Irving Oil. In the early 1970s, K.C. and his sons decided to invest $50 million to double the refinery's capacity and another $15 million in the Canaport deepwater facility to better handle the new supertankers. Their balance sheet was healthy, and they also had no difficulty borrowing both from Canadian banks and the international banking community.

The competition, once again, was convinced that Irving Oil was moving too fast and too big with its expansion plan. The crude oil market was anything but stable and, as John DeMont writes, "it was a gamble. Even the European contractors who worked on the refinery privately mocked the folly of expanding in the face of a worldwide oil glut."[32] But once again, K.C. Irving's business instincts would win the day. By 1977, Irving Oil had Canada's largest refinery, able to process 250,000 barrels of crude a day into a variety of products. It also came up with innovative ways to move products, agreeing to swap products with other firms so that Shell, for example, received its finished products to sell near the Irving refinery while Irving Oil received its products from other refineries, including Imperial Oil's, to sell in Quebec and Nova Scotia.

The big prize for Irving Oil, however, was its ability to expand its retail capacity in New England. The search never stopped for new retail sites in all regions. They pushed farther and farther into New England while never losing sight of possible expansion opportunities in Atlantic Canada and Quebec. With the refinery's capacity to produce 250,000 barrels a day, finding a market for Irving Oil's products was no small task.

The task became even more difficult in the late 1970s, when suddenly the world was awash in oil and gas products. Large firms had also expanded their refineries in the mid-1970s, with the result that capacity was far outstripping demand. By 1979, the Irving refinery was running at half its capacity and profits dropped sharply. Maybe this time the competition had it right and K.C. and his sons had overplayed their hand when expanding the refinery.

But things soon turned around. It will be recalled that the Ayatollah Khomeini led a revolution against the US-backed shah of Iran. The shah left Iran in January 1979 and the royal regime collapsed a few weeks later. The revolution's anti-Western perspective proved highly popular in Iran, and the crude oil market would soon feel the impact, sending shock waves everywhere oil was sold.[33] Crude oil production in Iran dropped by nearly 5 million barrels, or 7 percent of the world's oil production. Oil prices rose sharply from $13 per barrel in 1979 to $34 in 1980. Oil on the spot market sold for as much a $50 per barrel.[34] It was not long before Saudi Arabia and other oil producers decided to increase production.

The demand for finished oil products also surged. The Irving refinery immediately cranked up production after getting calls from all over the world looking to buy finished products. It now had the capacity not only to supply its own service stations, which at the time required eighty thousand barrels a day, but also to meet demand in the world market. Irving Oil sold the rest of its production to the United States, western Europe, Brazil, and as far away as Hong Kong. Irving Oil was now permanently on the world map as a reliable producer of finished petroleum products. Profits jumped exponentially, and once again K.C. Irving and his sons would invest the profits into growing their businesses.

LOOKING BACK

THE OIL AND GAS INDUSTRY IS NOT FOR THE WEAK OF HEART. It is highly competitive and, more than many other businesses, it has to cope with sharp and unpredictable swings in market conditions. Dealing with political crises, balancing supply and demand, and operating a refinery's demanding maintenance needs all require business savvy, financial resources, and nerves of steel. Irving Oil, from the start, has had to deal with sharp swings in profits and industry unpredictability. It has also had to compete against much larger and highly profitable firms.

K.C. Irving had decided, against the advice of industry experts, to locate his refinery in Saint John. K.C. never doubted his decision. Some industry experts also felt it was a mistake to launch an ambitious expansion program at the refinery when the world was awash in oil. Again, K.C. never doubted his decision. Because Irving Oil is a privately held business, it could deal with the ups and downs better than could publicly traded companies. K.C. could ignore the pressure of quarterly reports and shareholders.

He and his sons could do what they wished with the profits. They decided to use the profits to smooth the peaks and valleys of the oil and gas industry and, over time, to grow both their production capacity and their retail infrastructure.

Irving Oil continued to push hard to expand the number of its retail outlets. It never let up. In doing so, the Irvings kept operations lean, avoiding establishing several levels of management. If anyone in Newfoundland or Nova Scotia had an issue or a problem, a quick phone call to the Golden Ball in Saint John would soon sort things out.

One thing remained constant: the Irvings' decision to stick to Saint John and New Brunswick while growing their businesses. K.C. decided to build the refinery because he lived there. As we will see later, Arthur recently decided to build a new head office in Saint John for the same reason.

Notes

1 See, for example, Douglas How and Ralph Costello, *K.C.: The Biography of K.C. Irving* (Toronto: Key Porter, 1993).
2 Ibid., 77.
3 Ibid., 78.
4 Quoted from an interview Harrison McCain gave to James Downey, February 19, 2001, 17.
5 Quoted in Paul Waldie, *A House Divided: The Untold Story of the McCain Family* (Toronto: Viking, 1996), 38.
6 Ibid., 37.
7 Testimony of Otto Miller, as quoted in "Respondent's Memorandum of Fact and Law," in the archives of the Federal Court of Appeal. The federal appeal, *The Queen v. Irving Oil Limited*, is reported as 91 Dominion Tax Cases 5106 (E.C.A.) (Feb. 18, 1991).
8 Downey interview, 18–19.
9 Ibid., 17.
10 Harvey Sawler makes this point in his *Twenty-First-Century Irvings* (Halifax: Nimbus, 2007), 12.
11 Vernon Oickle, *I'm Movin' On: The Life and Legacy of Hank Snow* (Halifax: Nimbus, 2014).
12 Irving Oil, "How did our Big Stop story begin?" n.d., online at irving24.com/en/OurNetwork/BigStops/.
13 Oickle, *I'm Movin' On*.
14 Mike Dunn, "Archie Moore's Most Memorable Triumph," *BoxingScene*, July 23, 2004, online at boxingscene.com/archie-moores-most-memorable-triumph--1448; and Greg Smith, "Moore vs. Durelle 2: The Night Sugar Ray Robinson Got Lucky," *Sweet Science*, June 18, 2005, online at google.com/search?client=firefox-b-d&q=the+night+sugar+ray+robinson+got+lucky.
15 Ibid.
16 How and Costello, *K.C.*, 307.
17 Ibid., 77.
18 Ibid., 88.
19 Ibid., 140.
20 Arthur Irving, who attended the meeting, told me this.

21 Ed Shaffer, "Royal Commission on Energy," *Canadian Encyclopedia*, February 7, 2006, online at thecanadianencyclopedia.ca/en/article/royal-commission-on-energy.

22 How and Costello, *K.C.*, 142.

23 Ibid., 142–3.

24 Quoted in ibid., 141.

25 Ibid., 139.

26 Quoted in ibid., 138.

27 John DeMont, *Citizens Irving: K.C. Irving and His Legacy* (Toronto: McClelland and Stewart, 1992), 119.

28 The letter was reproduced in ibid., 119–20.

29 Waldie, *House Divided*, 234.

30 "Otto N. Miller, 79; former Chevron Corp. chairman," *Los Angeles Times*, February 6, 1988, online at latimes.com/archives/la-xpm-1988-02-06-mn-10542-story.html.

31 *Irving Oil Ltd. v. Minister of National Revenue* (1988), 16 F.T.R. 253 (TD).

32 DeMont, *Citizens Irving*, 125.

33 See, among others, Nikki Keddie, *Modern Iran: Roots and Results of Revolution* (New Haven, CT: Yale University Press, 2006).

34 Samantha Gross, "What Iran's 1979 Revolution Meant for US and Global Oil Markets" (Washington, DC: Brookings Institution, March 5, 2019).

CHAPTER 4

"WE'RE DOING IT ALL FROM NEW BRUNSWICK"

⌒——————————⌒

T HE TITLE OF THIS CHAPTER REFLECTS THE WORDS K.C. Irving said in an interview when asked why he did not move to Alberta and invest early in western oil exploration.[1] Arthur Irving said the very same thing to me on many occasions. Both K.C. and Arthur Irving have a deeply felt attachment to the Maritimes, something that is not always fully appreciated even by many Maritimers.

I have published extensively on economic development from an Atlantic Canadian perspective. As already noted, at the request of former prime minister Brian Mulroney, I also prepared a report to review the federal government's approach to promoting economic development in Atlantic Canada that led to the establishment of the Atlantic Canada Opportunities Agency (ACOA). I have documented, on a number of occasions, the negative impact national policies have had and continue to have on Atlantic Canada. I have also written extensively about the inability of our national political and administrative institutions to accommodate Canada's regional economic circumstances.[2] Unlike all other federations including the United States, Germany, and Russia, Canada does not have an upper house in its political institutions that speaks on behalf of all of the regions.

It is strange, if not unique, for a federation to have political power in its national institutions decided solely on the basis of the number of seats a political party holds in a single body—in the House of Commons in the case of Canada. This, even though Canada is the second-largest country in the world and has at least six distinct regional economies. Russia, the world's largest country, has an effective upper house—the Council of the Federation—that speaks on behalf of its regions. The same is true for other federations, including Australia, which, like Canada, has a Westminster-inspired parliamentary system.

K.C. and Arthur Irving have never hesitated to speak on behalf of their region's economic interests and point the finger at national policies to explain many of the region's economic challenges. Their willingness to stand up for Atlantic Canada, their business acumen, and their ability to pull against gravity explain my admiration for what they have accomplished. Both have made their views known whenever they saw federal government policies inhibiting economic development in our region. More to the point, we have all sung from the same hymn book. Like K.C. and Arthur, I have spoken on behalf of our region throughout my career. Their voices, however, matter much more than mine to far more people because they are responsible for thousands of private-sector jobs in my province and throughout Atlantic Canada.

OTTAWA IS THE PROBLEM

IN NEW BRUNSWICK, IT IS ALL TOO OFTEN THE CASE THAT once a Liberal, always a Liberal, and once a Conservative, always a Conservative. It will be recalled that Premier J.B.M. Baxter decided that K.C. was a Liberal because his father J.D. Irving was a known Liberal Party supporter. K.C. lost business with the provincial government in the early 1930s as a result.

The Liberal Party has held power in Ottawa for nearly sixty of the past eighty-five years. K.C., however, always went to Ottawa as a businessman, not as a Liberal, having learned in the early 1930s that business and politics often do not mix well. He went to Ottawa to pursue business opportunities, but, much more often, to address the negative impact that proposed federal government policies were having on his businesses and on Atlantic Canada. His biographers write that he never felt at home in Ottawa. They add that "he saw Ottawa as an instrument for the projection of the will of central Canada and as a source of difficulties for the Atlantic provinces."[3]

I have had numerous discussions with Arthur Irving over the past ten to fifteen years about business, politics, and Atlantic Canada. I do not know to this day if he is a Liberal or a Conservative. I recall talking with him about someone we both knew and who was a known supporter of the New Democratic Party (NDP). His observation: "He has probably thought long and hard about supporting the NDP. He has his reasons and I respect that." Though it was a private conversation with just the two of us in the room, he did not offer any negative or positive opinion about the NDP or its policies. I have often heard him say kind words about Liberal politicians, including Frank McKenna, and Progressive Conservative politicians, including David Alward. My sense is that party leaders and their policies matter more to Arthur Irving than do political parties.

In short, Arthur Irving looks at things from a business perspective. He has no interest in partisan politics. He, too, sees governments, particularly the federal government, as at times getting in the way of economic development in Atlantic Canada. In economic development and, in particular, in Canadian federalism, history repeats itself. K.C. fought hard for the construction of the Chignecto Canal. Sixty years later, Arthur fought for the Energy East pipeline. One can easily draw parallels between the two initiatives, given that both ended in failure, though both would have generated strong economic growth for the region had they been successfully pursued.

THE CHIGNECTO CANAL

TO MANY MARITIMERS, THE INABILITY OR, RATHER, THE unwillingness of the federal government to construct the Chignecto Canal speaks directly to what is wrong with Canada's national institutions, and makes the case that K.C. had it right when he argued that Ottawa is "an instrument for the projection of the will of central Canada."

We need to go back in history to gain a better understanding of how this came to be. At the time Confederation was being negotiated (1864–67), the railway and canals were the key components of the country's transportation system and economic development infrastructure. Canals in 1867 were viewed as a public good that held importance for both the military and commerce.[4]

Delegates at the Quebec Conference had their favourite projects, starting with those in Ontario and Quebec. Maritime delegates had the construction of the Chignecto Canal at the top of their list. Since railways and canals were the necessary ingredients of the day to establish the circumstances for economic success, the

Chignecto Canal presented enormous potential for the Maritime region. The first suggestion to build a canal across the Chignecto Isthmus, the narrow strip of land that separates Nova Scotia from New Brunswick, was by Jacques de Meulles as far back as 1686. Over the years, twelve major engineering reports and three Royal Commissions looked at the possibility of the 30.5-kilometre canal, and none disputed its feasibility.[5] At the 1864 Quebec Conference, there was an understanding between Canadian and Maritime representatives that the construction of the Chignecto Canal was part of the Confederation deal. There was consensus then, and for another one hundred years, that the Isthmus of Chignecto was a "barrier which has obstructed the full economic development of Canada, particularly that of the Atlantic region."[6]

But things took a different turn soon after Confederation. The building and rebuilding of canals remained a priority of the new federal government in Ottawa. The *Canadian Encyclopedia* explains it this way:

Following Confederation in 1867, inland transportation in Canada was given high priority by the new government. The 1870s and 1880s were years of active canal rebuilding and improvement. The bottleneck locks on the Grenville, the third of the Ottawa River canals, were finally rebuilt; a new Carillon Canal replaced the original canal and the Chute à Blondeau single-lock canal. All the locks on the Lachine and St. Lawrence River canals were rebuilt in this period to standard dimensions....The third Welland Canal, a major rebuilding of the second, was finished by 1887.[7]

Nothing is said about the Chignecto Canal. Yet, until the mid-1960s, Maritime MPs continuously reminded the federal government of the commitments made during the negotiations that led to Confederation. Amos Edwin Botsford, among other MPs from New Brunswick and Nova Scotia, told Parliament that delegates at the Quebec and London deliberations held the Chignecto Canal as an inducement to New Brunswick to agree to Confederation.[8] No one challenged his point.

Though Ottawa committed important resources to the building and rebuilding of canals soon after the country was born in 1867, and though the proposed Chignecto Canal figured in the discussions leading to Confederation, the canal never made it onto the government's to-do list. However, all the other major canals in Central Canada did. To deal with the various demands, the Macdonald government established a Royal Commission in 1870, chaired by Sir Hugh Allan, to look into canal-building and establish priorities.

The Allan Commission divided its recommendations into works of first, second, third, and fourth classes. The first class embraced projects where "the general interest of the Dominion" was evident, and therefore such projects should "be undertaken and proceeded with as fast as the means at the disposal of the Government will warrant."[9] The Chignecto Canal made it to the first-class group. The commission reported: "The evidence submitted points out with remarkable force and unanimity, the necessity of opening a highway for commerce between the Gulf of St. Lawrence and the head waters of the Bay of Fundy through the Isthmus of Chignecto dividing them."[10] The commission turned to expert advice on the feasibility of building the canal. C.S. Gzowski, the commissioner of canals, declared: "Having read all the existing reports referring to this Canal, and given the subject my very best consideration, I am perfectly satisfied that Mr. Keefer's plan is quite practicable, with or without a supply of fresh water; and that a Canal of the dimensions the Commissioners have decided on recommending, can be built for the amount estimated."[11]

All canals, except one, that were part of the Allen Commission's first-class group were quickly built. The Chignecto Canal was the one never built. There is evidence to suggest that the canal got caught up in "conflicts and jealousies" in the Ottawa bureaucracy, and although tenders were called for its construction, it stalled in the Ottawa system. Sitting in Ottawa, one could easily see the importance of the Rideau Canal to the local economy— one only has to look out the window. But things looked a lot blurrier when viewing the Chignecto Canal. For whatever reason, the Chignecto Canal never made it to the drawing board under the Macdonald government.

In 1873 the Mackenzie government came to office, and it allocated funds in its spending estimates for the construction of the Chignecto Canal, but the economic depression of the 1870s forced the government to cut spending, and the canal became a casualty.[12] MPs from the Maritimes did not lose interest in the canal, however, and they kept pushing for its construction for the next ninety years or so.

In response to ongoing pressure from the Maritime MPs, the Mackenzie government appointed another commission in 1875 to inquire into the feasibility of the Chignecto Canal. It is important to underline the point that the 1875 commission was only the second of many other commissions and reports on the canal carried out through to the mid-1960s. All reported that the construction of the canal was possible on "climatic and engineering grounds."[13] There were always reasons, however, not to proceed with the project. Mostly, they had to do with cost, though somehow cost was never a problem for the construction of any of the other canals on the Allan Commission to-do list.

The Maritime provinces decided that they could no longer wait for the federal government to make good on its commitment to build the canal. They asked leading engineer H.G.C. Ketchum to come up with a new proposal and to shop around for additional support. Ketchum raised funds from private sources, and obtained a charter in 1882 to establish the Chignecto Marine Transport Railway Company. The federal government agreed to pay an annual subsidy of $150,000 for twenty-five years on condition the project be in operation within several years. This would enable Ottawa to turn over responsibility for the construction of the Chignecto Canal to the private sector—something it did not do for the other canals on Allan's first-class list.[14]

Ketchum successfully raised funds in the United Kingdom and was able to commit $4 million to the construction of the Chignecto Canal. However, he did not have enough funds to complete the project on time. One of his British investors had to back out of the deal after the crash of the money market in England in 1890 and because some of the firm's investments in Uruguay and Argentina had gone bad.[15] By 1896 Ketchum had raised and spent $3.5 million on the project and had something like 80 percent of the work completed. He required another $1.5 million and about two more months' work to finish the project. The bill to extend the period for Ketchum to secure new funds was defeated in the House of Commons by a single vote of fifty-five to fifty-four.[16] The Senate, as has all too often been the case when dealing with important regional issues, played no role in the decision.

Maritime politicians still would not let the project die. The Maritime economy was continuing to lose ground to Central Canada, particularly at the turn of the twentieth century. One of the reasons for this was the prohibitive cost of moving goods from the Maritimes to a protected market in Central Canada. Many in the region looked to the Chignecto Canal as a solution or as a way for the region to remain competitive.

The rise of the Maritime Rights Movement and repeated calls by Maritime MPs to address the issue led the House of Commons to adopt the following resolution in 1929:

> Resolved, that in the opinion of this House, it is advisable that the government of Canada take immediate steps to further investigate said project as to feasibility, cost of construction, economic and national advantages to be gained by the construction of a ship canal across the Isthmus of Chignecto to connect the waters of the Bay of Fundy with the waters of the Gulf of St. Lawrence and further that the government be urged to make these surveys and investigations with the least possible delay.[17]

Two years later, the Mackenzie King government responded by establishing yet another commission to look into the construction of the Chignecto Canal. The commission tabled its report in the Depression years of the 1930s—not good timing. Regardless, it maintained: "As a result of our extended study we find that physically, the project is feasible."[18] It also concluded that the canal would have no negative impact on the region's fishery.[19]

The commission, however, had a number of reservations. One was cost, which it estimated at between $23 and $38 million, depending on the depth and width of the canal. Another was the canal's impact on Canada's railway system and loss of traffic. The commission reminded the government that the railway system was built at a considerable cost to taxpayers. Furthermore, the government was providing a subsidy to the region to provide railway services under the Maritime Freight Rates Act.[20] Still, the commission considered the possibility of developing water power by harnessing the tides of the Bay of Fundy, and concluded that it was possible to combine navigation and power projects along the canal. But the cost would be very high, adding another $8 million to the total cost of the navigation project.[21] The commission—both chaired and managed from Central Canada—noted that its hearing in the region was "not largely attended and the interest displayed in the inquiry was not extensive."[22]

The commission's staff was drawn from the Ottawa bureaucracy. George W. Yates, the commission's secretary, was the assistant deputy minister in the Department of Railways and Canals. Other staff members came from the department's engineering division. Very few of the members of the commission had any ties to the Maritime region. Arthur Surveyer, an engineer from Montreal, chaired the commission. Other members included David Robb of Amherst, Nova Scotia, and John F. Sowards of Kingston, Ontario. Robb, the lone Maritimer on the commission and who knew the region well, wrote a dissenting opinion, reported here by his colleagues:

> Having had special opportunities to examine not only the previous engineering reports, but to look into the physical features closely as a life-long resident of the locality, he is of the opinion that the Minudie-La Planche route would have considerable advantages over the Missiguash route recommended by the engineers and endorsed by his fellow commissioners....It is his belief that a canal on the Minudie-La Planche route could be built for much less than the present estimate.[23]

The commission did acknowledge that the total cost of building the St. Lawrence—Great Lakes canal amounted to nearly $260 million, much greater than the cost of developing the Chignecto Canal. It explained, however, that, "in the case of the Great Lakes, the canals are a national necessity; in the case of Chignecto a canal would simply be a refinement of present facilities and largely of local significance."[24] It never explained what it meant by a "refinement of present facilities" or how it could separate "national necessity" from "local significance."

This argument made sense to the chair, who was from Montreal, to the second member of the commission, who was from Kingston, and to all the commission's staff, who were from Ottawa. It did not make sense to the lone voice from the Maritimes. Sitting in Ottawa, the St. Lawrence Seaway is a national project while the Chignecto Canal was only a regional project. Sitting in New Brunswick, the Chignecto Canal is a national project while the St. Lawrence Seaway is a regional project designed to benefit Ontario and Quebec. The difference is that Ontario and Quebec have the political clout and bureaucratic influence to decide what is national and what is regional. Atlantic and Western Canada do not, as history has all too often demonstrated.

K.C. TRIES AGAIN

MARITIME POLITICAL AND ECONOMIC LEADERS WERE STILL NOT prepared to throw in the towel on the Chignecto Canal. It will be recalled that infrastructure spending was in vogue in the postwar period. Construction began on the Trans-Canada Highway in 1950. In 1951, Parliament passed the International Rapids Power Development Act to enable Canada to start navigation works on the St. Lawrence River from Montreal to Lake Ontario. In 1954, the St. Lawrence Seaway Authority, a Crown corporation, was established by an Act of Parliament to acquire lands and construct and operate a waterway between Montreal and Lake Erie. In the end, the cost was $470.3 million, with Canada assuming $336.5 of it and the United States $133.8 million. In 1959, the St.

Lawrence Seaway was completed, establishing a link between the Great Lakes and global markets.[25] Other initiatives were later launched, including a realignment of the Welland Canal to bypass the city of Welland, at a cost to Canada of another $300 million. Canada and the United States spent an additional $600 million on hydroelectric development.[26] These developments all had a negative impact on Maritime ports, notably Halifax and Saint John.

Corey Slumkoski has written that the St. Lawrence Seaway once again sparked interest in the construction of the Chignecto Canal. Like the Seaway, the canal could also provide a new source of hydroelectric power for the region by harnessing the Fundy tides. Studies showed that the canal would also shorten shipping routes between the continental interior and the eastern seaboard of the United States by some 640 kilometres.[27] Maritimers looked to past "massive" government investments in canals in Ontario and the St. Lawrence Seaway—all funded by "federal coffers"— and asked why government investments could not be committed to the Chignecto Canal as well. The view from the Maritimes was that federal government spending continued to be earmarked for projects of "national importance" as defined by Ottawa.[28]

Maritimers were paying careful attention to what Ottawa was doing in Central Canada and not doing in their region. C.C. Avard, editor of the *Sackville Tribune-Herald*, wrote, "Ontario has its canals, why not the Maritimes?"[29] New Brunswick MP Alfred J. Brooks rose in the House on June 9, 1948, to make the point that "it was all very well for Ontario to have pleasure excursions, scenic beauty and places for the boys to go swimming, but we in the maritime provinces are asking for canals which would be of some benefit to the maritime provinces and to the whole of Canada."[30] Progressive Conservative MP Percy Black from Nova Scotia declared: "The members of this house are not averse to spending $500 million in order to build the St. Lawrence canal, but Nova Scotia, Prince Edward Island and New Brunswick are given the brush off."[31]

Local business and community leaders established a Chignecto Canal Committee to promote the project,[32] and commissioned studies to make the case for the canal before the federal government. Support for the committee's work came from many quarters in the four Atlantic provinces, starting with the two adjoining communities—Sackville, New Brunswick, and Amherst, Nova Scotia—as well as local boards of trade, and leading businessmen from the region, notably K.C. Irving.

Local business leaders made the case that national tariffs and trade barriers made it difficult for them to sell their products in Central Canada and international markets. Arthur Irving told me that K.C. made the point that Maritimers had to push their products "uphill" to markets in Central Canada, while businesses in Central Canada had only to nudge their goods downhill to the Maritime provinces. The Chignecto Canal Committee argued that all sectors of the Atlantic economy would benefit from the canal: essentially, the canal would establish the required circumstances for economic success in the region, much like the St. Lawrence Seaway was doing in Central Canada.

The committee also noted the canal would generate new activities around large zinc and copper deposits in northern New Brunswick and in the forestry, fishery, coal, and manufacturing sectors. Since transportation disadvantages to the eastern seaboard of the United States and to markets in Central Canada would be considerably attenuated, the region's economic performance would substantially improve. This, combined with new sources of energy, would provide important economic benefits not only to the three Maritime provinces but also to Newfoundland and even Quebec and Ontario. K.C. Irving alone pledged to invest $100 million—about $815 million in 2019 dollars[33]—in new economic activities in the Bay of Fundy area alone if the canal was built.[34]

Given past experience, the committee was also careful to highlight benefits that would flow to Central Canada. The canal, it argued, would also open up new markets for Ontario- and Quebec-based businesses by cutting shipping costs between Central Canada and the eastern seaboard of the United States. The committees reminded Ottawa that, out of the ten surveys of the Chignecto Canal since Confederation, "all" had agreed that it "was feasible."[35] It reminded Ottawa that the 1870 Allan Royal Commission had divided its recommendations into works of first, second, third, and fourth classes, and that the first class included "all those works" that were in "the general interest of the Dominion" and should be "proceeded with as fast as the means" will warrant. As already noted, the Chignecto Canal was one of twelve placed in the first category.[36]

The committee listed, in detail, the benefits flowing from the Chignecto Canal:

1) The Chignecto Canal would provide a passage for ships between the Fundy Bay and Northumberland Strait areas, at a cost estimated by Foundation of Canada Engineering Corporation Limited at approximately $90 million.

2) The Canal would be the direct cause for the investment of over $105 million in new industries in the Fundy area....The stimulus this new investment would give to regional industry makes the Chignecto Canal a primary major development project of the Atlantic region. New plants constructed as a result of the existence of the Chignecto Canal would result

in a permanent increase in annual production of the Atlantic Provinces estimated at $280 million.

3) The construction phase of the Canal could result in a temporary increase of $300 million in Canadian incomes, of which $160 million might be spent in the Atlantic Provinces.

4) The net cost to Canada of this step to relieve the depressed conditions of the Atlantic Provinces could be more than counterbalanced by increased revenues from the region.

5) The Canal would be a natural extension of the St. Lawrence Seaway, linking it with a sheltered route for Atlantic coastal shipping. For the new waterway a laker-type boat could be used which would be cheaper to build and to operate than the ships normally used in ocean travel.

6) It appears probable that the very large tidal power potential of the eastern portion of the Bay of Fundy will be economically developed in the future. This can be achieved without conflict with the construction and operation of the Canal.

7) The Surveyer Royal Commission reported favourably on the project in the 1930's on climatic and engineering grounds, but, influenced by the depression, it recommended that construction of the Canal should stand in abeyance until more favourable conditions prevailed. Both the construction of the St. Lawrence Seaway and the present economic advantages of the Canal combine to make the project highly desirable now to aid the depressed economies of the Atlantic Provinces.[37]

As we know, Ottawa did not buy the committee's arguments. Lionel Chevrier, the powerful transport minister from Quebec, made clear his opposition to Chignecto at every opportunity. If the responsible minister—particularly one with Chevrier's influence—representing a province that was also home to the prime minister did not support a project that came under his jurisdiction in the 1950s (and before governing from the centre became how things work in Ottawa), the chances of the project's seeing the light of day were slim.[38] Chevrier was convinced that the Chignecto Canal would take away from his St. Lawrence Seaway project, and he embraced all arguments against the canal, insisting that the cost was too high.[39]

To add insult to injury, the federal government in the 1980s cancelled a $500-million-plus debt of the St. Lawrence Seaway, which never paid its way.[40] To a Maritimer, money is never an issue when it comes to building infrastructure in Central Canada, but it always is to Quebecers and Ontarians when it comes to the Maritime provinces, particularly when it might run counter to the economic interests of Central Canada.

K.C. Irving was told in a private conversation with leading federal politicians that, if re-elected, they would support the building of the Chignecto Canal. C.D. Howe also told him that in 1957, shortly before the Louis St-Laurent government fell.[41] John Diefenbaker told him the same story before his government fell in 1963.[42] Politicians tend to find it a great deal easier to make political commitments on the campaign trail than behind their desks once an election has been won and trade-offs have to be made—trade-offs that could offend the heavily populated provinces of Ontario and Quebec.

K.C. did everything he could to see the Chignecto Canal built. He gave a talk before the Board of Trade on the issue, something he very rarely did. The cost, according to engineers, would amount to $90 million, a modest amount compared to the St. Lawrence Seaway. For K.C., the lesson learned was that Ottawa will always look after the economic interests of Central Canada before those of Atlantic Canada. The Chignecto Canal might well have been a precursor of the proposed Energy East pipeline. The battle that K.C. fought in the late 1950s for the canal would look a lot like the battle Arthur Irving would fight sixty years later for Energy East.

ARTHUR AND ENERGY EAST

FRANK MCKENNA, ONCE NEW BRUNSWICK'S PREMIER AND later a successful Bay Street banker and insider, has never forgotten his Maritime roots. He was one of the first to voice his support for building or extending a pipeline to connect the oil-producing fields in Alberta to Canada's largest oil and gas refinery in Saint John. Others in Western and Atlantic Canada were quick to jump on the bandwagon.[43] McKenna and other Energy East supporters, including New Brunswick's two main political parties, saw it as a win-win situation for Canada, particularly for Western and Atlantic Canada.

The Energy East pipeline was to cost $12 billion (in 2014 dollars) and run from Alberta to New Brunswick over a 4,600-kilometre route.[44] The pipeline would open new markets for western Canadian oil producers by connecting them not only to New Brunswick but also to markets in India, China, Europe, South America, and Africa. Saint John is one of Canada's major ice-free deepwater ports. It is also the shortest route by sea to deliver western Canadian crude to India and points in between. Energy East would also replace much higher-priced imports from the Middle East and Africa with Alberta crude. Because Alberta producers do not have access to deepwater ports, it makes Alberta one of the world's cheapest sources of crude oil.[45] A senior executive with TransCanada Corporation explained that, "with one project, Energy East will give Alberta's oil sands not only an outlet 'to eastern Canadian markets but to global markets'...with a 1.1 million barrel per day pipeline, which will go a long way to removing the spectre of those big differentials for many years to come."[46] In short, it would be a win for Alberta, a win for New Brunswick, and a win for Canada because it would open up new markets for Alberta crude, thus generating jobs for Western and Atlantic Canadians and tax revenues for the federal and provincial governments.

Arthur Irving made it clear at every opportunity that "nothing would please us more than to get Alberta oil in bigger quantities than we are getting now....Alberta needs it, Ottawa needs it, New Brunswick is all behind it."[47] He could also have pointed out that the Progressive Conservative government and the Liberal opposition had passed a unanimous resolution in the New Brunswick legislature in support of Energy East. The proposed pipeline would replace much of the 550–600,000 barrels of offshore imported oil used every day in Eastern Canada with western Canadian oil. To signal its firm support for Energy East, and after weeks of negotiations, Irving Oil agreed to a fifty–fifty joint venture with TransCanada to build a terminal near the Saint John refinery. Irving Oil immediately began to spend money on plans for the terminal. It was also committed to invest another us$300 million to build it.

To be sure, Energy East would give Irving Oil less expensive access to crude, but it held other promises. Jeff Matthews, a senior Irving Oil executive, said that Energy East would open up a number of new "opportunities" not only for Irving Oil, but also for a number of firms in Western Canada.[48] As K.C. had done when the Chignecto Canal was under review, Arthur Irving made the point that the Energy East pipeline would give rise to a number of new economic development possibilities throughout Atlantic Canada. He made it clear that Irving Oil was prepared to do its part in pursuing these opportunities by investing in a series of new initiatives.

Energy East, however, would soon run into problems, and died while still in the planning stages.[49] In October 2017, TransCanada decided to drop plans for the Energy East pipeline, pointing to changed conditions for its decision. Many looked to Ottawa and politics, however, for an explanation. Jeffrey Jones explains that "[t]he National Energy Board review process was a tragedy of errors, with proceedings having to be rebooted with a new panel after members of the first one were discovered to have attended ill-advised meetings with TransCanada lobbyists."[50] New conditions were also later introduced to guide the review process, including adding upstream and downstream emissions. Thus, greenhouse gas emissions created both by extracting oil before it flows in the pipeline and by refining and burning after it leaves the pipeline would need to be evaluated. That effectively killed the project. The federal government could have intervened, but it decided not to.

The Justin Trudeau government had political problems with the Energy East pipeline project, at least in part because vote-rich Quebec had problems with the project, which did not square with the province's economic interests. Rather, the main beneficiaries would be Alberta, Saskatchewan, and New Brunswick. Saskatchewan premier Brad Wall urged Montreal mayor Denis Coderre to support the Energy East project, making the case that it was in the interest of the national economy and that it would generate revenues for governments at all levels. But Coderre dismissed Wall's position out of hand, tweeting "the respective populations of metropolitan Montreal versus Saskatchewan: four million compared to 1.13 million,"[51] effectively suggesting that premiers from smaller provinces and regions other than Ontario and Quebec have little standing in Ottawa. No mayor or elected politician from a large city or state in a federation with an effective upper house would be able to argue such a point with any hope of making it stick. But things are different in Canada, and there is little in our national political institutions to counterbalance the political clout of Ontario and Quebec. More to the point, Ottawa did not want to take on Quebec, for political reasons.

Alberta and New Brunswick politicians reacted strongly to the decision not to pursue the Energy East pipeline. Prime Minister Trudeau, however, was quick to evoke national unity concerns, and accused proponents of Energy East of "stoking national divisions."[52] Trudeau said nothing to Mayor Coderre about his response to Premier Wall's plea to support the pipeline. Trudeau and his close political advisers can count: Quebec has seventy-eight seats up for grabs while Alberta and New Brunswick combined have only forty-four. Three leading Quebec pollsters warned the Trudeau government that a "yes" to the Energy East project could create a perfect storm in the province, arguing that not only would it make winning the 2018 provincial election difficult for the Liberals; it could also "lead to a resurgence for sovereignty in Quebec."[53] Atlantic and Western Canada learned once again that national unity concerns are always about Quebec; they can never be about their regions.

Many in Western Canada insist that the Trudeau government does not give pipeline issues the attention they warrant. According to Gary Mason, "in the West, the pipeline is the biggest issue, one now enveloped in generations-old complaints. If the aggrieved party was Quebec, instead of Alberta, this matter likely would have been solved by now. (Mostly by ensuring Quebec got whatever it wanted). At least, that is the sentiment this clash has sown west of Ontario."[54] Mason could have added that this view is also widely shared in Atlantic Canada.

The perception is that Quebec, in the name of national unity, has held the sword of Damocles over the rest of Canada. Mathieu Bouchard, senior policy adviser to Justin Trudeau, explains: "If Quebeckers don't feel represented by the government for a period of time, unlike in other provinces, it becomes a question of national unity. We always have to be conscious of the fact."[55] According to Bouchard, that logic only applies to Quebec. He does not explain on what basis he could make the point "unlike in other provinces" or why the logic applies only to Quebec.

At the same time that TransCanada announced it was cancelling the project, in October 2017, it said it would write down about $1 billion in costs tied to the pipeline project.[56] Irving Oil also announced that it would write down costs of over $10 million from the US$300 million commitment it had made to build the terminal designed to receive crude from the Energy East pipeline.

It is difficult for most Maritimers, including politicians from both major political parties, to understand why Ottawa did not aggressively support the proposed Energy East pipeline. The reality is that pipelines do not promote a greater consumption of oil-based products—they simply change the source of the supply of crude. If not from Western Canada, oil products need come from somewhere else, notably the Middle East. It is worth repeating the point that the Energy East pipeline would have replaced crude imported from Saudi Arabia and elsewhere with crude produced in Alberta and Saskatchewan.

Jacques Poitras, in *Pipe Dreams*, outlines the advantages of Energy East. He points out that Saint John is home to a natural deepwater port capable of accommodating the world's largest supertankers, giving them economies of scale, and is also home to Canada's largest oil refinery. In addition, New Brunswick wanted the project. The pipeline would have created three thousand jobs in New Brunswick over nine years.[57] But that is not all. Pipelines are a great deal safer than other forms of transportation for moving crude, as Canada discovered in 2013 at Lac-Mégantic.

In the end, Arthur Irving and the New Brunswick government were no more successful in getting Ottawa to commit to Energy East than K.C. Irving and the New Brunswick government had been in getting Ottawa to move on the Chignecto Canal. Ottawa had no problem, however, approving the construction of a second pipeline linking Alberta to the coast of British Columbia. Ottawa even took the extra step of paying $4.5 billion to buy the Kinder Morgan pipeline.[58] Contrast this with Energy East, where the private sector was prepared to build all of the needed infrastructure without government funds. The difference between the two is political: Quebec and its seventy-eight seats are not in the way of the Kinder Morgan pipeline.

LOOKING BACK

SAY WHAT YOU LIKE ABOUT K.C. AND ARTHUR IRVING, BUT NO one can accuse them of playing the victim card. They are both hard-nosed businessmen. Both competed and won in a highly competitive setting in Canada, in New England, and in Ireland. They do not look for excuses when things go wrong—they simply get on with fixing them. As Arthur Irving says, "don't be worried, be concerned."

Like K.C., Arthur always has more important things to do than engage in conspiracy theories or come up with reasons to explain why things do not turn out as planned. Father and son simply learned to pull against gravity and win. This, while recognizing, as K.C. explained, that Ottawa is "an instrument for the projection of the will of Central Canada and as a source of difficulties for the Atlantic provinces."[59] K.C. summed things up nicely when he observed: "When these national—or federal—policies are changed, then the economy of the province of New Brunswick will change."[60] Arthur Irving has said the same thing to me and to others on many occasions.

All the more remarkable that they have been able to grow successful businesses capable of competing on two continents, all the while pulling against gravity. They also decided to stay in New Brunswick, to locate their head office in the province, and to build an oil refinery in Saint John, which has been described as "an unlikely place to build an oil refinery and marketing power-house."[61] The decision to remain and grow their businesses in New Brunswick is based not on economics, but on the fact that "they live there."

The point of this chapter is to make the case that, as K.C. was, Arthur Irving is a deeply committed Maritimer, always on the lookout to expand his businesses and generate economic development in his home province. Both were prepared to commit resources to economic development initiatives, provided that the federal government invested in infrastructure to support these initiatives—like the Chignecto Canal or, in the case of Energy East, at least give the green light for the private sector to build the infrastructure and pay for it. In both cases, Ottawa did nothing. In the case of the Energy East pipeline, one can only conclude that Ottawa would rather see Canada export crude at a cheap price than refine it in Saint John and continue to import crude from as far away as the Middle East. This, in turn, requires supertankers travelling nearly ten thousand kilometres. I am at a loss to understand how this is better for the environment or the economy.

Notes

1   Quoted in Jacques Poitras, *Irving vs. Irving: Canada's Feuding Billionaires and the Stories They Won't Tell* (Toronto: Viking Canada, 2014), 19.
2   See, for example, Donald J. Savoie, *Looking for Bootstraps: Economic Development in the Maritimes*, (Halifax: Nimbus, 2017).
3   Douglas How and Ralph Costello, *K.C.: The Biography of K.C. Irving* (Toronto: Key Porter, 1993), 131.
4   See, for example, Robert F. Legget, "Canals and Inland Waterways," *Canadian Encyclopedia*, last edited March 4, 2015, online at thecanadianencyclopedia.ca/en/article/canals-and-inland-waterways.
5   Donald E. Armstrong and D. Harvey Hay, *The Chignecto Canal* (Montreal: Economic Research Corporation, April 1960), 6; and Chignecto Canal Committee, *The Story of the Chignecto Barrier* (Sackville, NB, 1950).
6   Ibid., 5.
7   See, for example, Legget, "Canals and Inland Waterways."
8   Chignecto Canal Committee, *Story of the Chignecto Barrier*, 14.
9   Armstrong and Hay, *Chignecto Canal*, 6.
10 Canada, *Sessional Papers: Fourth Session of the First Parliament of the Dominion of Canada* (Ottawa: I.B. Taylor, 1871), 79.
11 Ibid.
12 See Chignecto Canal Committee, *Story of the Chignecto Barrier*, 8.
13 See Armstrong and Hay, *Chignecto Canal*, 5.
14 See Chignecto Canal Committee, *Story of the Chignecto Barrier*, 13.
15 Ibid.
16 Ibid, 6. For a contrary view, readers should consult C.R. McKay, "Investors, Government and the CMTR: A Study of Entrepreneurial Failure," *Acadiensis* 9, no. 1 (1979): 71–94. McKay maintains that the Ketchum proposal did not make economic sense.
17 Canada, *Report of the Chignecto Canal Commission* (Ottawa: Printer of the King's Most Excellent Majesty, 1939), 16.
18 Ibid., 5.
19 Ibid., 11.
20 Ibid., 9.
21 Ibid., 11.
22 Ibid.
23 Ibid., 12.
24 Ibid., 10.

25 "Seaway History," *Great Lakes St. Lawrence System*, n.d., online at greatlakes-seaway.com/en/seaway/history/index.html.

26 Gordon C. Shaw and Viktor Kaczkowski, "Saint Lawrence," *Canadian Encyclopedia*, February 17, 2009, online at thecanadianencyclopedia.ca/en/article/st-lawrence-seaway.

27 Corey Slumkoski, *Inventing Atlantic Canada: Regionalism and the Maritime Reaction to Newfoundland's Entry into Canadian Confederation* (Toronto: University of Toronto Press, 2011), 97.

28 Ibid.

29 G.S. Gzowski, quoted in ibid., 99.

30 Ibid.

31 Ibid.

32 Members of the committee included Mayor N.S. Sanford, G. Fuller, and A.R. Lusby of Amherst, NS, and Mayor H.A. Beale and E.R. Richard of Sackville, NB.

33 How and Costello, *K.C.*, 133–4.

34 Armstrong and Hay, *The Chignecto Canal*, 5.

35 Chignecto Canal Committee, *Story of the Chignecto Barrier*, 15.

36 Ibid., 8.

37 Armstrong and Hay, *Chignecto Canal*, 5.

38 I outline how the approach works in Donald J. Savoie, *Governing from the Centre: The Concentration of Power in Canadian Politics* (Toronto: University of Toronto Press, 1999).

39 Chevrier could make the point that the premier of Nova Scotia never publicly supported the Chignecto Canal proposal. See, for example, Slumkoski, *Inventing Atlantic Canada*, 105.

40 How and Costello, *K.C.*, 135–6.

41 Ibid., 129.

42 Author's consultations with Arthur Irving, various dates.

43 See, among many others, "How Alberta's oil patch teamed up with the 'little guys' for an end run around Obama," *Financial Post*, October 7, 2014, online at business.financialpost.com/commodities/energy/energy-east-keystone.

44 Jillian Bell, "Energy East pipeline: What you need to know," CBC *News*, January 26, 2016, online at cbc.ca/news/business/energy-east-pipeline-explained-1.3420595.

45 Jeff Lewis, "The Hub: Saint John end point of 'Energy East' readies for crude revolution," *Financial Post*, November 9, 2013, online at business.financialpost.com/commodities/energy/the-pipeline-that-could-turn-canadas-oil-diet-on-its-head.

46 Quoted in "How Alberta's oil patch teamed up with the 'little guys' for an end run around Obama."

47 Arthur Irving, quoted in Claudia Cattaneo, "Playing the piper," *National Post*, n.d., online at business.financialpost.com/playing-the-piper-in-an-exclusive-interview-arthur-irving-the-spotlight-shy-head-of-irving-oil-makes-the-case-for-energy-east-a-project-he-believes-isnt-just-good-for-his-company-but.

48 Ibid.

49 See Jacques Poitras, *Pipe Dreams: The Fight for Canada's Energy Future* (Toronto: Penguin Random House, 2018).

50 Jeffrey Jones, "Energy East pipeline: Best-laid backup plan goes awry," *Globe and Mail*, October 5, 2017.

51 "Montreal-area mayors' Energy East criticisms 'short sighted,' Notley says," CTV *News Atlantic*, January 22, 2016.

52 "Trudeau warns against 'national divisions' after Energy East pipeline decision," *Huffington Post* (Canada), October 7, 2017, online at huffingtonpost.ca/2017/10/07/trudeau-pipeline-decision_a_23236202/.

53 Jean-Marc Léger, Jacques Nantel, and Pierre Duhamel, *Cracking the Quebec Code: The 7 Keys to Understanding Quebecers* (Montreal: Juniper, 2016); and Derek Abma, "Quebec sovereignty could be ignited by pipeline decision, PQ win, says Léger," *Hill Times*, October 17, 2016, online at hilltimes.com/2016/10/17/quebec-sovereignty-ignited-pipeline-decision-pq-win-says-author/83985.

54 Gary Mason, "Why a pipeline could cost Justin Trudeau the next election," *Globe and Mail*, April 13, 2018, online at theglobeandmail.com/opinion/article-why-a-pipeline-could-cost-justin-trudeau-the-next-election/.

55 Daniel LeBlanc, "Trudeau adviser Mathieu Bouchard more than just PMO's Quebec guy," *Globe and Mail*, January 29, 2016, online at theglobeandmail.com/news/politics/globe-politics-insider/trudeau-advisor-mathieu-bouchard-more-than-just-pmos-quebec-guy/article28469010/.

56 Warren Mabee, "What really sank the Energy East pipeline?" *Canada's National Observer*, October 20, 2017, online at nationalobserver.com/2017/10/20/analysis/what-really-sank-energy-east-pipeline.
57 Poitras, *Pipe Dreams*, 8.
58 See, among others, "Kinder Morgan pipeline: Canadian government to buy project for $4.5 bn," *Guardian*, May 29, 2018, online at theguardian.com/world/2018/may/29/canada-kinder-morgan-pipeline-trans-mountain.
59 How and Costello, *K.C.*, 131.
60 K.C. Irving, quoted in "The Unknown Giant K.C. IRVING," *Maclean's*, April 18, 1964.
61 Quoted in Cattaneo, "Playing the piper."

CHAPTER 5

"GET TO WORK"

A RTHUR AND HIS TWO BROTHERS LEARNED ALL ABOUT business at a very early age. They went into business even before they were teenagers, under the watchful eyes of their father and their mother, Harriet Irving (née MacNarin). As is so often the case with mothers not getting the credit they deserve, Harriet Irving, by all accounts, was a model mother to the three boys and a model spouse to K.C. Irving.[1] Everyone who had any contact with her says she was a rock for both K.C. and her children.[2] Arthur Irving speaks only in glowing terms about his mother and her influence on his development. Douglas How and Ralph Costello write that K.C. and Harriet had a particularly strong marriage. Both were from small-town Kent County. K.C. often said that they never even had a quarrel and that she was an important factor in his business success.

Harriet Irving always kept a close eye on her three sons and, according to How and Costello, "they idolized her." She made sure they attended the local Presbyterian church. She helped the three boys with their businesses or other ventures. She once called a local Irving retail store during one of their summer visits to Bouctouche and asked the manager if he had telephone wire for her three boys because they wanted to string a wire to a neighbour's house. He did and quoted the price. She told him she was "afraid the boys would find it too high." The manager was able to find second-hand telephone wire at a much cheaper price. She told him "the boys would be delighted."[3] Evidently, the boys learned at a very young age the importance of saving a penny whenever they could.

Arthur Leigh is the second-born child. He is named after K.C.'s close childhood friend, Arthur Simpson, from Miramichi, New Brunswick, and his cousin and lifelong friend, Leigh Stevenson. Psychologists have sought to explain how birth order shapes personalities. Kevin Leman, in his *Birth Order Book*, argues that, once a role is filled by the first-born, the second-born will seek out a role that's completely the opposite.[4] Frank Sulloway maintains, in his widely quoted *Born to Rebel: Birth Order, Family Dynamics, and Creative Lives*, that second-borns handle disappointment well, have realistic expectations, tend to be highly independent, and are the least likely to be spoiled. He also explains that middle-borns are the most willing to wheel and deal.[5] Arthur never gave me the impression that he was much concerned about where he stands in the birth order. Growing up, and well into adulthood, he was very close to his younger brother Jack. He also tells me that he worked very well with both Jack and J.K.

As is well known, the brothers decided to go their separate ways in business. While working on this book, and unprompted, Arthur told me: "In business and in families, sometimes things go off the rails." In all my conversations with him, Arthur never had a bad word to say about his two brothers. Things went off the rails in business but not in their personal relationship. I note that, like the great majority of academics, I have a narrow focus on our field of research, admittedly too narrow in the eyes of many. In any event, I have never had much interest in family issues, no matter the family. It was the case when I wrote the book on Harrison McCain, and it is now, writing about the Irvings.

My discussions with Arthur Irving have always been about Irving Oil—how it began and its growth, his and Irving Oil's contributions to our region, and, occasionally, about politics, public policy, his ties to Bouctouche, and sports. I did not know his brother Jack well, and met him only a few times. I do know J.K., though not well. I know his son J.D. Irving better, as well as his grandson, Jamie Irving. J.D. and I have had many discussions over the years—always about business, politics, and public policy. He has never had a bad word to say to me about his uncle "Art."

Leaving aside Sarah and, to a lesser extent, his son Arthur Leigh, I do not know Arthur's other children. Kenneth was responsible for the business until 2010, when he retired for health reasons. I met Kenneth on several occasions at conferences and at a meeting in Ottawa we both attended. My conversations with Kenneth were also always about business and government, never about family matters. I always found him to be very polite, pleasant, and engaging in our conversations. In brief, though I do not know Kenneth well, he proved to be an easy person to like whenever we met. Arthur Leigh Jr. ran the real estate side of Irving Oil, until he decided to move on to other opportunities. The family member who plays a key leadership role at Irving Oil today is the daughter of Arthur and Sandra, Sarah Irving.

As noted earlier, my friendship with Arthur dates back only about fifteen years, so I have very little knowledge of Arthur's business or personal relations before that. I draw on published material and interviews for this period. In this chapter, I want to understand how Arthur learned the business from his father and how both went about growing it. I look at some major developments in the business when each of them was at the helm of Irving Oil.

LEARNING THE WAYS OF BUSINESS EARLY

THE THREE BOYS, AT A VERY YOUNG AGE, SOLD MAGAZINES SUCH as *Maclean's*, *Ladies' Home Journal*, and *The Saturday Evening Post* door-to-door to earn money. They did this not because their parents insisted, but because they wanted to make money on their own, much like their father did when he was young.[6] They also went into the egg business, buying a dozen hens and selling eggs in the neighbourhood. They later sold the hens after placing an ad in the local newspaper, and learned that advertising works.[7] Between the ages of eight and twelve, the boys expanded their chicken-selling business to Bouctouche and Moncton. They took care of their hens in Bouctouche in the summer months, and sold the hens at the market in Moncton or to a local grocer. They grew their business to the point where they had 150 chickens.

They learned a crucial business lesson from their father at a very young age: the importance of providing top service to customers. How and Costello report that K.C. Irving arrived home one day and saw two dozen eggs on the kitchen table. It was New Year's Eve. K.C. woke up one of his sons and asked why the eggs were on the table. He was told that the boys were to have delivered the eggs but forgot all about it. J.K., the older brother, said that they would make sure to deliver them the next day. That was not good enough for K.C.—a promise made to a customer had to be a promise kept. One of the boys had to knock on doors at 12:30 A.M. on New Year's Day to deliver the eggs.[8]

As history often shows, the children of the rich and famous do not always have the drive to pursue business success. Alan Farnham explains:

> Wealthy children lack that spark of want that sends other people scurrying to offices and factories each day....Why work? If you know where your next meal is coming from...why even get out of bed?....Some inheritors feel so intimidated by a forebear's accomplishments that they never attempt anything of their own.... Parents may have been too busy getting wealth to have taught heirs how to keep it.[9]

K.C. Irving would have none of this nor, for that matter, did Harriet and the three brothers. If his three boys wanted money, they would have to earn it by selling newspapers, magazines. and eggs to neighbours or at the market. That is also how J.K., Arthur, and Jack wanted it—to be in business and earn their keep. At school and at Acadia University, their parents made sure they would not become "too big for their britches." They did not have luxury items that would make them stand out from the crowd. All three spent their holidays working in one of the businesses. In the summer months, they were expected to work in the field and pull their weight like all the others—in short, no special treatment because they were the Irving boys.

The three brothers attended Rothesay Collegiate, a private school near Saint John. The school's headmaster, Dr. C.H. Bonnycastle, reports that Arthur had "a good mind," welcomed "whatever was going on, highjinks," and was "the author of minor mischief."[10] John DeMont writes that Arthur "was the most popular one in the family" at Rothesay Collegiate, where he "was a deadly rugby tackler, star forward on the hockey team and an avid member of the scout troop."[11]

Arthur followed his father and his brothers and enrolled at Acadia University. He was also known at Acadia as a strong athlete—one of the best players on the university's rugby team. He had a reputation as a "rabble rouser," and ran around Acadia and Wolfville with "a group of rowdy Cape Bretoners."[12] Arthur has fond memories of his Acadia days—in particular, of hanging out with his Cape Breton friends.

Arthur and his brothers knew from the very start that they were just putting in time at Acadia before going into the family businesses. Every summer break meant working on the front lines in one of them, so they would learn all of its facets. I asked Arthur about his days at Acadia. He said he enjoyed his time there and made friendships that lasted a lifetime. Former Acadia president Ray Ivany told me it is clear to him that "Acadia had a profound impact on Arthur Irving." I also asked Arthur why he left Acadia after only a few years. He was quick with the answer: "Well, Donald, you decided that your future was in education and you went to Oxford. I decided that my future was in business and I had the choice to go on at Acadia or learn about business from the best teacher available anywhere—my father. I went with the best teacher." He has no regrets.

Arthur would look to Irving Oil, J.K. to forestry and shipbuilding, and Jack to construction and real estate, to chart out a role in the family business. Unlike his two brothers, who would be involved in several sectors, Arthur focused his efforts on Irving Oil. That said, Arthur, like his two brothers, had an eye on and a say in all the Irving businesses. They and their father were the board of directors of all their businesses, and met regularly to go over all major developments in all facets of the Irving businesses.

As noted, Arthur likes the oil and gas business because it has a heavy "sales" component, and sales is what he enjoys most. Looking for new customers, searching for a deal, striking a deal, and looking after current customers motivates him more than anything. Arthur is the most outgoing of the three brothers, and thus sales comes naturally to him. He told me he wanted nothing more than to roll up his sleeves and get into business with his father. He insisted that the oil and gas business and sales were a natural fit. He added that his first day on the job was a very happy day—he got a Ford, quickly slapped the Irving diamond on the door, and off he went. He was out to hustle business, meet existing customers, seek new ones, and beat the competition.

Arthur has had little interest in newspapers from day one. He did, at one time, own a share of New Brunswick Publishing, which, in turn, owned the Saint John *Telegraph-Journal* and other newspapers. He eventually sold his share to J.K., and today he has no association directly or indirectly with any newspapers. He tells me that, even when he held a share in New Brunswick Publishing, he stayed away from the business. He once said that he rarely went into the *Telegraph-Journal* building, and when he did, he "got the hell out as quickly as I could." Art Doyle, the *Telegraph-Journal*'s publisher in the 1990s, confirmed this, and told me that Arthur Irving never once called him about either editorial or business issues.

Norbert Cunningham, who occupied several senior posts with the Moncton *Times & Transcript*, said that he too never once received a call from Arthur Irving about his work at the newspaper. He tells me he only ever received one call from a representative of the Irving family to influence content. It was about K.C. Irving's obituary. The family wanted to make sure that a certain sentence would remain in the published version. Cunningham reports that it was an "innocuous" sentence, and saw no reason to tamper with it. He does not recall the sentence.

Arthur Irving never believed that the newspaper business was worth the visibility, hassles, and controversies it invariably generates. This explains why he sold his share in the newspaper business several years ago. More to the point, Arthur never liked the newspaper business, and that is why he left it. Looking back, he tells me he has "absolutely no regrets."

But this might not tell the whole story. Politics and business are different in both important and unimportant ways. In business, reality is reality in that you compete, you win or lose, you turn a profit or not, you grab a bigger slice of the market or not; and the bottom line is unrelenting. In politics, perception is all too often reality, as many politicians will point out.

Many New Brunswickers still think of the Irvings in terms of a large business empire that dominates several economic sectors in the province in addition to owning all the English-language print media. To them, that amounts to too much economic and political power concentrated in too few hands. To the critics, this remains the case, even though the Irving empire is no more, with three distinct lines of business owned and operated separately by different Irvings. As recently as April 2019, one observer wrote that "the family controls all English-language newspapers in New Brunswick."[13] This observer had it wrong. Only one member of the family owns the newspapers. This is where perception comes in.

I readily accept what Arthur Doyle and Norbert Cunningham told me. I have known both for some time, and both always tell it like it is. It still leaves, however, a question unanswered. Publishers and journalists know whom they work for, and it takes courage to take the owners on in their own newspapers. They might not be told what to publish and what not to publish—but their gut likely guides them. I am hardly the first or the only observer to make this point.[14]

NOTHING IS MORE FUN THAN WORKING

Arthur Irving, like his father, can work up to sixteen hours a day, grab lunch on the run, and have dinner late in the evening. Like K.C., he has a single-minded purpose, and will pursue goals with energy and tenacity. As was the case for his father, Arthur is sober, unrelenting, and has loads of energy to burn. He too prefers operating away from the limelight and keeping things close to his chest. He, like other owners of privately held firms, sees no merit in opening the books or his operations for the world to see.

As already noted, I have known Arthur Irving only for the past fifteen years and Sandra for nearly twenty. John DeMont published his *Citizens Irving* in 1992, or some fifteen years before Arthur and I became friends. DeMont might well have been right when he wrote that Arthur Irving likes to fish for salmon, has a short fuse, and is "so tightly wound, you fear he is going to explode."[15] But that is not the Arthur Irving I know. The Arthur Irving I know does not fish for salmon, nor have I ever seen him "tightly wound" or feared that he would explode. DeMont, however, goes on to describe Arthur Irving in a way that resonates with me to this day. He writes that Arthur "has the energy of someone half his age," has no interest in alcohol or tobacco, has the "drive to win," is "tireless," and that "his enthusiasm can be contagious."[16] I have seen this first-hand. I recall stopping unannounced with him at an Irving service station in Nova Scotia. The plan was to transform the existing service station into a Big Stop. I was struck by several things—things that might well be of interest to aspiring entrepreneurs. Arthur Irving spoke with everyone as equals, and at no point did he pull rank. He showed a keen and genuine interest in the work of his employees, he asked question after question, down to the most minute detail. He made a point of asking for their views, had a genuine interest in their answers, and was careful to thank them at every turn.

Frank Gallant, an independent Irving Oil dealer in Moncton, had a problem in early summer 2019. The gas tanks by the side of his convenience store were over thirty years old and they no longer qualified for insurance. The solution: buy new tanks at a cost of $300,000. He put a telephone call directly to Arthur Irving and explained that he was closing in on seventy years old and did not think he could, or should, commit $300,000 for new tanks. He and Arthur had met thirty years earlier when Gallant started selling Irving gas.

Arthur Irving agreed, and said he would find a solution. Gallant tells me head-office officials at Irving Oil were not happy that he had gone over their heads and spoken directly with Arthur. This, however, indicates two things that matter a great deal to Arthur. First, the individual, whether a customer or a dealer, is key to business success. Second, if you provide top-quality service to individuals and you remain steadfastly loyal to your business associates and staff, you will outperform the competition. As promised, Arthur found a solution that worked for Frank Gallant at little cost to him.

Arthur Irving has the ability to move from broad strategic questions to the details of the day with ease. My experience with many business and government leaders is that some are excellent at defining a vision, a broad strategy for them and their staff to follow; others are excellent at looking after the details of the day, making certain that little is left to chance, and seeing that things run on time and on track. Some, not many, are strong at both; Arthur Irving is one of them.

I also have a sense that Arthur prefers to meet with front-line Irving Oil employees and customers more than with anyone else. Harrison McCain was the same way. He too enjoyed meeting "local folks" much more than bankers or company CEOS from away. This is likely due to K.C. Irving's influence, since both Arthur and Harrison cut their teeth in business under K.C.'s watchful eye.

To be sure, K.C. Irving was the driving force, the business genius who guided Irving Oil in its early years—the most difficult period for any business. It is Arthur Irving, however, who has grown the business to what it is today. He too has had to deal with numerous challenges in a demanding environment and highly competitive sector. Consider the following: Irving Oil remains a family business and, although it has no oil-production capacity, it runs Canada's largest refinery. Arthur tells me that Irving Oil did try its hand at searching for oil. It searched in several communities in all three Maritime provinces, but came up empty-handed every time. Irving Oil also joined Chevron in looking for oil in Alberta, but saw only modest success, and once again gave up on the search for crude.

A PRIVATE FIRM

AS WAS THE CASE FOR HIS FATHER, ARTHUR IRVING SEES NO merit in going public with Irving Oil, and he is convinced that a private company is much better suited to promote a long-term perspective. As I note on several occasions in this book, private firms are not subject to the constant pressure of quarterly results or the demanding transparency requirements that come from being publicly traded.

There are other reasons for maintaining a private status or even for public companies wanting to go private. Some high-profile publicly traded firms have gone private in recent years—Dell Computers and Kinder Morgan, among others, come to mind. It also will be recalled that the spectacular failures of Enron and WorldCom in the early 2000s gave rise to the US Sarbanes-Oxley Act in 2002 and other demands for greater transparency in publicly traded companies throughout the Western world. Canada was no exception. Publicly traded companies must now deal with demanding corporate governance requirements, strict financial controls, and numerous reporting requirements, the cost of which is high. Irving Oil, like other privately held companies, can avoid many of these costs. The extra time and funds freed from not having to attend to increasingly demanding reporting requirements can be used for other purposes.[17] That said, privately held corporations—and Irving Oil is no exception—do tailor administrative and financial requirements to square with in-house demands. In addition, Irving Oil must comply with governance requirements that corporations, notably banks, demand whenever they loan money. I also note that, starting with K.C. and continuing to this day with Arthur Irving, profits are largely reinvested in Irving Oil. This explains, at least in part, the firm's success in a challenging sector. This is not so easily done in publicly traded companies.

I can add another reason for not going public. I contend that, if Irving Oil were to go public, we would see the head office move out of Saint John within a decade. The decision to locate elsewhere would no longer be a question of "because I live there," but rather one of economic and business considerations and a matter of where the firm's top executives would want to live. The senior executives in a publicly traded company would look at several considerations—for example, low corporate and personal tax rates and employment and educational opportunities for their spouses and their children.

Perhaps because they had to deal with the pressure of quarterly performance measures and because their head offices were located far from their refineries, we have seen many oil refineries shut down in Canada in recent years. Imperial Oil shut down its Dartmouth refinery in 2013, Shell Canada closed its Montreal refinery in 2010, Petro-Canada did the same with its Oakville refinery in 2005, as did Gulf Canada with its Point Tupper, Nova Scotia, refinery in 1980. Many more have shut down in the United States, Europe, and Asia, including the 335,000-barrel-per-day Philadelphia Energy Solutions refinery in 2019, which threw a thousand workers, in addition to local contractors who did business with the refinery, out of a job.[18] Leaving aside the Sturgeon refinery located near Edmonton, there have been no new refineries built in Canada in over thirty years.[19]

Today's refineries are not only capital-intensive, they are also very expensive to operate. They require substantial investments in maintenance, and there is constant demand for new equipment to strengthen efficiency and meet environmental and safety standards.[20] Some of the refineries that are still in business have a checkered past but continue to limp along. It will be recalled that John Shaheen negotiated a deal with Newfoundland premier Joey Smallwood to build an oil refinery at Come By Chance in the mid-1960s. The refinery would import crude from the Middle East, produce a variety of products from its 100,000-barrel-a-day capacity, employ a thousand people, and export the bulk of its products to different locations in North America. That, at least, was the plan. Smallwood agreed to a $30 million loan to help with the construction and another $5 million in unsecured financing to begin work. Two senior members of his Cabinet, John Crosbie and

Clyde Wells, objected to the deal, however, and crossed the floor to sit as independents.[21]

To be sure, as history has shown, Shaheen was a much better promoter than a businessman. He boldly predicted the refinery would pay for itself within six years. It went bankrupt in three. Shaheen rented the *Queen Elizabeth II* to ferry 1,200 dignitaries from New York to Come By Chance to attend the refinery's official opening. Arthur Irving and Smallwood were aboard the luxury liner, where there was no shortage of fine food and alcohol. Arthur recalls having several discussions with Smallwood on the trip. Frank Moores and John Crosbie were also on board, and did not hesitate to claim political credit for the building of the refinery. Smallwood was appalled by their hypocrisy and, once at Come By Chance, he decided not to attend the ceremony. I note that Shaheen never paid the $1 million owed the *Queen Elizabeth II*'s owners.

The Come By Chance refinery has had a troubled existence from day one. It lost $58 million by 1974, and was still not operating at full capacity by 1976. The refinery went into receivership by the late 1970s with debts totalling $500 million, with Shaheen owing the province $42 million and the federal government another $40 million. It shut down for four years and Petro-Canada, then a Crown corporation, bought it for $10 million in 1980. Shaheen is reported to have said that Petro-Canada had "bought itself the biggest lemon in the world."[22]

Petro-Canada decided not to reopen it, instead selling to Bermuda-based Newfoundland Energy for just $1 in 1986. Newfoundland Energy upgraded the refinery, and began operations in 1987. In 2006, Harvest Energy Trust, of Calgary, bought the facility for $1.6 billion. The refinery was sold once more in 2014 to a New York–based merchant bank, Silverpeak Strategic Partners. Although it processes 115,000 barrels daily, the refinery has an uncertain future. There are days when the owners want to sell it because of higher production costs than those of its competitors, and other days when the owners claim they want to upgrade it. In late 2016, the firm announced that it had decided to lay off over 128 of its workers, explaining that the layoffs were necessary to deal with "economic pressures" that have "forced many refineries throughout the world to close."[23]

Irving Oil has been dealing with the same "economic pressures," but rather than shutting down its refinery or laying off employees and contracting the business, it expanded. Under Kenneth's leadership, it carried out an ambitious $1.5 billion upgrade in 2000. More recently, under the current management team, the company is growing on both sides of the Atlantic Basin. In short, workers at the Irving Oil refinery in Saint John are much more confident about the long-term viability of their jobs than those in Come By Chance, and for good reason.

I can add that, unlike the Come By Chance refinery or the recently closed Imperial Oil Dartmouth refinery, Irving Oil regularly launches expensive "turnaround," "upgrade," or "maintenance" projects designed to ensure the long-term competitiveness of its refinery. It carried out "Operation Falcon" in the fall of 2015, for example, investing $200 million and calling for three thousand additional workers to undertake the most ambitious turnaround initiative in its history. Operation Falcon aimed at improving safety, reliability, and competitiveness.[24] In doing so, Irving Oil injected a lot of money into the local economy.

As for the Come By Chance refinery, its New York–based investors recently sent out mixed signals.[25] Irving Oil, in the past, purchased some of its products from Come By Chance, particularly when it had to shut down its own refinery or parts of it, as it did in the immediate aftermath of a refinery explosion in 2018.[26]

In 2016, Irving Oil bought the 75,000-barrel-a-day Whitegate refinery. The refinery had been experiencing problems, losing $148 million in 2014,[27] but it turned a handsome profit in its first full year of operation under Irving Oil. Two years later, Irving Oil also bought the family-owned Top Oil, launched in Ireland as a coal company in 1800. The firm, now integrated with Irving Oil, is one of Ireland's leading suppliers of home heating oil and gas and diesel fuel.[28] Although it had strong revenues, the refinery registered a modest loss in 2018 because of tighter margins due to price differences between crude and refined products.[29]

It has not always been easy sailing for Irving Oil. As noted, it does not own its own sources of crude and, in the eyes of some observers, Saint John is hardly the ideal location to build an oil refinery. The city is well known as a "labour town," and it is also not easy to attract top talent there, given that New Brunswick has one of Canada's highest personal income tax rates. Both K.C. and Arthur have had to deal with high-profile labour-management issues. In brief, running an oil and gas business and building and operating Canada's largest refinery are not for the weak of heart. It takes strong business acumen and a capacity to make tough decisions.

MANAGING HUMAN RESOURCES

MANAGING HUMAN RESOURCES IS NEVER EASY. IF ANYTHING, the challenge is even more demanding for businesses operating away from larger urban centres. High-performing executives are always in demand, and it only takes a moment's reflection to appreciate that it is easier to attract them in large urban centres. Businesses in Atlantic Canada also have to deal with employees' expectations that national pay standards should apply in the region.

The federal government has a lot to answer for on this issue.

I have made the case elsewhere that it is not in the economic interests of Atlantic Canada to pursue national wage standards in all sectors. I argued in my *Visiting Grandchildren*, published in 2006, that the federal government should tailor its policies and programs to accommodate the region's circumstances and, at the same time, the region itself should recognize that it needs to adjust its expectations with regard to national salaries and wages. More to the point, they should not be determined by national pay scales applicable equally across Canada. In Atlantic Canada, salaries are higher than the region could generate if left to its own devices because of pressures for national parity in the federal government. A national salary scale is incompatible with the fact that Atlantic Canada's economy is different from that of, say, Ontario, and that regionally tailored policies are required. Moreover, a national scale is not compatible with private-sector practices in the regional economy. We know that 40 percent of Canadian manufacturers plan their pay based on regional differentials, an approach that is also widely employed in the United States. The pay for manufacturing employees is still higher, for example, in Fort McMurray, Alberta, or Windsor, Ontario, than in the Maritimes.[30]

To be sure, it is understandable that federal public servants in the Maritimes would prefer to have their salaries tied to national standards. I know this because a number of them contacted me to voice their strong disagreement with my position after I published *Visiting Grandchildren*. But their arguments must be weighed against the fact that no salaries are going in the Maritimes to the unemployed or to those who have left the region for better opportunities. Paying national salary levels makes sense if it is required to attract highly qualified people; otherwise it can create unemployment.

The central point here is that the federal government should follow the private sector, not lead it. That is, if the private sector decides it needs to pay national salary levels to attract certain skills, then the federal government should do the same. But the opposite also applies. Currently, the federal government inhibits economic development and job creation in the region by paying higher salaries and wages than does the private sector. If these were lower than the national standards, the region would also be more competitive in the public sector itself, and the case to locate more federal government units in the region would be strengthened. High salary levels can create an upward trend in salaries and wages and, by ricochet, reduce demand for labour and make a region less competitive.

Salaries of federal public servants are also relatively high even by national standards. The parliamentary budget officer reports that the average salary for federal public servants in 2013 amounted to $114,000 a year in total compensation.[31] In a comprehensive review, James Lahey, a senior Treasury Board Secretariat official, concluded that federal public sector employees enjoyed a premium of 8 to 9 percent over their private-sector counterparts, with the total compensation premium for federal public servants between 15 and 20 percent once non-wage benefits such as pensions are included.[32] Further, the average salary of federal public servants was in the ninety-fifth percentile of all services sector salaries in the same year.[33]

In November 2019, the federal government advertised an opening for an accounting operations manager in Fredericton. The position required experience in finance, accounting, and a degree from a post-secondary institution. The position pays up to $109,683, which was, at the time, under review. The position also provided for gold-standard benefits, including a very generous pension and other benefits beyond the reach of the great majority of private-sector firms in Atlantic Canada.[34] In September 2019, the federal government advertised a senior-level financial analyst position in Saint John paying between $69,908 and $96,580, in addition to generous fringe benefits.[35] I know of no private-sector position in Atlantic Canada that would pay anywhere near these salaries for similar responsibilities and comparable knowledge, experience, and skills. Costs, including salaries, wages, and qualified workers, matter to local businesses and aspiring entrepreneurs in their efforts to build viable firms. Salaries of federal public servants in the region tied to a national salary scale make it more difficult for local firms to attract quality staff.

LOOKING BACK

ARTHUR IRVING, LIKE HIS TWO BROTHERS, LEARNED THE WAYS of business from his parents at a very young age. If the boys had promised to deliver a dozen eggs by a certain time, the promise had to be kept, even if they had to deliver the eggs past midnight. Arthur, again like his brothers, did not go into business unwillingly. At a very young age, he decided that business was his vocation and that Irving Oil was where he would make his mark. He went at it with determination and enthusiasm. He learned by watching his father at work and, like his father was, Arthur Irving is always at the ready to take on the competition. To understand K.C., Arthur, and Irving Oil, one must appreciate how K.C. saw the world and how Arthur still sees it.

In getting into the oil and gas business, Arthur Irving had to learn all facets of business under the watchful eye of his father. Those who have worked with Arthur have told me that a number of things come naturally to him. They say that he is a natural-born salesman, that he never needs to be prompted to put in the extra effort, that he can go from dealing with broad issues to dealing with the details of the day with remarkable ease, and that he is always ready to put in long days to get the job done. They report that he also never shies away from competition—on the contrary, he welcomes it—or from making tough decisions.

K.C. looked, and Arthur Irving now looks, at Irving Oil as a family firm that has to compete against the world's oil giants. Irving Oil remains firmly planted in Saint John, New Brunswick, always pulling against gravity or against powerful economic and political power from away. It is worth repeating what Arthur had to say about his father, which speaks as much to his motivation as it did for that of his father. He insisted that, at work, there "was excitement every day. Every day there was something new....Every day was a new game. The score was three to two. We were two and the other guy was three....He got a big charge out of being successful."[36] That is the way Arthur Irving and Irving Oil also look at the oil and gas business. They are the little dogs looking for their share of the business in a world where big dogs eat first.

Notes

1 See, for example, Douglas How and Ralph Costello, *K.C.: The Biography of K.C. Irving* (Toronto: Key Porter, 1993), 71.
2 Ibid.
3 Ibid., 70.
4 Kevin Leman, *The Birth Order Book: Why You Are the Way You Are* (Grand Rapids, MI: Revell, 2009).
5 Frank J. Sulloway, *Born to Rebel: Birth Order, Family Dynamics, and Creative Lives* (New York: Vintage, 1997).
6 See, for example, How and Costello, *K.C.*
7 Ibid., 71.
8 Ibid., 72.
9 Alan Farnham, "The Children of the Rich and Famous," *Fortune*, September 10, 1990, online at money.cnn.com/magazines/fortune/fortune_archive/1990/09/10/73985/index.htm.
10 How and Costello, *K.C.*, 74.
11 John DeMont, *Citizens Irving: K.C. Irving and His Legacy* (Toronto: McClelland and Stewart, 1992), 141.
12 Ibid., 142.
13 Alain Deneault, "The Irvings, Canada's Robber Barons." *Le Monde diplomatique*, April 2019, online at mondediplo.com/2019/04/13canada.
14 See, for example, Toby D. Couture, "Without Favour: The Concentration of Ownership in New Brunswick's Print Media Industry," *Canadian Journal of Communication* 38, no. 1 (2013): 57–81.
15 DeMont, *Citizens Irving*, 147–8.
16 Ibid., 147, 149.
17 Marvin Dumont, "Why Public Companies Go Private," *Investopedia*, June 25, 2019, online at investopedia.com/articles/stocks/08/public-companies-privatize-go-private.asp.
18 Laila Kearney, Jarrett Renshaw, and Noah Browning, "PES refinery expected to shut down remaining units as crude dwindles: sources," *Reuters*, July 17, 2019, online at reuters.com/article/us-refinery-operations-pes-philadelphia/pes-refinery-expected-to-shut-remaining-units-as-crude-supply-dwindles-sources-idUSKCN1UC2ID.
19 Canada, *Canadian Refinery Overview—Energy Market Assessment, April 2018* (Ottawa: National Energy Board, 2018), 8.

20 Conference Board of Canada, *Canada's Petroleum Refining Sector: An Important Contributor Facing Global Challenges* (Ottawa: Conference Board of Canada, October 2011), 9.

21 Jenny Higgins with Melanie Martin, "The Come By Chance Oil Refinery," *Heritage Newfoundland & Labrador*, updated January 2018, online at heritage.nf.ca/articles/politics/come-by-chance.php.

22 Ibid.

23 Garrett Barry, "Come By Chance refinery owner lays off 128, citing economy," CBC *News*, November 10, 2016, online at cbc.ca/news/canada/newfoundland-labrador/come-by-chance-refinery-cuts-1.3843847.

24 "Irving Oil announces $200-million refinery project," *Oil & Gas Product News*, August 25, 2015, online at oilandgasproductnews.com/article/21412/irving-oil-announces-dollar200-million-refinery-project.

25 See, for example, "Come By Chance refinery sale falls through after pricetag squabble: report," CBC *News*, July 11, 2018, online at cbc.ca/news/canada/newfoundland-labrador/sale-come-by-chance-refinery-falls-through-1.4742057.

26 Bobbi-Jean MacKinnon and Elizabeth Fraser, "Following Saint John oil refinery blast and fire, Irving Oil to focus on cause," CBC *News*, October 10, 2018, online at cbc.ca/news/canada/new-brunswick/explosion-fire-saint-john-oil-refinery-1.4854460.

27 Barry O'Halloran, "Canadian group Irving Oil to buy Cork's Whitegate Refinery," *Irish Times*, August 3, 2016, online at irishtimes.com/business/energy-and-resources/canadian-group-irving-oil-to-buy-cork-s-whitegate-refinery-1.2743671.

28 Sean Galea-Pace, "Canada's Irving Oil to acquire Top Oil to expand into Ireland," *Business Chief*, August 21, 2018, online at canada.businesschief.com/leadership/2860/Canadas-Irving-Oil-to-acquire-Top-Oil-to-expand-into-Ireland.

29 "Arthur Irving posts Irish refinery losses," online at allnovascotia.com, December 4, 2019.

30 Virginia Galt, "Regional pay differences becoming common: study," *Globe and Mail*, November 16, 2004, online at theglobeandmail.com/amp/report-on-business/regional-pay-differences-becoming-common-study/article1007043/.

31 Julian Beltrame, "Public service salaries: Canada pays average bureaucrat $114,000, watchdog finds," *Canadian Press*, December 11, 2012.

32 James Lahey, "Controlling Federal Compensation Costs: Towards a Fairer and More Sustainable System," in *How Ottawa Spends 2011–2012*, ed. Christopher Stoney and G. Bruce Doern (Montreal; Kingston, ON: McGill-Queen's University Press, 2012), 84–109.

33 Statistics Canada, *Annual Estimates of Employment, Earnings and Hours 1991–2004*, based on the North American Industrial Classification System (NAICS–2002).

34 *Canada Government Jobs*, "Manager Accounting Operations, November 1, 2019, Employment in New Brunswick," online at canadagovernmentjobs.ca/3528/manager-accouting-operations/.

35 Canada, "Senior Financial Analyst, Saint John, New Brunswick" (Ottawa: Canada Revenue Agency, closing date 13 September, 2019), online at careers-carrieres.cra-arc.gc.ca/gol-ged/wcis/pub/rtrvjbpst. action?pi=3863BB41B6A41ED9AF9EBC1273EF8BD2, accessed September 2019.

36 Quoted in How and Costello, *K.C.*, 381.

CHAPTER 6

PASSING THE TORCH TO ARTHUR

A RTHUR IRVING JOINED IRVING OIL IN 1951. I ASKED him why he decided to go into the oil and gas business rather than, say, forestry. Was it his idea or K.C.'s? He tells me that it was a natural transition and that it was everybody's idea. Arthur wanted to get into the oil and gas business, and his father was very supportive of his choice, as were his two brothers. There was no agreement or disagreement, it just happened, and all sides were happy with the move. He also saw that there was a heavy sales component to the oil and gas business, and sales is what he enjoys most and what he is very good at. In short, it was a natural fit for Arthur to get into the oil and gas business, and everyone saw it.

Arthur tells me that his father's true passion was always trees. K.C. was focused on forestry, and he laid the groundwork for a highly successful business that has survived many twists and turns and remains prosperous today. In 1957, K.C. Irving was the first in Atlantic Canada to launch a tree-planting program; some sixty years later, the firm that he led for nearly three decades planted its one billionth tree.[1] K.C. planted his first tree in Black Brook, a small New Brunswick community. A year later, he started the firm's first tree nursery in Juniper, another small New Brunswick community.

I have flown over New Brunswick on many occasions, and one can easily spot Irving's forest land and that of the competition, or what is left of it. There are no zigzag roads on Irving's forest land—everything is in a straight line, everything is square where it needs to be and everything is in perfect order. Not so for the other forestry businesses—at least the few that own forest land and still operate in New Brunswick.

It is not much of an exaggeration to write that out-of-province forestry businesses that came to New Brunswick were little more than opportunists. They came, they exploited the resources, and, when things turned too demanding, they left town. I am thinking here of International Paper, Consolidated-Bathurst, Smurfit-Stone, Repap, and UPM-Kymmene in Miramichi. It will be recalled that Smurfit-Stone simply picked up and left Bathurst in 2005 with little forewarning, leaving three hundred workers out of a job and an eyesore in the middle of the town. Green Investment Group from the United States took over the site, sold its assets, and left town without even paying property taxes.[2] I invite the reader to visit Miramichi and Dalhousie, among other communities, and see the holes these businesses left behind—in some cases, not even bothering to clean up their mess. J.D. Irving (JDI) is still present in the province, however, and so is its head office. It operates several businesses in the forestry sector—from Saint John to Saint-Léonard, Madawaska, and many communities in between—and has expanded to other jurisdictions, notably in the state of Maine.

Though forestry was clearly K.C.'s passion, Arthur reports that his father could very quickly "switch gears" so that, when he had to focus on his oil and gas business, he could do so on a moment's notice. Arthur adds that K.C. identified and paid attention to the important issues at the right time, whatever the sector or the issue. Arthur learned the business by doing and by watching how his father operated. He did whatever needed to be done, and no task was too small or too large. By the time he became CEO in 1972, he had gained a full appreciation of Irving Oil and its operations from its refinery to its retail outlets and everything in between. He became CEO very quietly. The business world only learned of it when Irving Oil announced it had signed a memorandum of understanding to undertake an exploration program to look for crude in Nova Scotia. The agreement was signed by A.B. Bristow, Chevron's president, and Arthur Irving as chairman, president, and chief executive officer of Irving Oil. There was no grand announcement, not even a press release. Neither K.C. nor Arthur saw a need for it. As Arthur would put it, "there was no need to brag about it."

MOVING TO BERMUDA

MUCH HAS BEEN WRITTEN AND SAID ABOUT K.C. IRVING'S decision to move first to the Bahamas and then to Bermuda. He simply issued a brief and to-the-point statement: "I am no longer residing in New Brunswick. My sons are carrying on the various businesses. As far as anything else goes, I do not choose to discuss the matter further."[3]

K.C.'s decision to move coincided with Ottawa's decision to impose a capital gains tax and the New Brunswick government's decision to start taxing estates. Ottawa also served notice that it would lay charges against K.C.'s media ownership. A number of RCMP officers marched into Irving-owned newspaper offices with search warrants. They carried away nearly four thousand pages of material, and pored over them for about nine months. The federal government eventually charged K.C. Irving and his holding company with breaking competition law. It was a bitter, prolonged, and costly case for both sides. It also had deep political overtones. A Liberal senator from New Brunswick, Charles McElman, led the charge against the Irving papers. McElman made the case that the newspapers were incapable of properly covering their owner. K.C. Irving explained that he bought all the newspapers because he did not want them falling to out-of-province owners. He added that he did not take a salary from the newspapers, that he received no dividend, that all profits were reinvested in the papers, and that he never talked to anyone to influence editorial content. He only spoke to them about business decisions.[4]

For K.C. Irving, however, newspapers were just another business, and he always insisted that he had no interest in the papers' editorial content.[5] The case eventually made its way to the Supreme Court of Canada. Four years after K.C. left New Brunswick, the Supreme Court reaffirmed the decision of the New Brunswick Court of Appeal. The courts concluded that K.C.'s concentration of ownership of the province's newspapers entailed a substantial improvement in all the newspapers after he had purchased them, that there was "complete editorial autonomy by the respective publishers and editors," and that "the trial judge found no actual detriment to the public."[6] To many in the business community, the decision was a win not only for K.C. Irving, but also for free enterprise. To them, the decision told Canadians that no one, not the federal government, not even the courts, could take away what a business person had built and earned.[7]

I can easily imagine that the episode left a sour taste with K.C. Irving. He likely could not envisage that one could break the law by buying and successfully running a business. He probably struggled with the notion that Ottawa would spend millions of taxpayers' dollars pursuing a court case it had already lost before the New Brunswick Court of Appeal and would again before the Supreme Court of Canada. Harrison McCain once told me that he did not so much mind paying taxes, but that he did mind what the government did with them. From K.C.'s perspective, he had to pay a substantial sum of money to retain high-profile lawyers, including J.J. Robinette, to defend his business in court, but also cover, through taxes, some of the fees paid to government lawyers and outside counsel.

It was by many accounts the tax issue that was top of mind when K.C. Irving left New Brunswick for the Bahamas and then Bermuda, and what led him to ask existential questions about his businesses and his legacy. K.C. understood the implications. If he stayed, he or his estate would eventually have to give up a good chunk of his assets to pay the new taxes. What would it be: selling Irving Oil or his forestry business in order to pass on one or the other to his sons? He had spent a lifetime building these businesses, and likely felt it unfair that a good part of it would be sold to pay taxes to feed the government's insatiable appetite for revenues. He might well have also concluded that out-of-province buyers would take over the half of the business he or his estate would have to sell. If they did, he would have known, with history as a guide, that, over time, head offices from away would move senior management away from the province. History also suggests that they would have stripped away the best assets and sold them for profit that meant little to them but a great deal to the province.

K.C. said little, even after the fact, about his decision to move out of the province. His only comment: "There were a lot of things at that time."[8] He was later asked if he would return after the government of New Brunswick suspended its estate tax in 1974 but kept the legislation intact. He simply responded that he had no such plans.[9]

The three boys were by then close to or in their forties and ready to take over the businesses. Although K.C. stayed far away from day-to-day operations, this is not to suggest for a moment that he shied away from talking business with his sons. He was in constant communication with them, and spent a great deal of time in New Brunswick. While in Saint John, he stayed in an apartment on top of the JDI building on Union Street, across from the Golden Ball Building. He and his three sons talked frequently and met often.

The transition from father to sons was seamless. The three had, by then, gained extensive experience in the businesses—well over twenty years in all three cases. J.K. had seen growth in the forestry sector. The same can be said for Arthur at Irving Oil and Jack in the building and real estate sectors. The three had participated directly in managing and growing all of the businesses.

Arthur arrived at the wheel of Irving Oil at a critical moment in its development. The refinery was operating efficiently and, with hindsight, it was clear that the decision to build it was a wise investment. Irving Oil's retail capacity was also working well and growing. In short, K.C. had put in place all the ingredients for a highly successful business. It was now up to Arthur to build on this success and grow the company.

Children of highly successful entrepreneurs often feel the need to break from their parents' shadows. Arthur, however, saw that his father was extremely driven, consumed by his work, and widely respected by his staff and the community, and wanted to emulate that. As is well known, it is not always easy to be the child of a highly successful entrepreneur and, to be sure, K.C. was all of that and then some. Numerous books have been written about the challenges sons or daughters of highly successful parents face when tasked with leading a family business. Some are successful in growing the family business, but others are not.[10]

Some are also able to break away from their father's shadow; others are not. Arthur Irving must have known that all eyes were on him, wondering if he would be able to cut it and chart his own course. My sense is that Arthur did not give it much thought. He admired his father, still does, and adored his mother and still does. Never one to complicate matters, Arthur simply hit the ground running when he joined Irving Oil. He never stopped to debate the pros and cons of working in his father's shadow. He welcomed it. He was also never intimidated by his father's business success and accomplishments—quite the opposite, he applauded them, and was looking forward to being a part of it and carrying on the business. He told me that, at a very early age, he was anxious to get going, to help grow the business that his father had founded and guided for nearly fifty years. As already noted, he also told me that it was a very happy day when he was handed the keys to a Ford, slapped the Irving diamond on it, and hit the road selling oil and gas products.

ARTHUR IS A BUSINESSMAN

ARTHUR, LIKE HIS FATHER AND HIS TWO BROTHERS, IS A HARD-nosed, hard-driven, hard-working, and highly competitive businessman. He plays to win, and history shows that he has won more often than not. He took his father's legacy in the oil and gas sector and made the family business bigger and more successful. Irving Oil is substantially larger than it was when Arthur took it over in all aspects of the business, from refinery operations to sales, number of retail outlets, market share, and size.

Arthur has had a hand in all major developments at Irving Oil from the moment he joined the firm. When he landed in the CEO's chair, he knew all the ins and outs of the business, and he never lost sight of what was important, what remains important, and what is needed to grow the business. He, like his father, always strives to be "on top of his game." And for him, like his father, every day is a new day. It is worth repeating once more what Arthur said when the Atlantic Canada Plus Association honoured his father: "The score was three to two. We were two and the other guy was three. We had about ten seconds to play—and we had to win."[11]

ARTHUR AND HIS PEOPLE

WHILE WORKING ON THIS BOOK, I CONSULTED A NUMBER OF former and current Irving Oil employees and executives. Two things struck me. First, the message was consistent: what I heard in one interview, I very often heard again. Second, Arthur's sense of loyalty to staff works both ways. Senior Irving Oil executives are very loyal to him and his legacy.

Arthur Irving employed K.C.'s tried-and-true approach in taking over Irving Oil as its CEO. Long-serving Irving Oil employees tell me that when K.C. left in the early 1970s, he did not try to micro- or even macro-manage Irving Oil from away or from Bermuda. K.C. was there whenever Arthur called, but he left Arthur to run Irving Oil as he saw fit.

It might well be that K.C. felt no need to manage Irving Oil from away because he saw that Arthur was employing the same playbook he had used in growing Irving Oil to what it was by then. K.C. quickly saw that Arthur was also successful in managing and growing the business. Like his father, Arthur always underlined the importance of providing better service to customers than the competition, paying very close attention to details, dealing with everyone with respect and civility, hiring solid performers and being loyal to them, and reinvesting profits in growing the company. That was K.C.'s playbook, and it became Arthur's playbook.

Arthur had a consistent message to his people, a message he would repeat time and again: service is key. Irving Oil staff, in interviews, underlined on numerous occasions the importance of providing top service to customers. Furthermore, Arthur consistently pushed everyone to secure new customers, to wrestle customers away from the competition, and, once they were secured, to ensure they received the best service.

Arthur Irving has always made it a point of calling in, often unannounced, at his service stations. He enjoys doing this, particularly talking with his front-line people. They know what customers want and appreciate, and Arthur invariably meets them with a series of questions, with one question often leading to another. He repeatedly insists that the best way to find out what customers want and when change is needed is to talk with those who are serving them.

It was under Arthur's watch that Irving Oil launched its Big Stop concept. Big Stops are all about responding to the wishes of customers, and have been highly successful from day one. Arthur Irving opened the first Big Stop in 1984 in Aulds Cove, Nova Scotia. Today there are nearly thirty Big Stops located in the Maritimes, Ontario, and New England, and their number continues to grow.

A Big Stop is a constant beehive of activity. I stopped at two while working on this book. All have conversation pieces, large parking lots, very friendly staff, and easy access to gas and diesel pumps and some to fast-charging stations for electric vehicles. Harvey Sawler describes Irving Big Stops as mini Walmarts.[12] They are all that. I have seen things in Big Stops that one used to see in general stores in small communities, from work gloves to car and truck accessories.

Each Big Stop carries a name that speaks to the history of the community in which it is located. Salisbury, New Brunswick, adopted silver fox farming at the beginning of the twentieth century and is known as "the home of the silver fox." So the Big Stop there is named "Big Stop Silver Fox." The Big Stop in Lincoln, near Fredericton, is named "Blue Canoe" because of Fredericton's strong historical ties to canoe building.

One can easily see Arthur Irving's handprint on the Big Stop stores. They are all customer-centric. As an example, the Salisbury Big Stop offers the following: sixty truck-parking spaces; a 24/7 convenience store; five diesel lanes; six showers; Tim Hortons, Subway, and Big Stop restaurants; internet access; a laundry facility; CAT scales; a travel store; an ATM; a Big Scoop ice cream take-out; electric vehicle charging stations; and payphones.[13] At some Big Stops, it is possible for customers to leave comments on their website. Sawler explains: "Everything at an Irving Big Stop is well organized—a place for everything and everything in its place. And with every one they build, they learn how to organize things better, leaving no detail undone."[14] The restaurants and washrooms are clean, the food is excellent, and the staff's uniforms look like they just came back from the cleaners. In brief, everything is neat.

Truckers are "revered" at Big Stops. Trucking associations recommend Irving Big Stops because of the level of service and the reputation of their restaurants, where they make hot turkey sandwiches "with real turkey, covered in gravy and topped with peas."[15] One competitor had this to say about Irving Big Stops: "Their service stations are cleaner than most hospitals I've seen. Irving restaurants—with their fresh breads, home-made soups and pies—are consistently some of the best rural restaurants found throughout the Atlantic provinces and Maine."[16]

Arthur Irving kept a close watch and a hands-on approach as the Big Stop concept was being developed. John DeMont writes that "one manager remembers watching in awe as Arthur refused to open up a million-dollar Big Stop service station complex until he had personally checked the shower stalls for the truck drivers, to ensure that they were stocked with big bars of soap, rather than the tiny, hotel-room variety."[17] Again, attention to detail matters to Arthur Irving. It is as important as it once was for his father and as it is now for Irving Oil management.

The Big Stop concept works and it has paid large dividends. It is a masterpiece of retailing built by paying close attention to customers and to details. The result is that Big Stops have won the day with customers everywhere they have been built. Customers know they exist, if nothing else, by word of mouth. As Sawler concludes, "the packed parking lot shows that it works," and customers know about it, including "truckers from as far afield as California."[18]

Arthur Irving does not want to take credit for the success of the Big Stop. He insists that you need a top-performing team around you to succeed in business. He reports that, by the 1980s, the team noticed that the oil and gas retail business was shifting away from service bays to a mixture of retail gas and convenience store. Arthur and his senior team saw that it was time for Irving Oil to reinvent itself. The Big Stop was the answer.

ATTENTION TO DETAIL

AT THE RISK OF BEING REPETITIVE, THE IRVING OIL EMPLOYees I consulted report that Arthur Irving always pays very close attention to detail, much like his father did. No detail is too small or too trivial. Everything also has to be in order. The message remains in place to this day. I recall walking by the employee locker room at the Irving Oil refinery—it was remarkably clean, as were the uniforms, which were all hung up in perfect order.

Arthur Irving, while he was CEO, never hesitated to delve down to the most minute of administrative details. One senior executive who worked directly for him said that, for a long time, Arthur signed all cheques over $1,000. He would spend whatever hours were needed to look after pressing business matters, but would always find time to look after the details of the day and sign a multitude of cheques. This, the executive added, was not so much to control spending as to understand all parts of the Irving Oil operations. Signing cheques would lead him to ask questions about all aspects of the business.

That executive also told me that, when he went in to meet Arthur, he made certain he had answers to all possible questions. But he never felt intimidated—he reports that it is just not Arthur's management style. He told me that there is one golden rule in dealing with Arthur Irving: "Be straight with him and he will be straight with you. Play games with him or try to sidestep difficult questions, you will not last long in his office." Steve McLaughlin, a senior Irving Oil executive, recalls going in to tell Arthur that Irving Oil would be losing $300,000 on a case. He explained that he decided to soften the blow by telling him, "well, it is only $300,000." Arthur replied: "You should only use the word 'only' when it is your own money." The message was not lost on McLaughlin.

Darren Gillis, another senior Irving Oil executive, tells me that the most important lesson he learned from Arthur Irving is that business success is directly tied to how well you serve your customers, your loyalty to your people, and your level of tenacity in pursuing objectives. In one case, he reports that, while others would have long given up on securing the business, Arthur insisted on keeping at it, month after month, never accepting no for an answer in pursuing this one customer. The objective was to sell lubricant to a pulp and paper mill firm. Gillis explains that there is nothing more difficult than wrestling a heavy equipment customer away from the competition. These firms do not like to change lubricants for fear that it might hurt their heavy equipment. No matter, Arthur kept at it, until one day it was the customer who gave up and finally decided to go with Irving Oil. The customer is still with Irving Oil today.

Gillis also reports that Arthur has a contagious, positive, go-get-'em attitude—anything and everything is possible. Whatever it is, and however difficult it might be, Arthur Irving always thinks it can be done. In addition, Arthur has a well-known capacity for motivating people to outperform even their own expectations.

We saw earlier that Arthur Irving makes it a point of meeting his front-line people. As he told Gillis, it is best to meet the "oiler" first when you go on a ship, rather than the captain. The oiler is the junior worker on a ship, the person in the boiler room whose job is to keep the machinery going. Arthur insisted that this is the person who can tell you how the ship really works and if it needs repairs. When Arthur goes into an Irving service station, he immediately goes to the cashier and then the store manager—not the other way around like most business owners do.

Senior Irving Oil executives tell me they have seen first-hand Arthur's ability to ask question after question; at times, the questions come rapid-fire. They believe there are two reasons Arthur constantly asks questions. First, he wants to know everything about the business, and no detail is too small. Second, it is his way of sizing up staff. They also report that Arthur Irving is very often the last person to leave when visiting field operations, which speaks to his insatiable appetite to learn.

I asked a senior Irving Oil executive if he had ever seen Arthur lose his cool, as some publications have reported in the past.[19] "Yes," he responded, "but not as often as I have." He adds that it is likely impossible for someone running a sprawling business that operates in several jurisdictions, who has a very strong work ethic and a perfectionist bent, not to lose his cool.

Both Irving Oil executives and Arthur Irving very often refer to the important role the management team plays, with the emphasis on "team." Executives report that, consistent with Arthur's approach while CEO, when key decisions are to be struck, the practice was and is today to go around the table asking for everybody's opinion. The decision thus becomes the team's decision, and everyone is expected to put their shoulder to the wheel.

Arthur Irving ran a flat organization when he was CEO. He saw advantages in having a number of people reporting directly to him. It enabled him to gain insights into all facets of the business. He also never believed in having a closed-door approach to running Irving Oil. He saw and still sees merit in being challenged. He was also always one of the first to highlight new ideas to grow the business whenever anyone on the management team came up with them. He would make certain that such ideas would be put to the test, with everyone asked to voice their views. By all accounts, Arthur is not one to turn to or promote favourites. Promotions, with Arthur Irving at the helm, have to be obtained the old-fashioned way: they have to be earned.

THE BIG ISSUES

ARTHUR IRVING CAN MOVE WITH EASE BETWEEN DEALING WITH the details of the business and looking at broad public policy and complex business issues. He was an early and vocal supporter of the 1988 Canada-US Free Trade Agreement. It will be recalled that his father had also pushed hard for better trade arrangements with the United States. K.C. explained at every opportunity that "the Maritimes are closer to New York and Boston than to Toronto. That is the natural way for us to go."[20]

Arthur quickly saw the opportunity to grow Irving Oil's New England market with a free trade agreement in place. To be sure, the agreement made accessing a large market considerably less complicated for Irving Oil. It opened the door for Irving Oil to purchase more retail outlets, and made it easier to initiate acquisitions in the US oil and gas sector. As a result, Irving Oil substantially improved its infrastructure in New England to accommodate future growth. It now has, for example, a highly efficient terminal in Revere, Massachusetts, to receive, store, and distribute its products throughout the New England region.

Arthur Irving, working with his sons Kenneth and Arthur Jr., pulled the trigger on the previously mentioned ambitious $1.5 billion upgrade to the refinery in Saint John. The upgrade was designed to increase the refinery's efficiency and capacity to convert low-value fuel oils into higher-value transportation fuels—notably gasoline and diesel. It also strengthened the refinery's ability to process a wider range of light and heavy feed stocks. In addition, the expansion improved the refinery's environmental performance by reducing sulphur emissions.[21]

Irving Oil's practice is to invest significantly in regular maintenance turnarounds and other upgrades. Though costly, they are critical to a refinery's long-term viability. That explains why, at one time, there were six refineries in Atlantic Canada, but now the region is down to only two.

Steve McLaughlin, who has worked closely with Arthur Irving for three decades, explains why Arthur decided to make a major investment to expand the refinery and why he never hesitates to spend the necessary resources to ensure that it receives regular maintenance exercises. McLaughlin maintains that Arthur Irving is deeply committed to the region and that he is always ready to make the necessary investments to ensure Irving Oil stays in business and in the region.[22] It is important to note that the $1.5 billion upgrade in 2000 was hardly the only major investment to ensure the refinery's continued success. Another $150 million upgrade was carried out in 2003, which enabled the refinery to produce ultra-low-sulphur diesel. The refinery also became the first in Canada to produce high-octane gasoline without the use of lead additives. In addition, a $100 million upgrade was undertaken in 2011, this time to reduce the levels of benzene in gasoline as required by both US and Canadian government regulations.[23]

As we saw earlier, in 2015 Irving Oil initiated the largest refinery upgrade or "turnaround" in its history. The $200 million Operation Falcon initiative was strictly an Irving Oil investment, with no government money involved. It ran for eight weeks and created 2,700 jobs, with employees working around the clock to make certain that the projects were completed on time. The initiative, however, did not add new capacity to the refinery. Mark Sherman, who then ran the refinery, explains: "The scope and investment level represent our commitment to long-term operation in Saint John and in Atlantic Canada, and positions our company for future growth opportunities."[24] In short, the investment was designed both to keep Irving Oil one step ahead of the competition and to ensure its long-term viability.

It was under Kenneth's watch that Irving Oil teamed up with Repsol to establish a liquefied natural gas (LNG) terminal and regasification plant that saw, at one point, some 1,500 workers on the building site. The Spanish firm holds 75 percent of the shares and

Irving Oil 25 percent. They broke ground on the site in November 2005. The plan was to carry natural gas on a 145-kilometre-long pipeline to the Maritimes & North East Pipeline and across the St. Croix River north of St. Stephen to the large US market.[25]

Irving Oil got the better part of the deal. Repsol did not want to compete against Irving Oil in its market; it wanted to control the partnership. In return for taking control of the partnership, it would take all of the market risks. This was Repsol's call. Irving Oil, for its part, was guaranteed a return on capital, no matter the revenues. A court case launched by Repsol against the Canada Revenue Agency reveals that the Repsol-Irving Oil deal guarantees Irving Oil at least US$20 million a year in profits from the LNG terminal in addition to Repsol's paying rent to Irving Oil plus a fixed 14 percent equity dividend.[26]

The Canaport LNG began operations in 2008. It has had a difficult existence from day one because of market conditions. Low gas prices in the United States have meant that the plant operates at only between 20 and 40 percent capacity.[27] At one point, Repsol tried to sell its participation in the LNG operations and to combine its Saint John assets with others it had in Trinidad and Tobago and Peru in a package to Shell. Shell, however, balked at the Saint John operations. Repsol quickly wrote down the value of its Canaport LNG import terminal by $1.3 billion. The problem, in a nutshell, was that the United States did not need anywhere near the level of natural gas that was envisaged when negotiations first began on the LNG terminal.[28] Repsol looked at converting Canaport LNG into an export terminal, but dropped the plan after it was unable to find outside investors. It concluded that a "conversion was not currently economical," leaving the door open to another look down the road.[29]

It will be recalled that Irving Oil was also all set to go on building a terminal to receive crude flowing from the Energy East pipeline,

and teamed up with TransCanada Corp. to build the us$300 mil-
lion Canaport Energy East Marine Terminal. It will also be recalled
that Irving Oil spent over $10 million on engineering and design
before work came to a full stop.

The above is not a complete list of all the major initiatives
Arthur Irving and Irving Oil have pursued. In the 1980s, for example, Arthur Irving led the charge to buy Chevron's stake in the
Saint John refinery. He had a price in mind, and told it to family
members and senior Irving executives before he left for California.
They told him he would need to up the offer considerably, but
he went to California and got the deal done at the price he had
envisaged. Irving Oil is now the sole proprietor of the refinery. In
2004 came the building of the Grandview co-generation project,
designed to use natural gas to produce electricity and steam for
use at the refinery.[30] This made the production process less costly
and more environmentally friendly. The initiative also produces
power for the community.

Today Irving Oil is owned by a trust established for the benefit
of Arthur Irving's family. In establishing the trust, Irving Oil also
established a board of directors to oversee the company's operations and to achieve the benefits that governance requirements in
publicly traded companies provide.

TAKING A BACK SEAT ON
DAY-TO-DAY OPERATIONS

As the new millenium approached, Arthur Irving
gradually removed himself from day-to-day operations. By the
1990s, he no longer signed all cheques over $1,000 or delved into
the details of the day. His son, Kenneth Irving, took over as CEO
in 2000, followed by Mayank (Mike) Ashar (2010–13) and Paul

Browning (2013–14). Ian Whitcomb took over as president in 2015. The requirements of running Irving Oil are demanding, and no doubt they took their toll on Kenneth Irving, as he acknowledged in early 2017.[31] There was also a major adjustment for both Ashar and Browning, who moved from large urban centres in the United States and Western Canada to Saint John.

The adjustment was likely made more difficult by moving from publicly traded firms to a privately held family firm. The differences are considerable, as the Wharton business school has summed up: "Executives who hone their skills at the helm of private companies tend to be more driven, more bottom line–oriented and have much more flexibility than CEOs at publicly owned companies, who are constrained by their need to balance multiple objectives in a corporate ecosystem."[32] There are also important differences in accountability requirements between the two. The CEO of a privately held firm sees the owner often, or as often as the owner or owners want. The CEO of a publicly held firm has a board of directors and many shareholders to whom he or she reports. The board of directors meets every quarter and on a needs-only basis. This is not to argue that one is more difficult than the other. Rather, the point is that they are different—very different. It might well be just as difficult for a CEO in a privately held firm to make the transition to a publicly held firm as the other way around.

Arthur Irving, as chairman of Irving Oil's board of directors, is still involved in big decisions, but leaves day-to-day management to Ian Whitcomb. Whitcomb has strong ties to Irving Oil going back over thirty years, so he is well versed in the workings of this privately held family business. By all accounts, the relationship has worked very well since 2015. Has Arthur Irving remained involved over the years? Yes, on big decisions and on projects that matter personally to him; the building of the new head office is a case in point, as we will see. On decisions that deal with daily management issues, Whitcomb and his senior management team are given free rein to run the business and look after day-to-day operations as they see fit. They report both to Arthur and to the board.

Anyone who knows Arthur Irving knows that retirement is not for him. The write-up on his appointment to the Canadian Business Hall of Fame reads: "Arthur Irving enjoys his dogs, motorcycles, gardening and the outdoors."[33] He always fills his days with activities and his days have long hours. He is a motorcycle enthusiast. He showed me his collection of motorcycles, ranging from a Harley Davidson to an Indian, which those who know motorcycles tell me is *la crème de la crème* of motorcycles. When he left Irving Oil as its CEO, Arthur frequently went on extended visits with his motorcycle to New Zealand, Italy, and the United States. Senior Irving Oil executives tell me that he did this because he enjoyed motorcycling, but also because he did not want to hang constantly over the shoulders of those responsible for running Irving Oil.

Arthur Irving continues to attend to important issues at Irving Oil. He and his daughter Sarah are active members of the firm's board of directors in establishing Irving Oil's strategic direction, its operational goals, its management performance evaluation system, and in striking annual budgets. He has a strong relationship with Ian Whitcomb, who is also on the board. Arthur was also intimately involved in the decision to purchase the shares owned by Jack Irving's family, a move he labelled "an important day for the future of our company."[34] The move enables Irving Oil to strike strategic decisions free of considerations other than those that deal directly with the firm's business interests.

Arthur Irving has never stopped visiting Irving Oil's retail stores to meet with front-line workers. He also never stops looking for new business opportunities. I have seen him in action on many occasions, and I do not think it is possible for anyone or anything to hold him back. He has too much energy to go on idle for any length of time. He also takes delight in mentoring his daughter Sarah and showing her the ins and outs of the business, much as his father did for him. When he decides to sink his teeth into a project, he still goes all out.

LOOKING BACK

THE CHALLENGE FOR A SON OR DAUGHTER OF A HIGHLY SUC-cessful entrepreneur is to keep the business going and growing. Arthur Irving met the challenge and then some. One long-serving senior Irving Oil executive told me "Arthur grew the business to the point that his father would ask—'Now, Arthur, how did you do it?'" Arthur likely would answer by saying that he followed K.C. Irving's recipe: focus on the customers, look after details, work long hours, hire good people, do not be afraid to take risks, fight the big boys when you have to, and always reinvest profits into growing the company. This sums up Arthur's formula for business success.

Arthur Irving also had several fortunate developments that helped him grow the business. The Canada-us Free Trade Agreement cleared the way for Irving Oil to march into the rich New England market. When you combine tenacity, strong business skills, and work ethic with luck, you have a powerful brew for success, and Arthur Irving knows better than anyone how to make the recipe work.

Notes

1 J.D. Irving, Limited, Woodlands Division, "JK Irving plants company's billionth tree with sons Jim and Robert," press release, July 27, 2018, online at irvingwoodlands.com/jdi-woodlands-stories-billionth-tree-celebration.aspx.
2 Allison Roy, "Smurfit-Stone à Bathurst: la petite histoire d'un gros gâchis," *Acadie Nouvelle*, August 1, 2019, 5.
3 Quoted in Douglas How and Ralph Costello, *K.C. The Biography of K.C. Irving* (Toronto: Key Porter, 1993), 299.
4 Jacques Poitras, *Irving vs. Irving: Canada's Feuding Billionaires and the Stories They Won't Tell* (Toronto: Viking Canada, 2014), 42–3.
5 How and Costelle, *K.C.*, 295.
6 Andrew Paul Prokopich, "Regina versus K.C. Irving: A Case Study in Canadian Media Ownership" (MA thesis, University of Windsor, 1979), 75, online at scholar.uwindsor.ca/cgi/viewcontent.cgi?article=7727&context=etd.
7 John DeMont also makes this point in *Citizens Irving: K.C. Irving and His Legacy* (Toronto: McClelland and Stewart, 1992), 116.
8 Quoted in How and Costello, *K.C.*, 299.
9 Ibid., 300.
10 See, for example, Roy H. Park Jr., *Sons in the Shadow: Surviving the Family Business as an SOB–Son of the Boss* (Oakland: Elderberry Press, 2016).
11 Quoted in How and Costello, *K.C.*, 381–2.
12 Harvey Sawler, *Twenty-first-Century Irvings* (Halifax: Nimbus, 2007), 96.
13 "Irving Salisbury Big Stop," n.d., online at allstays.com/truckstops-details/92344.php.
14 Sawler, *Twenty-first-Century Irvings*, 97.
15 "Keep Truckin': Cardlocks and Truck Stops," *Canadian Fuels Association*, October 3, 2018, online at canadianfuels.ca/Blog/2018/October-2018/Keep-Truckin-Cardlocks-and-Truck-Stops/.
16 DeMont, *Citizens Irving*, 166.
17 Quoted in ibid.
18 Sawler, *Twenty-first-Century Irvings*, 98.
19 See, among others, DeMont, *Citizens Irving*.
20 Jacques Poitras, *Pipe Dreams: The Fight for Canada's Energy Future* (Toronto: Penguin Canada, 2018).

21 "Saint John Refinery, New Brunswick," *Hydrocarbons Technology*, n.d., online at hydrocarbons-technology.com/projects/saint-john-refinery-new-brunswick/.

22 Quoted in "Pumped and primed," *Atlantic Business*, June 23, 2016, online at atlanticbusinessmagazine.net/article/pumped-and-primed/.

23 "Saint John Refinery, New Brunswick."

24 Mark Sherman, quoted in "Pumped and primed."

25 Atlantic Institute for Market Studies, "Energy Irving/Repsol Partnership Plans to Send First Natural Gas Down Pipeline in March," October 23, 2008, online at aims.ca/in-the-media/energy-irvingrepsol-partnership-plans-to-send-first-natural-gas-down-pipeline-in-march/.

26 Bruce Livesey, "Company province, provincial company," *Globe and Mail*, February 26, 2016, online at theglobeandmail.com/report-on-business/rob-magazine/is-the-secretive-irving-family-ready-for-itscloseup/article28917978/.

27 See, for example, "Repsol holds onto Canaport LNG after Shell deal," *CBC News*, February 27, 2013, online at cbc.ca/news/canada/new-brunswick/repsol-holds-onto-canaport-lng-after-shell-deal-1.1336866.

28 Jeff Lewis, "Repsol writes down Canaport by $1.3B after failing to sell LNG terminal in blockbuster Shell deal," *Financial Post*, February 26, 2013, online at business.financialpost.com/commodities/energy/no-buyers-for-canaport-as-shell-picks-up-repsols-lng-stakes. See also Jennifer Winter et al., "The Potential for Canadian LNG Exports to Europe," *SPP Research Paper* 11, no. 20 (Calgary: University of Calgary, School of Public Policy Publications, July 2018).

29 Robert Jones, "Repsol scraps plans to convert Canaport LNG to export gas," *CBC News*, March 16, 2016, online at cbc.ca/news/canada/new-brunswick/repsol-canaport-conversion-scrapped-1.3493617.

30 Irving Oil, "The Irving Difference," n.d., online at theirving.com/default.aspx?pageid=9.

31 Eric Anderssen, "Irving family's fortunate son explains how he fell into a dark depression, and rose again," *Globe and Mail*, January 28, 2017, online at theglobeandmail.com/report-on-business/kenneth-irving/article33791019/.

32 Wharton School, "Public versus Private Company Managers: Which Are More Likely to Impact the Bottom Line?" *Knowledge @ Wharton*, University of Pennsylvania, October 15, 2008, online at knowledge.wharton.upenn.edu/article/public-vs-private-company-managers-which-are-more-likely-to-impact-the-bottom-line/.

33 "Arthur Irving," *Canadian Business Hall of Fame*, n.d., online at cbhf.ca/arthur-irving-oc-cbhf-class-2008.

34 Quoted in Jacques Poitras, "Jack Irving's family sells stake in major Irving Oil shakeup," CBC *News*, June 1, 2018, online at cbc.ca/news/canada/new-brunswick/irving-oil-jack-irving-buyout-1.4688059.

K.C. Irving leaving his office—Dock Street Building,
Saint John, NB, 1920s.

TOP: K.C. Irving at work—Dock Street, Saint John, NB, 1950s.
BOTTOM: Arthur Irving (left) and K.C. Irving—Sales Convention, 1960s.

TOP: (left to right) Jack, K.C. and Arthur Irving—Canaport, Saint John, NB, December 1969.
BOTTOM: (left to right) Harriet, Arthur, K.C., Jim, and Jack Irving.

TOP: Irving Oil Refinery, Saint John, NB.
BOTTOM: K.C. Irving was from the small New Brunswick community of Bouctouche (also spelled "Buctouche").

TOP: Arthur Irving, 2019.
BOTTOM: The Golden Ball Building in Saint John, NB, circa 1930.

• 183 •

TOP: The New Irving Oil head office in Saint John, NB, opened in 2019. BOTTOM: (left to right) Sandra, Sarah, and Arthur Irving—Irving Oil Picnic, 2019.

Arthur Irving, summer 2019.

TOP: (left to right) Sandra, Sarah, and Arthur Irving with the author at Fenway Park, Boston, 2019.
BOTTOM: The author (left) with Arthur Irving at a church in Scotland in 2018.

CHAPTER 7

LESSONS FROM THE IRVING SCHOOL OF BUSINESS

A RTHUR IRVING READILY AND HAPPILY ADMITS THAT he learned his business skills from his father. We saw earlier that he worked closely with him and attended virtually all key meetings that dealt with Irving Oil from the day he joined the company. He was even present, for example, at the Montreal Ritz-Carlton Hotel meeting when K.C. broke off negotiations with BP about building a refinery in Saint John. Given that Arthur was by his father's side when K.C. Irving grew Irving Oil, I asked Arthur to sum up the reasons for his father's business success. His response: "He was always on top of his game." The same can now be said about Arthur Irving.

One thing is beyond question: Arthur, his father, and his two brothers were and are successful businessmen. Arthur told me on many occasions that, for K.C. Irving, business was not about making money, but "about the chase, the competition and winning, and bringing jobs to the community." This is equally true for Arthur Irving. As I have already noted, both have looked to reinvest profits to grow businesses rather than buy personal luxury items.

What made them constantly strive to be on top of their game? How can one explain Irving Oil's remarkable success story going back to 1924? What is the curriculum at the Irving School of Business? What kind of employees succeed at Irving Oil?

One thing is clear. Arthur Irving, like his father and brothers, is a hard-nosed businessman who will never hesitate to go hard at the competition. Like them, he is highly competitive, pushes the envelope, works long hours, and does not stop until he wins the top prize. All four are known to be tenacious and to play to win everywhere, every time, and against everyone in competition with them. They always drive a hard bargain. Successful business people are, by definition, driven, hard-nosed, tough negotiators. It would be wrong to confuse their civility for weakness. If they are not driven and hard-nosed, then they must be lucky, or they must have the right product at the right time to succeed. Luck might explain some of K.C.'s and Arthur's success in business. But there is much more to it than luck. As Harrison McCain discovered when he worked for K.C. at Irving Oil, winning 90 percent of the prize is not enough; 100 percent is always better. The same is true for Arthur.

Arthur Irving is not much different from other highly successful businessmen. He is focused, goes after a goal with single-minded purpose, and often sees the business world as a zero-sum game, particularly in the oil and gas sector, where it is a case of "I win, you lose" or "if I don't win, someone else will." To be sure, the oil and gas sector has been and continues to be remarkably competitive.

Irving Oil has to go head-to-head with large, highly profitable global firms that also see the business world, particularly in their sector, as a zero-sum game. These large multinationals, such as Exxon and Shell, see Irving Oil for what it is—a small, regional, family-owned business limited to eastern Canada, New England, and Ireland. I remind the reader that the most profitable business in the world is in the oil and gas sector: Saudi Aramco, valued at $111.1 billion in 2018. These large firms have marketing capacities that dwarf Irving Oil's marketing and branding arm. Like K.C. and Arthur Irving, Irving Oil also has to be constantly on top of its game to hold and, better yet, expand its market share in such a highly competitive sector. How, then, does it stay competitive? Solid management is one reason.

THE IRVING SCHOOL OF BUSINESS

IRVING OIL HAS A DISTINCT MANAGEMENT STYLE, ONE THAT has its roots in a corporate culture shaped, in large measure, by K.C. and Arthur Irving and by the business habits of a family-owned company. Blaine Higgs, who held several senior executive positions while working at Irving Oil for thirty-three years and later became premier of New Brunswick, speaks to the requirements of the Irving School of Business. He reports that it includes hard work, attention to detail, and loyalty, which add up to a "family culture built on trust." Trust and success are always applauded at the firm. Higgs adds that there was never an Irving event "where people would not be recognized for building and growing and sustaining the company."[1]

I put the following question to a senior Irving Oil executive: what is the curriculum at the Irving Oil School of Business? He points to Arthur Irving as the main architect of the curriculum.

He insists that the very first thing one needs to know about the Irving School of Business is that Arthur "is extremely passionate about customers and Irving Oil employees." He adds that he learned from Arthur to be "as tenacious as a bull dog" and "never, ever, give up." This senior executive maintains that Arthur Irving always keeps things simple. He tells us to "start with honest, hard-working, and highly motivated employees and go from there." He adds that these employees "will deliver if you let them and if you motivate them." Arthur Irving, I was told by many other executives who have worked or still work with him, will never hesitate to ask questions. It does not matter with whom he is dealing, questions will be asked. The questions will often lead to other questions, which will always be relevant and to the point. Arthur decided long ago that there is always something new to learn in the oil and gas business and in running Irving Oil, and that the best way to learn is to ask questions.

I have seen this first-hand on a few occasions, when I stopped with Arthur at Irving service stations. He asked questions of everyone in an easy, never-challenging manner. An answer would often lead to another question. Current and former senior Irving Oil executives recommend that, if you know the answer, you should give it without "fluff," and if you don't, you should not try to bluff or make one up. As one former executive explained, "Mr. Irving's questions were straightforward and there was never any need to colour your answers." He added: "If you did not know the answer, you did not make one up. He could quickly see through BS or when someone was trying to buy time by going on about something that did not deal with his questions." That, he explained, was not the way to gain Arthur Irving's trust. "Straight up, no BS," he went on, "was the way to gain Arthur Irving's attention and confidence." Ross Gaudreault, who worked closely with Arthur from the 1960s to the late 1980s, says that the most important thing for Arthur was that staff had to be "honest, straight up. That was the key to gaining his confidence."

At management meetings, Arthur Irving would push managers to do more, to secure the extra sale or the new customer, much as his father did. A former Irving Oil employee, Pat Bates, recalls Arthur Irving asking one regional manager on more than one occasion if he had been able to wrestle a customer away from Imperial Oil in northwest New Brunswick. The manager finally came up with the answer: Yes, he had met with the customer and, yes, he had tried very hard to get the business. He reported, however, that the Imperial Oil customer told him: "You know, the Irvings have enough money, we don't need to give them any more." Arthur Irving was quick with an answer: "It is not about the money, it is about putting the puck in the net." It is not only about the money or even mainly about the money, it is about winning. The message was not lost on anyone at that meeting. If you are working at Irving Oil, you need to learn to put the puck in the net.

Arthur Irving, again like his father, makes a point of attending funerals of former employees. Bates recalls Arthur Irving walking down the hall one day, saying, "Boys, put your work down. So-and-so has passed away and we are all going to the funeral." That, Bates went on, happened on more than one occasion. Darren Gillis reports that the same happens today. I asked Gillis why Arthur Irving makes it a point to attend funerals of Irving Oil people. For Mr. Irving, he replied, "it is a question of loyalty. Employees have shown loyalty to Irving Oil and it is important for him to show loyalty back. For Arthur loyalty is always a two-way street." He adds, "Mr. Irving is always consistent about one thing: customers and employees matter a great deal to him, and I am not sure which ones come first."

I am hardly the first to write about the Irving School of Business. We know that employees who fit with Irving Oil's corporate culture and expectations are typically decisive, willing to take risks, hard-working, open to change, and demanding of their own performance.[2] They embrace a value that K.C. Irving first ingrained in his business in 1924: always provide better customer service than the competition.

Both K.C. and Arthur also embraced other values that now permeate Irving Oil. They include a strong work ethic, clean living, a high level of integrity, civility in dealing with everyone, no matter their standing in society, and tenacity. Clean living and staying away from alcohol and tobacco have long been associated with the Irvings. Ross Gaudreault recalls K.C. saying more than once that, "if God wanted us to smoke, he would have put chimneys on top of our heads." He added that "alcohol was out of the question everywhere, including in your expense accounts."

Arthur values black and white rather than grey. He looks for executives and managers who are decisive, sure-footed, able to carve out a path, capable of dealing with obstacles, and are passionate about their work. If he has to deal with errors, Arthur prefers dealing with those of commission, provided they do not eat up too much capital. Privately held firms often favour a bias for action, and see no merit in their people failing to act when they have a clear opportunity to do so. Publicly traded firms, in contrast, always have an eye on the next quarterly report and what the board of directors or the media will say if a senior executive makes a costly or high-profile error. Publicly traded companies, in short, can be much more risk-averse than privately owned firms, and they often favour a short-term perspective in order to respond to shareholders' expectations.

To be sure, not everyone is suited for the Irving Oil corporate culture and its untiring work ethic. Former Irving Oil employees who were not able to make the cut are unlikely to look in the mirror to understand why. They will blame Irving Oil for their lack of success with the firm rather than themselves. Those who make the cut, however, remain loyal and dedicated. As Joel Levesque, of Moosehead Breweries argues, "people who naturally have a strong work ethic and are exposed to the Irvings end up having nothing but admiration for them."[3]

In consulting an employment website that reports on work experiences at different companies, I found that the reviews for Irving Oil run the full gamut. One reviewer writes: "not hard work to do" at Irving Oil, "but ultimately overworked." Another reports that it is a "great place to work. There is a tremendous can-do spirit here. Senior leadership has a clear course and it is communicated clearly to all employees." On balance, there are many more positive comments than negative ones.

Ross Gaudreault recalls meeting with Arthur Irving and eight or nine other senior managers every Saturday morning between nine o'clock and noon. It was a more relaxed setting than a typical weekly meeting at the office, with everyone dressed in casual clothing. The Saturday-morning meetings were designed to take stock of what had transpired the week before and to plan the next week. But this is where key decisions were very often made. Gaudreault explains: "We did not operate with a budget. We decided what needed to be done and Arthur would OK the funds to get it done. That is the way we did business back then." He adds that everyone had a say, and when they walked out of those Saturday morning meetings, they all knew what they had to do in the coming week. Gaudreault further explains that, although Irving Oil is a large business, "we were running it like it was a small business." Arthur was in charge, and he had a hand in everything. Gaudreault still marvels at Arthur's level of energy. He says that he tried to talk Arthur into not signing every cheque of $1,000 or more and that he often sat in the office watching Arthur sign cheque after cheque while dealing with a multitude of issues and decisions.

IT'S OFTEN ABOUT PERCEPTION

PERCEPTION MATTERS WHEN LOOKING AT IRVING OIL. TO MANY New Brunswickers—and again at the risk of sounding repetitive—Irving Oil is a large, dominating business that wields substantial power over the provincial economy. To Arthur Irving, it is a relatively small family business trying "to compete with the big boys" on the world stage. I accept that, to the local convenience store owner, Irving Oil is a big firm managed by the big boys.

Richard Wilbur, a former professor of history at the University of New Brunswick, explains that K.C.'s phenomenal business success was a result of "his combativeness, his tenacity, his tendency toward the concrete and the physical rather than the abstract."[4] A conversation between K.C. and Lord Beaverbrook speaks to this. Lord Beaverbrook, a well-known art collector, invited K.C. to view a painting he had recently purchased. K.C. told Beaverbrook: "I recall reading somewhere that you paid $150,000 for this." Beaverbrook replied: "That's right." K.C. took a second look at the painting and said: "Just think how much pulpwood you could have bought with that."[5] K.C. clearly favoured the practical over the abstract, and how best to grow a business over the finer points of a work of art. I note that K.C. Irving and Lord Beaverbrook became good friends. They often visited each other in Saint John, Fredericton, London, and at Beaverbrook's winter home in the Bahamas.

First K.C., then Arthur, and now senior Irving Oil executives view the oil and gas sector as a David-and-Goliath struggle, with Irving Oil always David. Consider the following. Exxon Mobil generates nearly $270 billion in revenues every year, has vast oil and gas resources, produces 4.1 million barrels of oil a day, employs over 75,000 people, and operates in fifty-eight countries.[6] Shell has revenues of $388 billion, 82,000 employees, operates in over seventy countries, and produces about 3.7 million barrels of oil a day.[7] Closer to home, Suncor (which owns Petro-Canada) operates refineries in Alberta, Ontario, and Quebec, produces 732,000 barrels of oil a day, has revenues of over $15 billion annually and over 12,000 employees, and operates in all ten provinces.[8] It will be recalled that Ottawa created Petro-Canada as a Crown corporation in 1975 and that its growth, at least in part, was fuelled by taxpayers. Irving Oil, meanwhile, does not own oil and gas resources, operates in only five Canadian provinces, New England, and now Ireland, has a total workforce of 4,000, and a retail infrastructure of over 1,100 service stations.

That does not tell the full story. As we will see later, it is a great deal easier to attract top-flight talent in a large urban centre with lower income tax rates than to a small urban center like Saint John, New Brunswick, in a province with one of the highest personal income tax rates in Canada. Calgary, home to Canada's oil and gas industry, was long able to attract leading executives because of its high-quality civic institutions and because of Alberta's lower income- and consumption-tax rates. From the perspective of the small convenience store in New Brunswick, Irving Oil and its Circle K outlets are Goliath, easily capable of dominating the local market and with a purchasing power that dwarfs that of the small store owner. But things look very different from Irving Oil's head office on King Square in Saint John.

For Irving Oil executives, the competition is not the local convenience store but the big boys from away, and you need to be on top of your game to compete with them. Irving Oil managers must constantly put their best foot forward and learn to manage operations efficiently. They do not have the financial resources or the kind of elaborate management structure that Shell or Exxon have. In short, to compete, Irving Oil has to operate with a lean and efficient management team and has to provide a better level of service to customers.

Even as they try to compete with large global firms, Irving Oil executives also need to consider their firm's impact on the local economy. Senior managers sitting in head offices in, say, Toronto or Calgary have no such concern. The distance between them and the local store owner is a lot bigger than the distance between senior Irving Oil managers in Saint John and small Maritime communities. This adds another challenge to the curriculum at the Irving School of Business. Irving Oil managers have to learn to work closely with local communities and local service station-operators while they hone their management skills to compete with larger and financially stronger firms.

The owner of a Moncton-based manufacturing firm told me that his business has been running extremely well since he hired a top manager as his vice-president of operations. I asked him: "Who is he or she, and where does he or she come from?" His response: "He came to me from the Irvings, wanting to move to Moncton." The new executive had learned his management skills at the Irving School of Business, and he had proven to be a bolt of energy when he arrived at the firm. I asked the owner what made this manager different from the others. His response: "There is just no desire to come up short; he is straight-up, knows what needs to be done and does it. There is simply no pussyfooting with him." He added that this individual has a strong work ethic, never wastes time on things that do not matter to the business, and makes certain that everyone is pushing in the same direction. In brief, like other graduates of the Irving School of Business, he looks to the concrete, the physical, rather than the abstract, and he knows what it takes to compete.

LEAN IS ALWAYS BETTER

STARTING WITH K.C. AND CONTINUING WITH ARTHUR, THE Irving approach to management underlines the importance of simplicity, concreteness, and productivity. They have always avoided turning their organizations into large, bloated bureaucracies. They have also avoided businesses they do not understand—"always sticking to one's knitting," as Arthur Irving once told me. They value front-line managers who are able to seize the moment and quickly move initiatives forward. The organizational distance between top management and front-line managers is deliberately kept short. If a quick decision is needed, it can be made.

Ian Whitcomb, Irving Oil's president since 2015, once told me that Irving Oil managers need to value teamwork; if they don't, there is simply no place for them in the organization. Flying solo is not valued at the firm. More to the point, there is only room for team players at Irving Oil.[9]

Irving Oil employees learn very early on—going back to K.C. Irving and the first days in business—that the customer is king. It is also a key component of the curriculum at the Irving School of Business: always remember to make sure to provide a markedly better level of service to customers than the competition does. If Irving Oil managers are not prepared to work by this dictum, they are unlikely to succeed with the company. Furthermore, they must learn to turn to front-line employees to gain a better understanding of what customers value or want.

For those who think that all businesses look to their front-line employees for ideas on how best to serve their customers, I have a personal story that suggests otherwise. In 2013, I published *Harrison McCain: Single-Minded Purpose*, which was distributed by Chapters stores, among others. I was visiting their Moncton location, where the book had been placed in the "biographies" section. I noticed that there was a "local interest" table with books with a variety of titles dealing with New Brunswick. I asked a Chapters employee why my McCain book was not on that table. His response: "Yeah, it should be, but we don't have a say about that. The decision on where to place books is made by a computer at head office somewhere in Toronto." I asked: "Can't you talk to someone in Toronto?" He was quick with a reply: "Have you ever tried to talk to a computer?" I am a frequent visitor to the local Chapters store, and I know that the book never made it to the "local interest" table. The head office and its computer were not able to see that Harrison McCain was from Florenceville, New Brunswick, and that I live in Moncton, only seven kilometres from the store.

The public sector has little capacity or perhaps little desire to turn to clients to gain a better understanding of what they wish to see. One of the shortcomings that I have identified in the federal public service is that there are too many management levels—anywhere between seven and eleven, depending on how one counts and on the type of organization—between the top of a departmental organization and front-line workers. This is in sharp contrast even with the Roman Catholic Church, which has five levels between the pope in Rome and local parish priests.[10] The problem for the federal public service is that, all too often, there is a disconnect between those at the top and front-line workers. Those at the bottom do not always know what is expected of them, with the result that many are kept busy turning a crank that is not attached to anything.[11] I recognize, however, that the public and private sectors are different in every way, and that one ought to be careful in drawing comparisons between the two.

Still, Irving Oil has precious few workers kept busy turning cranks not attached to anything. I admit that this is also true for other businesses in the goods-producing sector. Irving Oil not only has a flat organization, the flow of information also moves easily between front-line workers and senior management. If they wish and if there is a need, front-line workers can quickly access and speak to any management level. As we saw, Arthur Irving has always made a point of deliberately connecting with front-line workers. This is widely known inside the organization, and has become part of the corporate culture and expectations. Stories of Arthur Irving suddenly arriving unannounced at service stations continue to make the rounds throughout the Irving Oil organization to this day.

To sum up, the management structure at Irving Oil is flat and lean. Leaving aside the physical beauty and the cost associated with the new head-office building, Irving Oil also has a parsimonious culture. The culture dates back to when Arthur patiently sat down and signed every cheque of $1,000 and over. The message is not lost on Irving Oil managers and staff. It has become part of the Irving Oil corporate culture and the Irving School of Business curriculum.

IT'S ALSO ABOUT THE
SAFETY OF EMPLOYEES

WITHIN MINUTES OF ARRIVING AT THE IRVING OIL REFINERY in Saint John, the importance of safety is made clear. I invite readers to consult various websites of firms that report on how management and employees view safety measures.[12] Irving Oil ranks high on safety compared with many other firms, notably those in the oil and gas sector. Irving Oil has full-time people whose mandate is to look after the safety and health of its employees.[13] The safety of employees is always an important part of all Irving Oil in-house publications. In its October 2019 *People Matters* publication, Irving Oil reported that it had gone five years without a "lost-time" injury at its network of terminals in Atlantic Canada and New England. The network employs two hundred people.[14] The publication also has a report card detailing how well the company is doing on safety in all areas of the business.[15]

Management reports that Irving Oil has a solid safety record, and it has the data to back up the claim. Mark Sherman, former manager of the refinery, points out that safety is a "core value, everyone working at our Refinery is accountable for their personal safety and the safety of others." He adds that the work "is never so urgent or so important that we compromise the environment, health or safety."[16] I note that the Saint John refinery's safety record compares very favourably with the other North American refineries.

In October 2018, a massive explosion at the refinery rattled workers and nearby residents. It occurred in the middle of a "turnaround" initiative, which meant that there were approximately two thousand people on the refinery site at the time of the explosion. The incident occurred because of a malfunction in the refinery's diesel-treating unit.[17] This led management and staff to initiate a full-scale review of safety procedures at the refinery. Senior Irving Oil officials report that the review led to a number of new or strengthened measures.

GOOD DEEDS AND GIVING BACK

SENIOR MANAGEMENT, GOING BACK TO ARTHUR IRVING, HAS encouraged Irving Oil employees to give back to their communities or to good causes, and Irving's people have responded. The number of requests for donations is always greater than available resources. Irving Oil has established a Donations and Sponsorship Review Committee that brings together representatives from across the organization to coordinate and ensure contributions are aligned with priorities tied to education, the environment, and helping families.

Apart from the many donations to local communities—at both a company and employee level, and on both a monetary and volunteer basis—the company has long-standing relationships with corporate social responsibility (CSR) partners including Ducks Unlimited, the New England Aquarium, and, notably, seven partner hospitals across the regions where Irving Oil and the CSR partners operate. Since 2002 Irving Oil has also provided fuel gift cards to over sixty-five thousand families travelling between home and hospital. The program, called Fuel the Care, is an initiative of which Irving Oil employees are especially proud. This is separate from the substantial contributions Arthur and Sandra Irving and the Arthur L. Irving Family Foundation make every year, as we will see in Chapter 9.

Irving Oil also has an in-house publication to keep employees abreast of developments within the firm. There is a section on the employee giving program, "Good Energy in Action," that reports on the various efforts to contribute to local communities and causes. In the third quarter of 2018, 65 percent of Irving Oil employees in Canada participated in the Good Energy initiative, as did 58 percent in Ireland and 56 percent in the United States. They accumulated nearly eleven thousand volunteer hours both during and outside work time supporting 419 causes, including Saint John community food banks, the Canadian Cancer Society, and local hospitals.[18] And, as we saw earlier, Irving Oil has other means to encourage its employees to give back to their communities and causes.

MANAGEMENT

Irving Oil was recognized as one of Canada's top one hundred employers for four years running, from 2016 to 2019, and one of Atlantic Canada's top employers. In the case of the Canadian ranking, the process is managed by the editors of "Canada's Top 100 Employers" at Toronto-based Mediacorp Canada. It is a national competition open to all companies that have their corporate head offices in Canada and to public-sector organizations. Candidates are assessed against eight criteria: physical workplace; work atmosphere and social aspects; health, financial, and family benefits; vacation and time off; employee communications; performance management; training and skills development; and community involvement.[19] Irving Oil was one of 7,500 organizations to submit an application, and was given an A grade on four of the eight criteria, including an A+ for community involvement. It also got an A for physical workplace (I suspect that this will go up to A+ when the new building comes into play), for health and family benefits, and for training and skills development. The same criteria are employed in establishing "Atlantic Canada's Top

30 Employers." Here, the process is managed by *Atlantic Business* magazine out of St. John's, Newfoundland.

This is no small achievement given that Irving Oil has had to deal with important management challenges in recent years. Senior management now has to manage operations in several jurisdictions, some of which have faced difficult political issues, including, for example, how Ireland will fit in the new Europe as Brexit plays out. To be sure, the oil and gas sector is not an easy sector to navigate as the debate on climate change continues to gain currency everywhere. Management at Irving Oil also has to deal with a wide array of issues, from running Canada's largest oil and gas refinery to how best to deal with its small retail outlets in remote communities.

I asked a senior Irving Oil executive if the firm had put management training opportunities in place. "Yes," he responded, and explained that Irving Oil looks to individual managers and sees what is needed for them to reach their full potential. It can tailor a course, assign someone to a special task, or slot a manager into a position for a set period to expose him or her to new challenges or to gain experience in a different part of the organization. In brief, Irving Oil does not have a one-size-fits-all approach to management development, opting instead to develop the potential of individual executives and managers to the firm's management requirements.

Senior Irving Oil executives report that managers never lose sight of the need to promote an entrepreneurial edge at all levels of the organization. That, according to one senior executive, is one of Irving Oil's basic approaches to management. He explained: "We keep pushing for gaining new markets, new customers, and securing a greater chunk of the business from our existing customers, if a greater chunk is to be had. This is everyone's business."

LOOKING BACK

LONG-SERVING SENIOR IRVING OIL EXECUTIVES I CONSULTED insist that Irving Oil has a distinct management culture. They say that the culture is firmly anchored in some unshakable beliefs that they trace back to K.C.'s and Arthur Irving's tenures as CEO. They have a point. However, I recognize that executives and managers always tell the story the way they want it told.

At the top of the list of current and former Irving Oil executives is the strongly held belief that success in business is directly tied to the quality of service to customers. This is now ingrained in staff that have been with Irving Oil for any extended period. In an interview with a business magazine, senior Irving Oil executive Darren Gillis explained: "We believe in giving our customers an exemplary experience, from the moment they arrive at our site. This means paying great attention to every detail—from clean washrooms for our customers to having the fluffiest white towels and clean showers for our professional truck driver customers."[20] Attention to detail mattered a great deal to K.C. Irving, as it does to Arthur Irving and continues to do at Irving Oil. In short, it is an important component of the curriculum at the Irving School of Business.

Perhaps because both K.C. and Arthur always felt as though they were the underdogs battling more powerful forces, whether large global firms or the federal government and its preoccupation with the two vote-rich central provinces, tenacity has also become another hallmark of the management culture at Irving Oil. Arthur has always given the extra effort in pursuing economic opportunities, and senior executives at Irving Oil have all learned to do the same.

Ian Whitcomb underlines the importance of another key management requirement at Irving Oil when he says that there is only room for team players. This became clear in my interviews with current and former Irving Oil employees. Again, perhaps because they feel as though they are the underdogs, everyone I talked with made the point that they all have to push in the same direction to ensure success, knowing that they have to compete against large, well-endowed global firms.

I also saw, both when touring the refinery and in my discussions with Irving Oil employees, that management places a great deal of importance on the safety and health of employees. Here, it might well be that running a refinery carries far more safety risks than is the case for many other businesses. At Irving Oil, safety is top of mind for management, as it likely is for any business that operates a refinery. This commitment generates two-way loyalty between workers and management. Arthur Irving has often, and unprompted, underlined the importance of safety when discussing work at the refinery.

There is an underlying factor that has had a profound influence in shaping the curriculum at the Irving School of Business, and it cannot be overstated. The differences between a privately held family business and a publicly traded company are immense, and they matter a great deal for how the business is run. To be sure, privately held businesses have many advantages for management. The relationship between management and the shareholders is clear, as are accountability requirements. Decisions can be made a great deal more easily and more quickly in a privately held business than is the case in publicly traded companies. It is also easier to promote an "us versus them" attitude at all levels in the business, an attitude that is evident at Irving Oil. In addition, the owner-shareholder is a great deal more accessible when it comes to feedback than is the case for large publicly traded companies.

TWENTY-FOUR HOURS

ONE REVIEWER OF THE MANUSCRIPT OF THIS BOOK TOLD ME "it would be interesting to know what Arthur Irving does in twenty-four hours." I did not know Arthur Irving when he was Irving Oil's CEO, but those who worked with him at the time report that Arthur never stopped from early morning to late into the evening. In the words of a former senior Irving Oil executive, "he just never stopped and he had us going strong day in, day out."

The one thing that can be said about Arthur's day is that there is no such thing as a "typical day." As he said about working with his father when he accepted the Atlantic Canada Plus honour on his behalf, "every day was different." Every one of Arthur's days is filled with activities from morning to night. He is an early riser, and typically begins the day with exercises. From there, it depends. There can be a series of meetings in Toronto, Boston, or Saint John. He always fills his days so there are precious few idle hours. He will set up visits to regional operations, to large customers, and to staff meetings. He will take stock of commitments made to community or university projects, frequently visiting Acadia University or Dartmouth College. He has a careful diet, and has never once turned to alcohol or tobacco. He can end his day by watching a hockey game. Typically, his day begins around 6 A.M. and ends after 10 P.M.

Here's just one example. November 5, 2019, was just another very busy day for Arthur Irving, who had arrived in Saint John from business meetings in New York late the night before. He was up at 5 that morning and in the gym by 5:30. He had breakfast, and then met Sarah and other Irving Oil executives at the airport at 7 A.M. for a flight to Quebec City. From there, the group went to Drummondville to visit existing dealers, talk to front-line staff, check on standards, and make sure that the facilities were clean.

One Irving Oil executive told me that, at one point, Arthur walked away from the group to go meet a truck driver. He and the driver, who was from Newfoundland and Labrador, talked for fifteen minutes or so about where he was from, his truck route, and what he was hauling.

The group then explored new business opportunities and possible new sites in the Drummondville area and also looked at sites held by the competition. Next, it was off to Quebec City to look at potential sites for service stations. Afterwards, there was a dinner meeting with dealers at which both Arthur and Sarah spoke. The group returned to Saint John on the same night, arriving around 10. A few days later, Arthur, Sarah, and a few senior Irving Oil executives were on their way to take stock of operations in Ireland. No matter the day, Arthur always has the future of Irving Oil top of mind.

LOOKING AHEAD

IRVING OIL WAS BORN IN NEW BRUNSWICK. K.C. REMAINED IN the province, as has Arthur Irving. There is every indication that Arthur wants to keep Irving Oil in New Brunswick and in the family. His decision to build what is arguably Atlantic Canada's most elegant and exquisite head office in Saint John speaks to his desire to anchor Irving Oil in New Brunswick for the long term. More is said about this and Irving Oil's head office in the next chapter.

Arthur has stayed the course first established by his father in building Irving Oil. He learned from his father what makes a successful business tick: a deeply felt loyalty to customers and employees. My sense is that Irving Oil's current president, Ian Whitcomb, and Sarah Irving, vice-president and chief brand officer, have every intention of pursuing growth at Irving Oil by embracing the same values that Arthur did—values that go back to 1924.

I have had a number of conversations with Arthur and Sarah Irving and Ian Whitcomb about Irving Oil and its future. Four themes invariably come up when talking about management at Irving Oil: customers and employees are at the core of their approach to management; safety at all Irving Oil operations is a priority; community support and good deeds are important regardless of whether Irving Oil gets any credit for the support—indeed, in most cases, it downplays its support to various communities and causes—and looking for ways to respect the environment is key. This while remaining committed to the region by anchoring its head office in New Brunswick.

Notes

1   Blaine Higgs, quoted in Bruce Livesey, "Company province, provincial economy," *Globe and Mail*, February 26, 2016, online at theglobeandmail.com/report-on-business/rob-magazine/is-the-secretive-irving-family-ready-for-itscloseup/article28917978/.
2   See, for example, Harvey Sawler, *Twenty-first-Century Irvings* (Halifax: Nimbus, 2007), 77–8.
3   Ibid., 77.
4   Richard Wilbur, "K.C. Irving: The man who built an empire—but why?" *Financial Post*, November 17, 1973.
5   Quoted in John DeMont, *Citizens Irving: K.C. Irving and His Legacy* (Toronto: McClelland and Stewart, 1992), 58.
6   Adam Taylor, "If ExxonMobil were a country, its economy would be bigger than Ireland's," *Washington Post*, December 13, 2016, online at washingtonpost.com/news/worldviews/wp/2016/12/12/if-exxonmobil-were-a-country-it-would-be-the-worlds-41st-largest-economy/.
7   Shell, *Annual Report and Form 20-F 2018*, March 13, 2019, online at reports.shell.com/annual-report/2018/servicepages/download-centre.php.
8   Suncor, *Annual Report 2018*, February 27, 2019, online at suncor.com/en-CA/investor-centre/financial-reports/annual-disclosure.
9   John DeMont also makes this point in *Citizens Irving*, 166.
10 Donald J. Savoie, *What Is Government Good At? A Canadian Answer* (Montreal; Kingston, ON: McGill-Queen's University Press, 2015).
11 Donald J. Savoie, *Whatever Happened to the Music Teacher: How Government Decides and Why* (Montreal: McGill-Queen's University Press, 2013), 160.
12 See, for example, indeed.ca.
13 See, for example, Irving Oil, "Environmental Health and Safety Project Coordinator," *Linkedin*, July 2019, online at ca.linkedin.com/jobs/view/environmental-health-and-safety-project-coordinator-at-irving-oil-1374274111.
14 Irving Oil, "Products & Terminals group marks important safety milestone," *People Matters* 4, no. 2 (2019): 6.
15 Ibid., 11.
16 Irving Oil, "Irving Oil's Refinery Surpasses Record Safety Performance," press release, May 15, 2012, online at irvingoil.com/en-CA/press-room/irving-oils-refinery-surpasses-record-safety-performance.

17 Kevin Bissett, "Irving Oil says refinery safe after 'malfunction' shakes Saint John," BNN *Bloomberg*, October 9, 2018, online at bnnbloomberg.ca/irving-oil-says-refinery-safe-after-malfunction-shakes-saint-john-1.1149028.

18 *People Matters* (Saint John, NB: Irving Oil, May 2019), 18–19.

19 See, among others, Diane Jermyn, "Canada's Top 100 Employers redefine how people work and live," *Globe and Mail*, December 14, 2017, online at theglobeandmail.com/report-on-business/careers/top-employers/canadas-top-100-employers-redefine-how-people-work-and-live/article37326224/.

20 Quoted in "Pumped and primed," *Atlantic Business*, June 23, 2016, online at atlanticbusinessmagazine.net/article/pumped-and-primed/.

CHAPTER 8

NO BETTER PLACE
THAN THE MARITIMES

OBVIOUSLY KNEW, AT A VERY YOUNG AGE, WHO K.C. IRVING was. I also knew that he had three sons at his side in business. My Bouctouche roots, if nothing else, told me that. And I saw that the Irving businesses kept growing through good times and bad.

The sons followed in their father's footsteps in many ways. They too shied away from public visibility and kept things very close to their chests. They still do. Like everyone else, I heard that they stayed away from alcohol and tobacco, that they were untiring workers, and that they were highly accomplished businessmen. However, I knew little else about them until I became friends with Sandra Irving and, later, with Arthur and Sarah Irving. As noted earlier, although I do not know J.D. Irving nearly as well, I have had many discussions with him and his son Jamie over the past ten years or so.

I did not realize until I got to know them better, however, the extent to which they are deeply committed Maritimers—far more than I, and likely many Maritimers, ever imagined. I now know that this strong sentiment can be traced back to K.C. Irving. I readily admit that I discovered K.C. Irving's deeply felt commitment to New Brunswick and Atlantic Canada only while carrying out research for this book.

I suspect that it was a highly motivating factor in K.C.'s business success. To be sure, Arthur has not lost his fervour for this deeply felt commitment to the region. If anything, it has only grown. Arthur Irving directed the expansion of the Saint John refinery to make it the biggest in Canada. He also led the charge at Irving Oil in its efforts to bring Energy East to the Maritimes. In addition, he oversaw the construction of the head-office building in Saint John, down to the most minute detail. He has stayed firm over the years about locating all major head-office activities in Saint John when economic circumstances might well have suggested otherwise.

THE REFINERY

SEVERAL YEARS BEFORE I STARTED WORK ON THIS BOOK, I WAS invited to tour the Irving Oil refinery. I readily admit that I knew and still know precious little about oil refineries and how they operate. Still, I was in awe of this engineering marvel. This is what I now know about the Irving refinery. It is the largest in Canada, capable of processing over 300,000 barrels of crude a day. The next largest is in Lévis, Quebec, capable of processing 235,000 barrels, followed by the Strathcona refinery in Edmonton, at 191,000 barrels.[1] The Irving Oil refinery accounts for about 15 percent of all the oil processed in Canada on any given day and 75 percent of all gasoline exports from Canada to the United States.[2] It is also one of the most efficiently operated refineries in North America.

The Irving Oil refinery produces a full range of products, including gasoline for automobiles, jet fuel, home heating oil, kerosene, butane, propane, and heavy crude oil for asphalt. The process to make these products is very intricate, particularly to the untrained eye. I can only provide a glimpse of the process by writing that the refinery is made up of units for distillation, cracking, reforming (molecular rearrangement), product treating, steam and hydrogen production, sulphur recovery, and tanks for blending and product storage.[3] The refinery enables Irving Oil to produce numerous lubricants and chemical products that are sold around the world.[4] An army of workers watches over operations, deciding when to shift resources from one product to another and running one of the largest end-to-end blending and packaging facilities in North America. Irving Oil can now tailor many products to source not only its own sales outlets, but also many private labels.

The high-tech facility is also home to two in-house laboratories. The first, which employs forty people, operates twenty-four hours a day, seven days a week, testing products to ensure they meet the exact specifications customers require. The second laboratory is tied to the manufacturing process, and looks after blending and packaging.[5] The plant is also connected to a state-of-the-art distribution centre. When I toured the refinery, I saw a number of highly skilled workers sitting at computer terminals, some monitoring the spot price of crude oil and others making sure that things were running on track. I also saw many signs, at every turn, suggesting that Irving Oil attaches a great deal of importance to the health and safety of its workers.

The refinery, built in a long straight line that stretches a kilometre and a half, is different from most other refineries, which are built in a more tightly concentrated area.[6] This not only makes it easier to expand the refinery, it also helps control fires and promote safety. Irving Oil was able to limit the damage to the refinery in the major fire of October 2018 because of the way it was built. This is in sharp contrast to the fire that shut down the Philadelphia Energy Solutions oil refinery in June 2019.[7] That refinery had much more closely spaced structures.

As already noted, the Saint John refinery was expanded in 1971 and again in 1974. In 2000 Irving Oil completed another ambitious $1.5 billion upgrade. As I walked the length of the refinery, I kept thinking back to the story Arthur had told me about the Montreal meeting between K.C. and BP Petroleum when K.C. explained in four words why he insisted on a Saint John site: "Because I live there."

It is the only reason New Brunswick could one day become home to Canada's largest refinery. No publicly traded or privately held corporation from away would have looked to Saint John sixty years ago to locate a refinery, as BP's decision made clear. It is in Saint John because K.C. Irving decided it should be there, and it is now the largest and arguably the most successful refinery in Canada because Arthur Irving decided to invest in its development, rather than simply run the refinery for a profit and then take the profits and run.

In contrast, Imperial Oil announced on July 21, 2011, that it would shut down its Dartmouth, Nova Scotia, refinery. The refinery was opened in 1918, employed two hundred workers and a similar number of local contractors, and was able to process 88,000 barrels of crude a day. Imperial Oil decided to shut it down because it could not find a buyer and the refinery could no longer compete.[8] Unlike Irving Oil, Imperial Oil decided not to upgrade its Dartmouth refinery or to carry out, every several years or so, expensive and time-consuming maintenance projects. Instead, it took the profits generated by the refinery and invested them in its other operations. Head office, as always, made that call. Imperial Oil had a choice location, or at least it seemed a much better location than Saint John, to operate a refinery. BP, in its failed negotiations to build a refinery with K.C. Irving, had identified Halifax among other sites. Halifax-Dartmouth has a year-round port, although not as welcoming for supertankers as the Saint John port. It also has easy access to the US eastern seaboard, is able to receive crude from the Middle East, and is a larger urban centre, presumably better able to attract top executive talent and skilled workers, than Saint John.

The Irving refinery employs sixteen hundred people and exports a growing percentage of its finished products to the United States. As we have seen, Irving Oil upgrades its refinery on a continuing basis. These periodic maintenance initiatives and annual fall turnaround activities are costly and employ up to three thousand skilled workers. Irving Oil also operates the Irving Canaport Marine Terminal, the first deepwater crude terminal in the Western Hemisphere to receive supertankers and with more than six million barrels of storage capacity.[9] Combined, the refinery and the Canaport Marine Terminal represent one of Canada's great engineering marvels, bringing together Canada's largest and most efficient refinery with a highly sophisticated transportation-unloading complex.

The bulk of the incoming crude to the refinery comes by ship. Canaport was opened in 1970, and is located a short distance from the refinery. It exists exclusively to receive crude to supply the refinery, and is connected to an underwater pipeline of over one kilometre in length that transfers the crude from a floating buoy to which tankers attach for unloading. The pipeline connects to a number of storage tanks onshore. The tanks in turn are connected to the refinery through pipelines that bridge the eight-kilometre journey.[10]

THE INFRASTRUCTURE

K.C. IRVING DECIDED TO BUILD THE REFINERY IN SAINT JOHN because, as he explained and as I have noted several times, "I live there." The thinking then was that a better business decision would have been to locate it elsewhere. But that was then. With hindsight, building the refinery in Saint John increasingly looks like an inspired business call.

The refinery is located less than one hundred kilometres from the US border. The US Northeast is a rich market of one hundred million people where Irving Oil now sells 80 percent of its products.[11] Moreover, the region is "desperately short of local refinery capacity," and it has little choice but to import the bulk of its petroleum products from offshore refineries.[12] There is no refinery in New England or New York, and one has to go to New Jersey, where they have five oil refineries, all of which are smaller than the Saint John refinery (the biggest, the Bayway refinery, has a 230,000-barrel-a-day capacity).[13] Because of Irving Oil's location, its products have only a short distance to travel to reach this market. Ships from the Irving Oil refinery can reach Boston in a little over twenty hours and New York in thirty-seven. This compares to six days from the US Gulf Coast to Boston, or sixteen days by pipeline.[14] Distance will only matter more in the years ahead, and the refinery's short distance to the New England market will continue to favour Irving Oil over its competitors. Kenneth Irving summed things up nicely when he said, "In a future where every act of consumption will incur cost based on environmental impact, distance will be a major factor in displacing barrels that come from much further away."[15] This is just one of several reasons the Energy East pipeline made sense.

Saint John, with the arrival of supertankers, has become a choice location for a refinery. Its deepwater port is the best year-round, ice-free port between Saint John and Louisiana. It has a water depth of 128 feet at low tide. Notwithstanding the powerful tides of the Bay of Fundy, supertankers have been able to move in and out without an oil spill. The infrastructure enables Irving Oil to buy crude from all over the planet. The world's largest ships can call on the Canaport Terminal whenever they want, attach their cargo to a floating buoy, and pump crude into a hose to move it to a row of large tanks that bear the Irving name. It is now widely recognized that the ability to access supertankers year-round gives the Saint John refinery a comparative advantage over many other refineries in Canada and the United States.

Large refineries tend to locate near waterways, which enables them to receive crude and ship finished products by tankers and supertankers. US refineries have a comparative advantage in part because of lower-priced US crude oil, which has resulted in large increases in the US production of oil, natural gas, and natural gas liquids in recent years. Between 2008 and 2013, the United States went from being the world's largest net importer of refined petroleum products to the world's largest net exporter of refined petroleum.[16] Irving Oil has to compete in the global market. It has to buy its crude because it has no production capacity of its own. This is why the Energy East pipeline, which would have enabled it to buy Canadian crude rather than importing it from the Middle East or West Africa, held strong appeal. Killing Energy East did not mean that Canada would consume less oil and gas; it meant that, instead of being able to tap into Canada's oil production, we would continue to have to import crude from other parts of the world.

Irving Oil's easy access to the New England market gives it a strong comparative advantage. But there is more to it than that. Irving Oil has strong management and is privately owned, which makes it easier to plan for the long term and reinvest profits in the firm. Instead of circling the wagons in an effort to hold on to what it has, the company has decided to expand to other markets.

GOING TO IRELAND

IRVING OIL, FROM ITS SAINT JOHN HEAD OFFICE, ALSO OVERSEES the operations of another refinery located in Ireland, some four thousand kilometres away. This is a new twist for New Brunswick, given that the province has many operations run by businesses with head offices located in other parts of the world. Still, Irving Oil's Saint John head office has been able to run successfully, from a distance, a refinery and an oil and gas retail firm in Ireland.

As mentioned earlier, Irving Oil bought the Whitegate refinery from Phillips in 2016. Industry observers reported that Phillips was losing money running the refinery—as much as US$280 million in one year (2014).[17] The city of Cork, where the refinery is located, was worried about potential job losses at the time, but Arthur Irving tells me that Irving Oil has been able to turn things around at the refinery over a relatively short period. The refinery processes up to seventy-five thousand barrels of crude per day, drawing supply from the North Sea and elsewhere. It employs 160 individuals and also retains contract workers. Arthur Irving declared, "It's a good day for our company and we're looking forward to welcoming the Whitegate team to Irving Oil."[18]

The concern in Ireland was that a large multinational would buy the refinery and then decide to shut it down since it was small and in need of an upgrade. Irving Oil, a relatively small family business, at least by global standards, saw things differently, to the relief of the local community and the refinery's employees. Irving Oil saw an opportunity to expand across the Atlantic, and quickly reassured the 160 workers that their jobs were secure.[19]

A few years later, Irving Oil acquired Tedcastle, an energy marketing and distribution group of companies based in Ireland and operating under the Top Oil brand. The two-hundred-year-old Dublin-based firm sold 1.3 billion litres of fuel annually before Irving Oil acquired it. Top Oil had 180 dealers located throughout Ireland and a network of home oil outlets. The Top Oil service stations are green, as are the trucks, and are all easily identifiable. They have a strong presence on Ireland's motorways. Arthur Irving called the purchase a "historic day" for Irving Oil. Sarah Irving added that "all of us are really happy to welcome the Top Oil team to the family at Irving Oil."[20] It was a case of a family selling its business to another family-owned business.

The purchase of Top Oil fits nicely with the acquisition of the Whitegate refinery. The two can now build on each other's successes. The task of Irving Oil's senior management was to ensure a smooth transition for the two firms as well as their smooth integration with Irving Oil.

THE MARITIMES AT THE CENTRE OF THINGS

IRVING OIL CAN NOW PURSUE NEW MARKETS IN NEW ENGLAND and Ireland. But the heart of the operations remains in Saint John, New Brunswick. To be sure, the move to Ireland and the expansion of the business in New England required new investments.

At the same time, however, Irving Oil remains focused on Atlantic Canada. It decided, for example, to invest $80 million to reopen the Halifax Harbour Terminal. The investment, all privately funded, was earmarked for existing assets—hence the term "reactivation project." The assets include storage facilities, loading equipment, a jetty, and supporting infrastructure. Arthur Irving indicated that Irving Oil always "enjoyed doing business in Nova Scotia," and was prepared to continue to make important investments in the province.[21] A few months later, Irving Oil announced an agreement with Valero Energy Inc. to purchase four inland storage facilities located in Port Hawkesbury, New Glasgow, Yarmouth, and Bridgewater.[22]

Early on, Irving Oil was—and remains—an active participant in promoting the natural gas industry in Atlantic Canada. It was one of the first firms to invest in natural gas by committing to purchase, over time, $1 billion of the Sable Offshore Energy Project's natural gas production.[23] The Saint John refinery also uses natural gas in several capacities that include developing on-site co-generation capabilities. Irving Oil teamed up with a partner, TransCanada Energy Corp., in a power redevelopment project using natural gas for co-generation.[24] As noted earlier, the project produces two forms of energy—electrical power and steam.

In July 2018, Irving Oil acquired from Ultramar thirteen sites and twenty-three branded retail outlets across Atlantic Canada, with eight of the thirteen acquired sites located in the greater Halifax area. I note that there is a difference between owning the service station and sites and managing stations (the retail brand) for a different owner.

A year earlier, Irving Oil announced that it had completed a $20 million privately funded investment to upgrade its marine terminal in St. John's, Newfoundland and Labrador. The upgrade included a new fuelling berth and improved harbour logistics. In unveiling the investments, Irving Oil reminded Newfoundlanders that it had been proudly serving their province since 1949.[25]

Irving Oil also tried its hand at finding crude in all three Maritime provinces. The reader might be interested to know that New Brunswick is home to one of the oldest oil-producing regions in the world. One of the first wells in North America was drilled in 1859 on the east side of the Petitcodiac River, outside Moncton, but only a small quantity of oil was produced. In the 1980s, however, Irving Oil teamed up with Chevron to search for crude in the Moncton sub-basin. The partnership drilled three other exploration wells in the area, and what has been described as a "sub-commercial natural gas discovery" was made near Moncton in 1985. The partners, however, decided that it was not sufficiently viable, and abandoned and cemented the wells in 1993. The partners made several other attempts in New Brunswick, Nova Scotia, and Prince Edward Island, but nothing came of them.

THE BUILDING

ANYONE LOOKING FOR EVIDENCE THAT IRVING OIL REMAINS deeply committed to New Brunswick need look no further than its new head office in Saint John. It is a jewel of a building—modern, handsome, expensive, located smack in the middle of Saint John, next door to the Imperial Theatre (built in 1912), and a few steps away from the historic Admiral Beatty Hotel.

Irving Oil, like all highly successful businesses, does not make major decisions lightly, especially costly ones. It decided that the time had come to build a new head office within easy walking distance from the Golden Ball Building.

The new head office is a remarkable building in many ways. It also gives a charge of energy to uptown Saint John, which was in great need of one. No expense was spared in erecting this state-of-the-art building. The building accomplishes a number of things. It brings under one roof virtually all the Saint John–based Irving Oil employees, at least those not employed at the refinery. It houses the most modern of amenities from health-care facilities to meeting places and work stations. Everyone who enters the building is struck by its physical beauty, the way it is laid out, and its cutting-edge facilities.[26]

To be sure, I appreciate the building's elegance—who would not? However, the building holds a far more important message for me. In committing the funds to erect an eleven-storey building, the company established a mark for years to come: Irving Oil's head office is in Saint John to stay for the long term. I note that, other than Irving Oil, the market for such a building in Saint John is virtually non-existent. At the time the building was going up, Saint John had the highest office vacancy rate in New Brunswick, at 21.5 percent.[27] This is clearly a case of action that speaks louder than words.

Irving Oil broke ground for the new building on June 6, 2016. Over fifty local firms were employed to construct the building, and the 317,323-square-foot structure took three years to build. The first three floors each have 30,138 square feet, the fourth floor has 24,003 square feet, and floors five to eleven have 21,366 square feet. The building required over two thousand tons of structural steel, eight thousand cubic metres of concrete, and about eleven thousand pieces of limestone. The limestone is from the same quarry that provided the cladding for the Empire State Building in New York. There are 275 stairs in the atrium staircase and 553 exterior windows. The head office is home to about a thousand employees, though the number changes from day to day.

I went with Arthur Irving and landscape architect Alex Novell to look at a number of office buildings in Boston and Toronto while they were still exploring options on how best to shape the outside of the building. I was of no help. I looked around the Boston and Toronto skylines, and all I saw were tall buildings covered with cement or glass—nothing complicated for me. It was either one or the other. I learned, however, that glass buildings are cheaper to build but come at a cost to the environment. Studies now reveal that glass towers are devastating to birds, killing them by the thousands. So, from the start, Arthur made it clear that he wanted "no part of a glass and steel building." He insisted on a classical style, one that would blend in with Saint John's historic King's Square. Once a vision of the building was set, a search was completed for the best architects for the project. After the company selected Toronto-based B+H Architects and FCC/EllisDon Joint Venture, Alex Novell worked closely with Arthur Irving and senior Irving Oil executives on the design of the new building. Arthur insisted on having, to the extent possible, local contractors and local products in the building.

Alex Novell outlines how Arthur approached the project, which speaks to Arthur's management style. First, Arthur continually asked questions about all things and everything. Alex has the sense that, at times, Arthur did this to make certain everyone understood clearly what he wanted. Second, he carefully picked the team to work on the project. He had the following criteria: team members had to be the best in their field and able to work well as a team, always keeping their egos in check. He insisted that everyone on the team should have his or her say. At meetings, he would ask everyone, no matter their rank, to voice an opinion. He consistently showed civility in his dealings with everyone, no matter their role. Anyone who works with Arthur has to be impressed with his level of energy. Alex adds: "He simply exhausted everyone around him."

Arthur Irving made certain that he would be part of every important decision and, at times, even less important ones to be made in building the new head office. Irving Oil employees who were involved in designing and building still marvel at the time and effort, detailed knowledge, and commitment Arthur brought to the project.

Arthur Irving attached a great deal of importance to the exterior of the building. I now understand why. This was not a decision to be made lightly, given that he was overseeing a building built for the ages. It was his commitment to the future of Irving Oil and to Saint John as home of the head office. As K.C. Irving's mother had told him, time and again, if he was going to do something, then do it right. K.C. passed that lesson on to Arthur. Arthur certainly took the advice to heart when he set out to build the new headquarters. Alex Novell reports that Arthur, as he always does on projects important to him, invested a great deal of time and effort in planning the project before it got to the design stage. Alex reveals that Arthur did the same when it came to the K.C. Irving Environmental Science Centre and the Harriet Irving Botanical Gardens at Acadia University.

The outside of the building was important to Arthur for a variety of reasons. First, he wanted it to blend with its surroundings and, in particular, to respect the culture and history of Saint John—notably, the scale and historic nature of King's Square.[28] Second, the outside of a building speaks directly to the quality of the building. Third, it is the first thing visitors see as they walk up to it. The outside of the building is stunning, and enhances the historic nature of King's Square. An eleven-storey glass tower simply would not work well in that setting.

The limestone-clad stately building does two things: it stands out in uptown Saint John and it complements King's Square—to be sure, no small achievement. Arthur Irving had a hand in selecting the quarry from which the high-grade granite was taken. It was important because it is the limestone that gives the building its classical look.

The building was also designed to meet demanding environmental standards, is registered with the Canada Green Building Council, and looks to meet LEED (Leadership in Energy and Environmental Design) standards that are recognized by 152 countries as the mark of excellence for green buildings.[29]

Inside, the building is no less impressive. The ground floor is spacious, with a central atrium that shoots up the eleven floors. There is also a large piece of granite on the ground floor. Arthur and I sat on it, admiring its quality. He told me that the Toronto architects said they would find the granite in an Ontario quarry. Arthur's reply was, "No, we will find it in a New Brunswick quarry." The architects persisted—they pointed out that the New Brunswick quarry was closed. Well, Arthur replied, "we will open it." Again, the architects persisted: "You do not have the tools to access the granite." And again Arthur would not back down: "No problem, we will find the tools." The granite piece is from a New Brunswick quarry.

Arthur got what he wanted. There is a strong New Brunswick and Atlantic Canada presence throughout the building. The furniture, including the coffee tables and harvest tables, were made in Saint John and Fredericton, New Brunswick, Charlottetown, Prince Edward Island, Crousetown, Nova Scotia, and Paradise, Newfoundland and Labrador. The wood panelling comes from Lunenburg, the wrought iron fencing from New Glasgow, the atrium staircase from Borden, Prince Edward Island, and the granite plinth from Hampstead, New Brunswick.

The decor is kept simple and uncluttered, as is the furniture. The ground floor brings you back to the early days at Irving Oil.

There are gas pumps with glass tops and old signs that one could have seen on the first Irving service station in Bouctouche.

Large windows run up both sides of the building. The view from the eleventh floor is both stunning and overwhelming. From one side of the building, one sees the port and uptown Saint John. On the other side, one looks out at the refinery. From Arthur's office, one looks across the Bay of Fundy to Nova Scotia. Every effort is made to have natural light flow in on all floors. There is a roof skylight on the eleventh floor and an outdoor terrace on the fifth.

The offices are essentially all the same size. Arthur Irving's office is no bigger than the offices of the other senior leaders. The offices are not small but also not overbearing. The boardroom, however, is another story. It is spacious, elegant, and has refined furniture. It also holds a deep historical tie to K.C. Irving and the early days of Irving Oil. The walnut panelling was first moved from K.C.'s original office on Dock Street to the Golden Ball Building and then to the new head office. As one would expect, the building is wired to accommodate the most advanced communications and information technology requirements.

The building houses a gym, fully furnished with modern equipment, that is open to all employees at all hours. When I visited the building, the gym was packed. In addition, the Irving Oil headquarters has a health centre staffed with professionals, and is accessible to all employees. There is also a nicely designed and spacious café.

I note, once again, that Arthur Irving had a hand in all aspects of the planning and construction phases of the building. He takes great pride in showing components of the building that are homegrown or New Brunswick–made. He insisted on Atlantic Canada products whenever they were available or could be made locally.

The building is now home to over one thousand Irving Oil employees who were previously spread out in five buildings. Ian

Whitcomb speaks of the "efficiency of having our entire team in one building," and the ability to promote better coordination among the various units.[30]

It is hardly possible to overstate the impact of the Irving Oil head office on uptown Saint John. The move doubles the number of Irving Oil employees working in the uptown area. It means that these one thousand employees will make numerous shopping trips to uptown boutiques; they will also purchase nearly 175,0000 lunches and some 140,000 coffees every year.[31]

LOOKING BACK

As a long-time student of regional economic development and someone who spent a good part of his career promoting the economy of Atlantic Canada, I take great satisfaction in seeing a head office located in Saint John, New Brunswick, responsible for large operations in New England and now Ireland. This chapter has documented some of the investments Irving Oil has made and continues to make in Atlantic Canada. It is not a complete list; there are many more in all four Atlantic provinces.

I underlined the move to Ireland because it matters for New Brunswick, for the Maritime region, and for all of Atlantic Canada. It sends out the signal that the Irving Oil head office is quite capable of managing a growing and complex set of operations in several jurisdictions. It also promotes a different mindset in our region. Rather than seeing businesses in the province being managed from away, the region sees one of its own businesses managing important operations in other parts of the world.

Arthur Irving's decision to invest in a new head office for Irving Oil also sends a number of important messages. First, it signals that he and Irving Oil have full confidence in Saint John's, and the

Maritime region's, economic future. Second, Arthur Irving laid down a marker, not through words but through actions, in initiating an expensive investment that cemented Saint John as the head office for Irving Oil for the long term. Third, it tells Irving Oil employees that their work is important and that the firm is prepared to house them in a modern state-of-the-art building. Fourth, the fact that all executive offices are the same size tells the executives to check their egos at the door and that teamwork is highly valued.

This chapter and this book underline the point that entrepreneurs are key to New Brunswick and Atlantic Canada's economic future. Governments can never be the driving force. I have spent my career working on two themes, the workings of government from a Canadian and comparative perspective, and economic development, largely from an Atlantic Canada perspective. I wrote in the preface that it is the entrepreneurs who propel economies forward. Governments, notwithstanding their large and costly bureaucracies, are not up to the task of identifying economic opportunities. All too often, they are excellent at giving the appearance of progress and change while standing still. The following makes the case.

In October 2019, I met a successful entrepreneur from away who decided to invest in apple orchards near my home village just outside of Bouctouche. He had already planted more than five hundred thousand apple trees, and had plans to plant another five hundred thousand. He also has apple orchards in the United States, Chile, and India. He will be exporting, in a few years, $200 million worth of apples annually from New Brunswick. He plans to be the world's biggest apple grower and to see his Bouctouche operations become the most productive and important part of the business.

I asked him, "Why did you decide on Bouctouche?" He replied that he had asked leading agriculturalists to identify the best possible sites around the world for growing apples. They identified the Bouctouche region as one of the best, and the following explains why. The soil around Bouctouche is rich and ideally suited to grow apples. The area is within a few kilometres of the Northumberland Strait and the Atlantic Ocean, which means that his apple orchards will enjoy more frost-free days than other Canadian sites. He could buy land in Bouctouche a great deal cheaper than elsewhere, including possible sites in Italy that also have well-suited soil to grow apples. He plans to export all of his products, and Bouctouche gives him relatively easy access to the port of Halifax. The bulk of his orchards are located on an old buffalo-raising farm, which made the already-rich soil even better suited to growing apples.

Here is the issue. An entrepreneur based in British Columbia and a few consultants were able to identify Bouctouche as an ideal location to grow apples and see a number of economic opportunities that could flow from it. The government of New Brunswick has 150 public servants working in the economic development field, and the Atlantic Canada Opportunities Agency (ACOA) has a few hundred more located in New Brunswick. Together they could not identify these opportunities. If it were not for this entrepreneur, the land would have remained dormant. But that is not all. Hundreds more public servants are employed in federal and provincial departments of agriculture and natural resources in New Brunswick, and many more in Ottawa. They too completely failed to see the economic opportunity.

I have had discussions with senior federal and provincial public servants about this case. All see the point, but they argue that public servants are not in the business of taking risks. They sit in judgment of economic development opportunities that entrepreneurs identify. One public servant told me that this responsibility rests with the department of agriculture. Another said that ACOA, at one point, had a unit that looked at such opportunities but it has been disbanded. These arguments only make sense to career government officials.

I note that the entrepreneur who moved to Bouctouche to grow apples did not receive any government funding from either Ottawa or Fredericton to develop his project. If public servants cannot identify development opportunities, and if their role is largely limited to sitting in judgment of what entrepreneurs can identify, it follows that their ability to promote economic development is limited. It also suggests that governments should look at streamlining their economic development departments and agencies by asking if they need such a high number of public servants to sit in judgment of what entrepreneurs do or are planning to do. Failing this, governments should undertake a fundamental rethink of their role in economic development. The above explains, in part, why I hold that Atlantic Canadians need to look to entrepreneurs and the private sector to grow their economy.

Notes

1   "Canadian Refineries," *Oil Sands Magazine*, updated November 2, 2019, online at oilsandsmagazine.com/projects/canadian-refineries.

2   "Pumped and Primed," *Atlantic Business*, June 23, 2016, online at atlanticbusinessmagazine.net/article/pumped-and-primed/.

3   Readers who wish a more detailed understanding of how the refinery operates should consult New Brunswick, *Facility Profile: Irving Oil Refining G.P. Saint John Refinery* (Fredericton: Department of Environment and Local Government, Impact Management Branch, September 2014), 3.

4   Irving Oil, "Discover Irving Oil," n.d., online at irvingoil.com/en-CA/ discover-irving/operations.

5   Darren Gillis, at Irving Oil, provided this information on November 15, 2019.

6   Douglas How and Ralph Costello, *K.C.: The Biography of K.C. Irving* (Toronto: Key Porter, 1993), 142.

7   Jarrett Renshaw and Jessica DiNapoli, "Unit at Philadelphia refinery completely destroyed in fire: sources," *Reuters*, June 23, 2019, online at reuters.com/article/us-usa-refinery-blast/unit-at-philadelphia-refinery-completely-destroyed-in-fire-sources-iduSKCN1TOOSZ.

8   Jeff Lewis, "Imperial Oil faces up to $280-million hit in second quarter due to N.S. refinery closure," *Financial Post*, June 19, 2013, online at business.financialpost.com/commodities/energy/imperial-oil-refinery-dartmouth.

9   Irving Oil, "Discover Irving Oil."

10 I had the good fortune to visit Canaport with friends in 2016, when I was given a briefing on its operations.

11 See, for example, Claudia Cattaneo, "Playing the Piper," *Financial Post*, n.d., online at business.financialpost.com/playing-the-piper-in-an-exclusive-interview-arthur-irving-the-spotlight-shy-head-of-irving-oil-makes-the-case-for-energy-east-a-project-he-believes-isnt-just-good-for-his-company-but.

12 Gordon Pitts, "Irving Oil: Eyeing growth in a time of declining demand," *Globe and Mail*, September 22, 2008, online at theglobeandmail.com/report-on-business/irving-oil-eyeing-growth-in-a-time-of-declining-demand/article660058/.

13 "Oil refineries in the United States," *InflationData*, online at inflationdata.com/articles/oil-refineries-united-states/, accessed September 17, 2019.

14 Irving Oil, "Corporate Overview," *TradeWinds*, n.d., online at tradewindsnews.com/incoming/article262903.ece5/binary/about%20 irv%20aboutirv.

15 Pitts, "Irving Oil."

16 See, for example, Nicholas Sakelaris, "How the shale boom translates into big profits for US refineries," *Dallas Business Journal*, June 5, 2014, online at bizjournals.com/dallas/news/2014/06/05/how-the-shale-boom-translates-into-big-profits-for.html.

17 Rachel Cave, "Irving Oil to buy Ireland's only refinery from Phillips 66," *CBC News*, August 3, 2016, online at cbc.ca/news/canada/new-brunswick/irving-oil-refinery-ireland-phillips-66-1.3705331.

18 "Irving Oil to buy Ireland's only refinery," *Globe and Mail*, August 3, 2016, online at theglobeandmail.com/report-on-business/industry-news/energy-and-resources/irving-oil-to-buy-irelands-only-refinery-from-phillips-66/article31253142/.

19 Irving Oil, "Irving Oil confirms agreement in place to acquire Whitegate Refinery in Ireland," press release, August 3, 2016, online at irvingoil.com/en-CA/press-room/irving-oil-confirms-agreement-place-acquire-whitegate-refinery-ireland.

20 "Canadian-owned Irving Oil announces successful acquisition of Irish company Top Oil," *Cision PR Newswire*, January 31, 2019, online at prnewswire.com/news-releases/canadian-owned-irving-oil-announces-successful-acquisition-of-irish-company-top-oil-300787363.html.

21 Irving Oil, "Irving Oil announces successful commission of its Halifax Harbour terminal," press release, October 20, 2016, online at irvingoil.com/en-CA/press-room/irving-oil-announces-successful-commission-its-halifax-harbour-terminal.

22 Irving Oil, "Irving Oil announces expansion of its terminal network in Nova Scotia," December 5, 2016, online at irvingoil.com/en-CA/press-room/irving-oil-announces-expansion-its-terminal-network-nova-scotia.

23 Irving Oil, "Corporate Overview," *TradeWinds*, n.d., online at tradewindsnews.com/incoming/article262903.ece5/binary/about%20 irv%20aboutirv.

24 Irving Oil executives provided me this information.

25 Irving Oil, "Irving Oil completes expansion of St. John's Marine Terminal—$20-million investment adds a second fuelling berth for offshore customers," press release, June 7, 2017, online at newswire.ca/news-releases/irving-oil-completes-expansion-of-st-johns-marine-terminal---20-million-investment-adds-a-second-fuelling-berth-for-offshore-customers-627011141.html.

26 Cherise Letson, "A Look Inside the Construction of the New Irving Oil HQ," *Huddle*, April 4, 2017, online at huddle.today/a-look-inside-the-construction-of-the-new-irving-oil-hq/.

27 Rachel Cave, "Saint John's vacant offices rate highest in province at 21.5%," CBC *News*, March 1, 2017, online at cbc.ca/news/canada/new-brunswick/saint-john-vacant-office-rate-highest-1.4005753.

28 See Mulvey and Banani International Inc., "Irving Oil Headquarters," n.d., online at mbii.com/succes_stories/irving-oil-headquarters/.

29 See "Pumped and Primed."

30 Irving Oil, "Our team. Our home—Irving Oil unveils new head office," press release, February 17, 2016, online at irvingoil.com/en-CA/press-room/our-team-our-home.

31 OSCO Construction Group, "Project Update: Irving Oil Home Office," *Connections*, spring/summer 2017, online at oceansteel.com/Resources/Docs/connection/Connect-Spring2017.pdf.

CHAPTER 9

SUPPORTING COMMUNITIES

I AM A MARITIMER FIRST IN ALL THINGS. I MAKE IT A POINT TO buy groceries from Sobeys, chocolates from Ganong, gas from Irving Oil, potatoes from New Brunswick or Prince Edward Island, french fries from McCain, and the list goes on. I earlier documented why head offices of major firms are important to a regional economy, and there is no need to go over the same territory here.

There is another reason I always look to Maritime-owned firms first for my purchases. I have been an active participant in several fundraising efforts, including three campaigns for my university, one for the Stan Cassidy Centre for Rehabilitation, and another for the Atlantic Cancer Research Institute. I note that Atlantic Canadians are generous. Notwithstanding their have-less status, all four provinces outperform Quebec and three outperform Ontario, with New Brunswick performing at the same level as Ontario when it comes to volunteering and giving to charitable causes.[1]

I learned a great deal from these fundraising experiences. First, the initial reaction of many I solicited was to come up with a reason, any reason, not to give. I heard it all, from digging up old feuds to nothing short of ridiculous reasons for not giving. One high-profile individual from my community said he would not contribute to one of my university's fundraising campaigns unless he got a free parking pass so that he would not have to pay whenever he visited the campus. Another told a friend he would not give to the university because it too firmly embraces the status quo. He said he would rather give to a widow with young children. I doubt he has ever helped a single widow. I have often heard similar stories when comparing notes with others who have been actively engaged in fundraising efforts.

I also learned not to rely on public sector employees to join in the effort. I point the finger at senior federal and provincial public servants with their above-average salaries and generous fringe benefits. They rarely show up to participate. I also point the finger at our medical community. Physicians, especially medical specialists, some of whom make over $500,000 a year, do not show up to help. Most of them got their education—at least, their undergraduate degrees—from New Brunswick universities. During our last university fundraising campaign, none of them came to lend a helping hand and only two made a contribution.

We invariably knock on the doors of local businesses, large and small, to raise funds. I do not ever recall asking Shell, Exxon, or even Petro-Canada to contribute, at least not to my university. We always turn to Irving Oil, JDI, Sobeys, Oxford Frozen Foods, and McCain Foods, and they always give. I wish Maritimers would think about this when they shop for groceries and gas.

CONSERVATION: DUCKS UNLIMITED

LEIGH STEVENSON, K.C.'S COUSIN AND CLOSEST FRIEND, encouraged Arthur Irving to get involved with Ducks Unlimited. Arthur explains that Stevenson "loved hunting, the outdoors and his dog. Uncle Leigh was one of Ducks Unlimited Canada's first directors and I was honoured when DUC asked me to be a director. At that time, DUC was still a small organization funded by Ducks Unlimited [in the United States]."[2] Arthur Irving was the Canadian president of Ducks Unlimited in 1986–87.

When Arthur joined Ducks Unlimited Canada in 1976, there were only a small group of directors and a handful of employees. Stewart Morrison, a past chief executive officer at Ducks Unlimited Canada, gives full credit to Arthur Irving for the organization's growth. He explains: "The thing about Arthur is that he's so enthusiastic. He's a doer. He's positive and energetic. He's the kind of person who's always thinking about how things could be made better."[3] Ducks Unlimited Canada has grown by leaps and bounds since 1976, and Arthur Irving has played an important role in its growth. Moreover, while contributing to Ducks Unlimited, Arthur always made sure that Atlantic Canada would be part of that growth.

Fredericton is now home to a state-of-the-art hub for wetland learning. The Ducks Unlimited Conservation Centre is housed in a sandstone-and-cedar-shingle building overlooking the St. John River.[4] The organization's New Brunswick branch headquarters is made of sandstone from Memramcook, flooring from trees that were felled because of Dutch Elm disease in the area, and furniture built from local wood. Irving Oil was a major contributor to the building of the Conservation Centre.

The centre sits on a choice location on the north side of the St. John River, across from the Beaverbrook Art Gallery and the

New Brunswick Legislative Assembly. Geoffrey Harding, the manager of major projects at Ducks Unlimited, reports that Arthur not only selected the site, but he also ensured that the property, which belonged to Irving Oil, was donated to the organization. It is apparent that Arthur took great interest in building the centre, down to the most minute detail. He also contributed financial resources, but no one knows how much, not even Geoffrey Harding. This is hardly the first time that Arthur Irving has kept the amount of his financial contribution to an initiative a secret, as we will see below in the case of Acadia University.

Arthur's contribution to Ducks Unlimited extends far beyond his role in building Fredericton's Conservation Centre. As he does in all things, he also brought a "can-do" attitude. Ducks Unlimited Canada, for a long time, was little more than an extension of its American counterpart. It received the bulk of its resources from the US operations, and quietly went about doing its work restoring grassland and watersheds, largely in Western Canada, Ontario, and Quebec. It did not seek a high public profile because it saw no reason for it. Arthur Irving pushed to see Ducks Unlimited Canada gain a higher profile and become more involved with communities. He told Harding: "If you do not wave your flag, no one else will." The organization now has a number of events that not only serve to raise funds, but also give the organization strong visibility in many communities across Canada.

Canada and the United States joined forces in 1986 to promote the conservation of North American waterfowl. Mexico signed on to the agreement in 1994. The plan reads in part: "The maintenance of abundant waterfowl population is dependent on the protection, restoration and management of habitat. The persistent loss of important waterfowl habitat should be reversed."[5] Ducks Unlimited Canada reports that Arthur Irving was an important driving force in seeing the plan come to life. He used his contacts in Canada and the United States to push the Canadian and US governments to sign the agreement. By all accounts, the agreement has been highly successful, generating investments by both the public and the private sector. The *Journal of Wildlife Management* called on three senior officials to assess progress made between 1986 and 1999. They concluded that, "[s]ince 1986, partners have contributed over $1.4 billion to deliver conservation on about 2 million [hectares] throughout North America. During the same period of time, most waterfowl populations have experienced a dramatic recovery, with many species currently at or above population levels identified in the Plan."[6] .

CONSERVATION: THE BEAUBASSIN RESEARCH STATION

In 2012, Arthur Irving invited me to visit the Beaubassin Research Station in Aulac, New Brunswick. I was impressed. It sits at the very centre of the Maritime region, on the border of New Brunswick and Nova Scotia, and on a clear day one can see Prince Edward Island from the eastern edge of the Isthmus of Chignecto. The Beaubassin area is where the Chignecto Canal would have been built. The Acadian village of Beaubassin was burnt down in 1750, and was one of the sites from which Acadians were expelled to faraway lands. The Mi'kmaq also have a deep history with Beaubassin.[7]

I was immediately smitten by the Beaubassin site. I quickly saw its historical significance and the important message it holds: English, Acadians, and Mi'kmaq working together to let bygones be bygones. Beaubassin was the capital of French-ruled Acadie between 1678 and 1684. I also saw the possibility of having the three Maritime provincial governments come together at Beaubassin to map out a strategy for greater cooperation and eventually perhaps Maritime union.

Arthur led the effort to establish the centre, and paved the way for a partnership between Irving Oil, Acadia University, and Ducks Unlimited. The centre has already produced excellent research on, among other issues, climate change, how human activity affects lakes in the region, and how birds move across landscapes on multiple stages of their migratory journeys.[8]

Walking around the Beaubassin site with Arthur, I observed that people need to know this place exists. Arthur talked about an official opening. "Great," I said. "Then we should get the prime minister to open the site, and I will see what I can do."

I knew that the prime minister at the time, Stephen Harper, had a family connection to Moncton and Beaubassin. I met Harper before he became prime minister when the Institute for Research on Public Policy celebrated its thirtieth anniversary. I reminded him that he had "Maritime roots" through his grandfather. He acknowledged this, and said that his grandfather's disappearance in the 1950s remains a mystery to his family. The story is well known to elderly Monctonians, but not to many Canadians. The senior Harper was attending to his principal duties at Prince Edward School in Moncton in January 1950 when he disappeared one afternoon, never to be seen or heard from again. To this day, no one knows what happened to him, and my wife's uncle remembers walking the Moncton area marshes with his father, looking for his school principal, "Poof" Harper.[9]

My wife's family also has ties to Harper. His grandfather taught my wife's uncle, Ron Dempsey. In addition, Stephen Harper's father, Joseph Harper, went to school with her mother, Corena, who has fond memories of him. She reports that "Jos" was a very good student, very intelligent, and well-liked by everyone.

Stephen Harper also has a family connection to Beaubassin. The first Harper to settle in North America came to Beaubassin from Yorkshire in the mid-1770s. Christopher Harper built a home within walking distance of both Fort Beauséjour-Cumberland and where the Beaubassin Research Station now sits. The Harpers, like the other Yorkshire families who had immigrated to the area, remained loyal to the British Crown during the American Revolution. The political situation in the region became dicey at the outbreak of the revolution, and it was not clear which side American Planters, who had moved to Nova Scotia after the Acadian expulsion to take over the abandoned farm land, would take.

Colonel Jonathan Eddy, with the support of the us Congress, led a small force to Nova Scotia to "add another stripe to the American flag."[10] He recruited local patriots, Acadians, and Indigenous people, and besieged Fort Cumberland. They burned homes around the fort that belonged to the Loyalists, including Harper's house. Harper escaped to the fort with his family and watched his house burn to the ground.

I wrote to the prime minister on April 16, 2012, to remind him once more of his ties to Moncton and Beaubassin and to ask him to open the Beaubassin Research Station. I explained that the redevelopment of Beaubassin involved the construction of a state-of-the-art research station and conference centre on the site of Île-de-La-Vallière/Tonge's Island, where the French governor once lived. I added that Île-de-La-Vallière was recognized as a Canadian historical site in 1925 and Beaubassin in 2005, that they sit in the middle of one of the most historically important regions of North America, and that this location speaks to Canada's history in a way that few others can. I pointed out that, given Christopher Harper's role at Beaubassin, it was only fitting that one of his descendants would, as Canada's prime minister, formally open the site. I also noted that there was no government money in carrying out the redevelopment efforts.

I received a telephone call from his office shortly after to say that the prime minister had a strong interest in opening the centre. I asked his assistant if he could relay a message to the prime minister. "Could you please tell him that the Acadians had nothing to do with burning down his ancestor's home in 1776!" I added that others were responsible, but not Acadians. I have no idea if the assistant relayed the message, but I do know that he had a good chuckle.

Prime Minister Harper did open the Beaubassin Research Station on a warm August day in 2012. He also visited the site where his ancestor's home once stood, and unveiled a plaque paying tribute to Beaubassin's history. In his speech, Harper said that he was happy to visit Beaubassin, "where First Nations, Acadians, and English peoples established themselves and played an important role in shaping Canada."[11] Beaubassin is now a temporary home to researchers and students from several universities from the region looking to make a contribution to wetland and environmental research.

EDUCATION: ACADIA UNIVERSITY

ARTHUR IRVING WAS AT THE FOREFRONT OF THE FAMILY EFFORT to establish the K.C. Irving Environmental Science Centre and the Harriet Irving Botanical Gardens at Acadia University. Ray Ivany, Acadia's former president, calls the buildings iconic and indicates that very few people understand the magnitude of their impact. I cannot possibly do justice to the centre in this book, and I urge readers to tour the buildings or, if this is not possible, to visit online at kcirvingcentre.acadiau.ca. I have been very fortunate in my career to be able to study at Oxford University, to be elected a visiting fellow at All Souls College, Oxford, to be a visiting professor at Harvard, Duke University, and the London School of Economics, and to participate in many conferences at a number of universities in Canada, the United States, the United Kingdom, Brazil, and France. I have never seen a campus facility as impressive and inspiring as the K.C. Irving Environmental Science Centre and the adjoining Harriet Irving Botanical Gardens.

Arthur selected well-known architect Robert A.M. Stern to design the Environmental Science Centre. Stern is a founding partner of the firm that bears his name and a former dean of the Yale School of Architecture. Stern has designed iconic buildings throughout Europe and North America, including the Wasserstein Hall at Harvard Law School, the George W. Bush Presidential Center in Dallas, the Comcast Center in Philadelphia, 30 Park Place in New York, and numerous projects for Walt Disney World. Arthur told Stern to look at the best university buildings in Europe and North America and design a better one for Acadia University. Together they visited many of them. One can easily identify a British influence at the K.C. Irving Environmental Science Centre, particularly in the Harriet Irving Botanical Gardens.

Arthur, alongside Sandra Irving, had a hand in shaping the broad contours of both buildings, and then immersed himself in the fine details when construction began. He even stood in the bucket of the boom truck as it went up and down a hill on the Acadia campus to select the precise location for the centre. It is a choice location in the middle of the campus. From the K.C. Irving Environmental Science Centre, one looks to University Hall, an impressive historic building. From the back patio, one can see the historic Blomidon Inn, which dates back to the 1880s.

The centre, with its oversized presence on campus, is a unique blend that speaks to the interests of researchers and students alike and puts Acadia University on the map in terms of environmental studies. No expense was spared to build what Ray Ivany calls the "grand building that binds students to one another and to the campus." He adds that he saw on many occasions "students queuing to get in this building."

The 65,000-square-foot structure only has top-quality materials, from its individually cast bricks and slate roof to its limestone trim. Furthermore, the interior decor and furniture of the centre is as exquisite as its exterior facade. Whenever possible, Arthur Irving insisted on buying local products.

Kelvin Ogilvie, a former Acadia University president, worked closely with Arthur in the planning and construction phases. Ogilvie maintains that Arthur was the driving force in shaping the broad outline of the building and in looking after the details of the construction. Ogilvie told me that Arthur Irving said from day one that the building had to be about students—a meeting place for them. He stuck to this point from start to finish.

A large meeting room, filled with natural light, sits in the middle of the centre. The room is an ideal place for students to gather. The K.C. Irving Environmental Science Centre also contains state-of-the-art research laboratories, greenhouses, a conservatory, and controlled environmental facilities. In addition, it houses a fully accessible, completely wired, 124-seat auditorium, a library and video conference centre, classrooms, lecture rooms, meeting spaces, and conference rooms. The centre has generated numerous accolades and awards, including being named one of the "Most Eye-Catching Campus Buildings in Canada" by the *Huffington Post* in 2015.[12]

The Harriet Irving Botanical Gardens lie adjacent to the centre and occupy six acres of Acadia's campus. They are home to several unique habitats of the Acadian forest region and to living specimens of endangered species. The entrance to the gardens opens onto an English garden setting where only plants native to the Acadian forest can be found. There is also an experimental garden where research is carried out in several plant beds with different soil types. The gardens even include a medicinal garden showcasing a collection of plants used by Indigenous peoples and early European settlers. There is much more to the Harriet Irving Botanical Gardens, and readers are urged to consult publications that explain in depth the gardens and their contents.[13]

Ogilvie reports that Arthur Irving was directly involved, with landscape architect Alex Novell, in all aspects of the creation of the botanical gardens as well. When researchers planning the garden uncovered a very rare plant in a local bog that is part of the Acadian forest, Arthur personally saw to it that the plant be removed carefully only in the dead of winter so as not to damage other plants in the bog.

One can only begin to imagine the cost of either the centre or the garden. We may, however, never know. A student once asked Arthur Irving the total cost of building both. Arthur, in turn, asked: "Do you give a present to your girlfriend at Christmas?"

"Yes," responded the young man. Arthur then replied: "Well, does she ask how much you paid for it?"

I asked Arthur why he does not wish to reveal the cost of building the centre and botanical gardens. His response: "That is not the important part. The important part is that we have two great facilities at Acadia that are making very important contributions. This is what really matters." To this day, Kelvin Ogilvie does not know how much Arthur and his two brothers, J.K. and Jack Irving, contributed to both initiatives. Arthur never told Ogilvie and he also never complained about the cost. Invoices were sent and paid, no questions asked. "But," Ogilvie explains, "that is how Arthur

Irving does things." He says he can think of a number of other occasions when Arthur intervened to help an individual or a cause without ever drawing any attention to himself or claiming credit.

It is rare, indeed, for a benefactor to decide not to disclose the amount he or she contributed to a fundraising campaign or a major initiative. In virtually all cases, the contributor will ask to tie the contribution to a media campaign to highlight the amount and its importance. This has been my experience whenever I served on fundraising campaigns. Philanthropic studies also suggest that anonymous giving by wealthy donors is the exception rather than the rule. One argument against anonymous giving is that, when donors highlight their gifts, it sets an example for others to follow. However, there are also a number of advantages to anonymous giving and anonymous receiving. One is that anonymous giving enables recipients to pursue objectives with less encumbrance and allows them to concentrate on their responsibilities instead of looking to the presumed objective of the donors.[14] By refusing to disclose the cost, Arthur made certain that discussions about the K.C. Irving Environmental Science Centre and the Harriet Irving Botanical Gardens would focus instead on their imposing presence, their physical beauty, and their contributions to science.

Harvey Gilmour, former director of development at Acadia, reports that one of his most frustrating experiences while at the university was that he was not allowed to talk about Arthur Irving's contributions to the university. The topic was off-limits because Arthur did not want to bring attention to them. Gilmour also reports that Arthur got directly involved with Acadia's fundraising efforts and knocked on many doors.

Arthur Irving decided early on that the new environmental science centre and botanical gardens would never be a drain on the university. As is well known, some donors give large sums of money to universities to have their name on a building, and consider the job done. The university is then left to maintain this infrastructure, often at a substantial cost. Arthur set a goal to create an endowment to look after the centre and gardens in perpetuity. In the end, sufficient capital was raised to fund the ongoing maintenance of the centre and botanical gardens. I know of no other such fund, at least tied to a university in Atlantic Canada, that looks after the maintenance requirements of one of its buildings.

Gilmour points out that Arthur also has a special knack for raising funds. They went to see the chief executive officer of one of the five big Canadian banks. On the way to the meeting, Arthur asked, "How much money should we ask for?" Gilmour told him that the bank was not known for giving to universities, "so we should ask for $100,000." They both made the pitch for the bank to support Acadia University, and then Arthur asked for $1 million. Both the bank CEO and Gilmour "gulped." The CEO "hummed and hawed a bit," and then said, "Well, I think that we can make it happen."

Gilmour also makes the case that Arthur Irving is not well understood by many. He had read, as I have, that Arthur Irving was "impatient" and could be "difficult." Gilmour insists that nothing could be further from the truth. He reports that Arthur never missed a meeting when he was chancellor at Acadia. He participated fully in the discussions and never once lost his patience. Meetings on a university campus can test anyone's patience—I can attest to that!

Gilmour also reports on a development that speaks to Arthur Irving's values. Arthur decided that, before the official opening of the K.C. Irving Environmental Science Centre and Harriet Irving Botanical Gardens—and before any dignitaries would even get a glimpse—he would invite the workers to tour the building and gardens. The day before the official opening, Arthur Irving toured the premises with electricians, plumbers, bricklayers, and others, along with their families, to see their masterpiece before anyone else. Gilmour reports that it was a special day, an emotional moment he will always remember.

Arthur Irving became chancellor at Acadia when Ogilvie was president. Ogilvie tells me that Arthur had a way to connect with students. He recalls when Arthur first spoke at convocation: "no speech, no notes, he just spoke from the heart. He connected. Here was a captain of industry speaking to them from the heart. The students gave him a standing ovation." The one problem Ogilvie had with Arthur was getting him to accept to wear the chancellor's robe. "It was not an easy task. Arthur Irving felt that the robe was much too pretentious and he resisted wearing it. I was only able to win him over after I secured the help of his wife, Sandra."

Arthur and Sandra Irving have made other important contributions to Acadia. They established the Arthur Irving Academy Foundation in 2014. The academy has three functions: it offers scholarships to undergraduate and graduate students to attend Acadia, it allocates research grants to support research carried out at the K.C. Irving Environmental Science Centre and the Harriet Irving Botanical Gardens, and, over many years, has provided funding for a full-time director of research.[15]

The academy has established the Arthur Irving Scholarships, which are among the most generous at Acadia. The Irving scholars can be from any region in the country, and they come from West Vancouver to Newfoundland and Labrador and points in between. Students need to provide a five-hundred-word essay outlining their interest in environmental science and the value of scientific and environmental research. Applicants must also demonstrate a history of community service and extracurricular activities. The scholarships are aimed to fund 100 percent of a student's undergraduate education at Acadia. Graduate scholarships are also awarded.

The Arthur Irving Academy also has provided generous grants to carry out research on environmental issues. The research needs to be tied to the work of the K.C. Irving Environmental Science Centre or the Harriet Irving Botanical Gardens.

THE ARTHUR L. IRVING INSTITUTE
FOR ENERGY AND SOCIETY

ARTHUR, SANDRA, AND SARAH, AS WELL AS THE ARTHUR L. Irving Family Foundation and Irving Oil, decided in 2016 to establish an institute on energy and society at Dartmouth College in Hanover, New Hampshire. The institute will be housed in a new building strategically located between the Tuck School of Business and the Thayer School of Engineering on the Dartmouth campus.[16]

The institute's research focus is to find ways to develop sustainable sources of energy. It looks to all disciplines and offers themes for researchers to pursue. The 2019 theme, for example, encouraged "critical reflections on the social implications of our individual and collective energy choices." The institute also strongly encourages "collaborations across disciplines" in its work, and calls for "meaningful collaborations" across disciplines.[17]

Why, one might ask, would Arthur Irving and his family want to have an institute that bears Arthur Irving's name and supports research that calls for "critical reflection" on energy choices? Arthur Irving and Irving Oil are well aware of the debate around fossil fuels and climate change. They are not by any means climate change deniers. They accept that climate change is one of the most important issues facing the world and that human activity is its main cause. They have never discredited climate science, nor do they intend to. The decision to create the Dartmouth energy institute speaks to their willingness to be part of the solution. Arthur explained why he supports the institute: "When my dad started Irving Oil in 1924 he sold Ford cars—at that time they started with a crank. Today we are talking about driverless cars and other advanced technologies. The world is always changing and the future is impossible to predict but I can't think of anything that will play a larger part than energy. The world will be powered by different sources in the future. We are confident that Dartmouth will help shape whatever the energy future will be."[18] More is said in the next chapter about climate change and the challenges ahead for Irving Oil as it deals with the growth in sales of both electric vehicles and plug-in hybrid cars.

Dartmouth College is an Ivy League university that ranked twelfth on the U.S. *News & World Report* list of top full-time MBA programs in 2019. We saw earlier that, in the same year, *Forbes* magazine ranked Dartmouth's Tuck School of Business sixth in its rating of the best business schools in the country.[19] In deciding to support the Arthur L. Irving Institute for Energy and Society and in providing 50 percent of its funding, Dartmouth College highlighted Irving Oil's contribution to the environment. It also underlined Irving Oil's contributions to Ducks Unlimited, and made the point that the firm was one of the first in the oil and gas sector to invest in emissions-control technology to improve its environmental performance, and that it led the way in lowering sulphur content in both transportation and home-heating fuels. More to the point, climate change deniers who are in the oil and gas business are not in the habit of launching an energy institute to promote "critical reflection" or to lead the way in the oil and gas sector by investing in emissions-control technology.

Additional contributions have also been made to Dartmouth College to support scholarships for Canadian students and the development of the Sandra L. and Arthur L. Irving '72a P'10 Professorship of Economics. In partnership with the Tuck School of Business, the Irvings also help fund undergraduate studies in business.

In the fall of 2012, Charles Grant, from Nova Scotia, was one of the first students to receive an Irving scholarship at Dartmouth. Two other students, both from Atlantic Canada, were also awarded the scholarship in the same year. Grant, a goaltender on the Dartmouth varsity hockey team, explains that many scholarships at Dartmouth are from anonymous donors, but that shortly after being awarded his scholarship, he learned that Arthur Irving and his family were responsible for funding it.

Arthur and Sandra took things a step further, and decided to establish personal relationships with the students they support at Dartmouth. Charles Grant reports that they made a point of meeting these students every semester, or three times during the academic year. Grant often stopped to visit Arthur and Sandra on his way to and from Dartmouth College and his home town in Nova Scotia. I asked him to define Arthur in a few words. His response: "Generous, down to earth, and very proud to be a Maritimer."

MEDICAL RESEARCH

THE ARTHUR L. IRVING FAMILY FOUNDATION HAS ALSO CONtributed to health research. In 2014, the Hutter Family Professorship in Medicine in the Field of Cardiology at the Massachusetts General Hospital and Harvard School of Medicine in Boston was established. Additionally, Arthur and Sandra have sponsored the Cardiac Performance Program at Mass General. I spoke with Dr. Adolph M. Hutter, who told me that Arthur and Sandra are ideal donors: "They are generous, they know what they want, they are very knowledgeable, they know how to listen, they know when to intervene, they understand the challenges, and they know how to hold us to account." He also reports that they never lose interest in the initiatives they support and always come back with insightful questions.

In 2017, Arthur, Sandra, and Sarah supported two new initiatives at the hospital: the David P. Ryan, MD Endowment Chair in Cancer Research, and the Arthur, Sandra, and Sarah Irving Fund in Gastrointestinal Immuno-Oncology. The goal for the latter is to push back the frontiers of knowledge and define "treatment options for patients with gastrointestinal cancers and other cancers, particularly in immunotherapy."[20] Furthermore, the Arthur L. Irving Family Foundation recently funded the establishment of a Cancer Immunology Symposium and a Cancer Immunology Innovation Retreat. They have also funded the H. Royden Jones, Jr., MD Chair in Neuroscience at the Lahey Hospital & Medical Center. Jones, a leading neurologist, was a friend of the family until he passed away in 2013.

It will be recalled that a large-scale earthquake devastated Haiti in January 2010. About 1.5 million people were displaced and approximately 250,000 were killed. Buildings collapsed, roads became impassable, and nearly four thousand schools were damaged or destroyed.[21] The Red Cross made a worldwide call for help at the time. Arthur Irving quietly responded by sending two planeloads of doctors, nurses, and medical supplies to help care for the injured.[22]

Arthur and Sandra Irving, the Arthur L. Irving Family Foundation, and Irving Oil have made additional substantial contributions to educational and health institutions. Some of these contributions are well known; many others are not.

THE UNIVERSITY OF TORONTO

IN 2015, THE ARTHUR L. IRVING FAMILY FOUNDATION DECIDED to launch the C. David Naylor University Fellowships at the

University of Toronto. The initiative is designed to support the development of strong leaders who demonstrate both academic excellence and community commitment. To qualify for the fellowship, the student has to demonstrate a track record of academic achievements at the highest level, have been admitted to the first year of a master's or doctoral program at the University of Toronto, and be a graduate of a university located in Atlantic Canada.[23]

I spoke with Billy Johnson, a PhD student in English literature. He was one of the first to be awarded the David Naylor fellowship. He grew up in Nova Scotia and New Brunswick, and tells me that he heard about the Irvings on countless occasions but had never met any of them. He was struck by two things when he first met Arthur Irving: "how down to earth he is" and "how committed he is to Atlantic Canada." He explained that Arthur Irving "wanted to know where in Atlantic Canada I was from, where my father was from, where my mother was from, and where I grew up. He knew very well all the communities in Atlantic Canada that I talked about."

Vincent Auffrey, from Pré-d'en-Haut, New Brunswick, was also awarded a David Naylor fellowship in 2018. He is doing a PhD in the history of science at the University of Toronto. Arthur Irving spoke to me about Auffrey, and Auffrey did the same about Arthur Irving. Arthur told me he was very impressed with Auffrey, particularly his determination to return to the Maritimes and, more precisely, to his home community after his studies. Auffrey told me there are two things that impressed him about Arthur. First is his deep commitment to, and knowledge of, the Maritimes. He reports that Arthur went into a detailed discussion about Beaumont, a small New Brunswick hamlet. Beaumont, at one point, could boast of having some of the best quarries in North America. Stones from these quarries can be found in heritage buildings from Ottawa to New York. Auffrey said that another thing that struck him is that "Arthur Irving is so down to earth, so easy to talk with. I was impressed."

MORE SUPPORT TO COMMUNITIES

ARTHUR AND SANDRA IRVING, IRVING OIL, AND THE ARTHUR L. Irving Family Foundation have supported universities in all four Atlantic provinces. They made a significant financial contribution to establish a community practice clinic at the Atlantic Veterinary College in Prince Edward Island. In addition to Acadia, they have funded student scholarships at Memorial and Dalhousie universities as well as at the University of New Brunswick. The foundation also made a substantial financial contribution to the University of New Brunswick in 2019 to promote the Harriet Irving Library Research Commons, and another donation for the Harriet Irving Rose Garden.

The foundation has also made major donations to St. Francis Xavier University in Antigonish, Nova Scotia, in support of Irving Family Scholarships at the Brian Mulroney Institute of Government and an additional amount to establish the Irving Research Mentorship Endowment Fund at the McKenna Centre. Irving Oil gave Dalhousie University a major gift toward an auditorium in its engineering centre and another to its scholarship fund. It made an important donation to Fredericton's Saint Thomas University for a track and field scholarship and gifts to Saint John's Rothesay Netherwood School toward its outdoor education program. The foundation and Irving Oil made a major donation to the Université de Moncton in 2019 in support of student activities, including a scholarship fund for students at the Edmundston, Moncton, and Shippagan campuses. It was the single biggest contribution made to the university since it was established in 1963. It will be recalled that, shortly after the university was established, K.C. Irving gave $500,000—the school's first major donation.

The Arthur L. Irving Family Foundation and Irving Oil have also supported a number of fundraising efforts outside the education sector. The foundation gave support to the Beaverbrook Art Gallery for the Harriet Irving Gallery. It made a significant gift toward the construction of an arena in Richibucto, New Brunswick, and Irving Oil gave land to both Richibucto and Tracadie to build municipal parks. The foundation recently made a significant contribution to the Saint John Regional Hospital Foundation's Stay Strong Program to help cancer survivors regain their health.

The above tells only part of the story. We know that the foundation made a substantial donation to the University of New Brunswick–Saint John to establish the Hans W. Klohn Commons. It has also struck partnerships with a number of community cultural groups in Saint John to assist the Imperial Theatre, Symphony Saint John, and the Saint John Theatre Company. Irving Oil has, over the years, also supported minor hockey throughout Atlantic Canada.

In September 2019, Irving Oil contributed $2 million to the capital campaign for Saint John's multisport facility. In return, it got naming rights to the facility. The CBC's comments page, however, had far more negative comments about this than positive ones. One individual, for example, wrote that it was a scheme by the Irvings to reduce their tax bill. This person clearly has never contributed to a fundraising effort; if he or she had, it would be obvious that one always saves more money by not giving. Put another way, there is no money to be made by giving to a fundraising effort. I speak from experience. Another individual, however, summed things up nicely: "The Irvings: They're damned if they do and damned if they don't. If ever a family was in a no-win situation, it is the Irvings. For more proof scan most if not all of the comments on this story."[24]

Arthur Irving, the Arthur L. Irving Family Foundation, and Irving Oil have made still more contributions, many of which we will never know about. In many cases, and as already mentioned, Arthur Irving does not want to bring attention to himself when making donations. The same is true of other Irvings. J.K. Irving and his family and the late Jack Irving and his family also made substantial contributions to education, health, and community-led fundraising efforts, nearly all of which were in Atlantic Canada.

LOOKING BACK

ARTHUR IRVING AND IRVING OIL GO ABOUT THEIR WORK AS quietly as possible. That was the way K.C. Irving worked, and that is how Arthur Irving prefers it.

As I have already noted several times, there are advantages to running a business without having to comply with the reporting requirements with which publicly traded firms have to contend. But there are also some disadvantages. It becomes a modus operandi in all things. The result is that, all too often, the good the firm does enjoys only limited visibility in the community. Arthur Irving thinks people should look at the K.C. Irving Environmental Science Centre and the Harriet Irving Botanical Gardens for what they are, for their physical beauty, and for what they mean for students at Acadia. He does not believe anyone should spend any time trying to determine the financial contribution he made to the projects. In this sense, he is rare. In nearly every case, donors with whom I have worked on fundraising campaigns insist on doing the opposite.

Arthur, Sandra, Sarah, the Arthur L. Irving Family Foundation, and Irving Oil have all made substantial contributions to health-care and educational institutions. Some of these donations are well known, others less so, and still others not at all. Starting with K.C. Irving, it is in the Irving DNA to not draw attention to themselves, to keep things close to their chests, and to avoid bragging. This works in business, in developing business strategies and an edge against the competition. But it makes it difficult for people and communities to gain a full appreciation of the contributions Arthur Irving and his family have made to help grow the region's health-care and educational institutions and, more broadly, the region's economy.

Notes

1 See Martin Turcotte, "Volunteering and Charitable Giving in Canada," cat. no. 89-652-X2015001 (Ottawa: Statistics Canada, January 30, 2015), 16.

2 Quoted in Chelsea Murray, "The Irving Commitment," *Conservator* 34, no. 1 (2013): 28.

3 Ibid.

4 Ducks Unlimited Canada, "Ducks Unlimited Conservation Centre," n.d., online at ducks.ca/places/new-brunswick/ducks-unlimited-conservation-centre/.

5 "North American Waterfowl Management Plan: A Strategy for Cooperation, May 1986" (Washington, DC; Ottawa: United States Department of the Interior and Environment Canada, 1986), online at fws.gov/migratorybirds/pdf/management/NAWMP/OriginalNAWMP.pdf.

6 Byron K. Williams, Mark D. Koneff, and David A. Smith, "Evaluation of Waterfowl Conservation under the North American Waterfowl Management Plan," *Journal of Wildlife Management* 63, no. 2 (1999): 417.

7 See, among others, Naomi E.S. Griffiths, *From Migrant to Acadian: A North American Border People, 1604–1755* (Montreal; Kingston, ON: McGill-Queen's University Press, 2004).

8 Canada, Research Support Fund, "Supporting Ecological Research in Beaubassin" (Ottawa, June 13, 2016), online at rsf-fsr.gc.ca/news_room-salle_de_presse/support-soutien/beaubassin-eng.aspx.

9 See, for example, Lawrence Martin, "A family tragedy that Stephen Harper has not forgotten," *Globe and Mail*, July 8, 2009, A6.

10 See, for example, Régis Brun, *Fort Beauséjour–Fort Cumberland: une histoire/A History* (Memramcook, NB: Société du Monument Lefebvre, 1991), 18–23.

11 "Harper opens Ducks Unlimited centre in Aulac," *CBC News*, August 29, 2012, online at cbc.ca/news/canada/new-brunswick/harper-opens-ducks-unlimited-centre-in-aulac-1.1200314.

12 Acadia University, "National accolades for K.C. Irving Environmental Science Centre," press release, October 9, 2015, online at acadiau.ca/home/news-reader-page/national-accolades-for-kc-irving-environmental-science-centre.html.

13 See, among others, Acadia University, "Endangered plants," Harriet
    Irving Botanical Gardens, n.d., online at botanicalgardens.acadiau.
    ca/9293.html.
14 For an excellent discussion on the topic, see Paul G. Schervish, "The
    Sound of One Hand Clapping: The Case for and against Anonymous
    Giving," *Voluntas: International Journal of Voluntary and Nonprofit
    Organizations* 5, no. 1 (1994): 1–26.
15 Acadia University, "The Arthur Irving Academy," K.C. Irving
    Environmental Science Centre, n.d., online at kcirvingcentre.acadiau.ca/
    IrvingAcademy.html.
16 Dartmouth College, Arthur L. Irving Institute for Energy and Society,
    "Dartmouth announces creation of the Arthur L. Irving Institute for
    Energy and Society," press release, n.d., online at irving.dartmouth.edu/
    news/2016/09/dartmouth-announces-creation-arthur-l-irving-institute-
    energy-and-society.
17 Dartmouth College, "The Arthur L. Irving Institute for Energy and
    Society—Request for Proposal: Investing in Our Energy Futures, Spring
    2019" (Hanover, NH, 2019), online at irving.dartmouth.edu/sites/
    irving_energy.prod/files/irving_energy/wysiwyg/rfp_spring_2019_
    2-18-19_final.pdf.
18 Ibid.
19 Dartmouth College, Tuck School of Business, "MBA Program Rankings,"
    n.d., online at tuck.dartmouth.edu/news/in-the-media/mba-program-
    rankings.
20 Massachusetts General Hospital, "Awards and Honors November 2017,"
    November 10, 2017, online at https://www.massgeneral.org/news/article/
    awards-and-honors-november-2017.
21 See, for example, World Vision, "2010 Haiti earthquake: Facts, FAQs
    and how to help," n.d., online at worldvision.org/disaster-relief-news-
    stories/2010-haiti-earthquake-facts.
22 Huddle, "Sandra Irving being honoured with Canadian Red Cross Power
    of Humanity Award," November 4, 2019, online at huddle.today/sandra-
    irving-being-honoured-with-canadian-red-cross-power-of-humanity-
    award/.

23 University of Toronto, School of Graduate Studies, "C. David Naylor University Fellowships endowed by a gift from the Arthur L. Irving Foundation," press release, n.d., online at qa-www.sgs.utoronto. ca/awards-funding/scholarships-awards/c-david-naylor-university-fellowships-endowed-by-a-gift-from-the-arthur-l-irving-foundation/.

24 "Irving Oil captures naming rights for Saint John field house," CBC News, September 16, 2019, online at cbc.ca/news/canada/new-brunswick/saint-john-field-house-irving-oil-1.5285570.

CHAPTER 10

NEW CHALLENGES

MANY HAVE BEEN PREDICTING THE DEMISE OF THE Irvings and Irving Oil since K.C. Irving first went into business. It will be recalled that New Brunswick business tycoon Howard P. Robinson is reported to have said that he would "chase that fellow Irving back to Bouctouche." K.C. Irving stayed in Saint John, and bought Robinson's house on Mount Pleasant Avenue. In their 1973 book on the Irvings, Russell Hunt and Robert Campbell compared Irving enterprises to a dinosaur— that they had become too big to survive changing times—and concluded that they "cannot adapt to change."[1] That was nearly fifty years ago. The various Irving businesses have not only adapted well to change; they have also kept growing.

On the face of it, however, the challenges ahead are particularly daunting. Some observers are already writing the obituary of the oil and gas sector. They note that the competition to attract young talent will be increasingly demanding, and the pressure to reduce costs and to compete against low-cost and low-tax jurisdictions will not let up. As is well known, there is also a shift away from fossil fuels in many jurisdictions and sectors. I asked Arthur Irving if he and Irving Oil were thinking about how best to meet the challenges ahead. He answered with two words: "Every day."

That said, and at the risk of stating the obvious, I take full responsibility for this book—in particular, for this and the next chapter. For these, I could not draw from books published on the Irving businesses, which do not deal with issues I raise here because, for the most part, such issues did not seem important at the time.

Interviews I carried out with current and past Irving Oil employees dealt with the past, with how Irving Oil grew into a highly competitive environment, and with the Irving School of Business. Here, however, I draw on current management literature that deals with the challenges now confronting the oil and gas sector. I decided in these concluding chapters to explore these issues by drawing on my own work and on how I see things in the years ahead for the oil and gas sector, for Irving Oil, and for my region.

THE ROOTS OF THE OIL AND GAS SECTOR

It is widely believed that the oil and gas industry has been a major contributor to climate change. What is less known is that the Maritimes—and one Maritimer, in particular—played a pivotal role in the birth of the industry. Abraham Gesner, born in Cornwallis, Nova Scotia, invented kerosene oil, and was granted the first patent for distilling bituminous material. While he was in New Brunswick, he discovered, or rediscovered, "the veins of solid Bitumen in Albert County, which he used in his experiments in distillation." The *Canadian Encyclopedia* calls Gesner "a founder of the modern Petroleum Industry."[2]

Gesner moved to Saint John in 1838, and served as the first government geologist in a British colony. He collected a wide array of specimens, which helped to build the collection now on display at the New Brunswick Museum. He moved to New York to pursue opportunities with his "coal oil" invention that could illuminate a room. He worked on ways to distill and refine bitumen to remove impurities that gave the product a foul odour. In 1854, he was awarded three US patents and started a commercial enterprise to refine bitumen. J.D. Rockefeller bought the Gesner operations—and eventually Rockefeller would take over Imperial Oil in Canada.[3]

Abraham Gesner, living in Saint John in the 1840s, and K.C. Irving some eighty years later, could never imagine the role the oil and gas sector would come to play in the economy. The sector accounts for 11 percent of Canada's gross domestic product and employs directly and indirectly some 819,500 Canadians.[4] Canada is the world's sixth-largest energy producer, the fifth-largest net exporter of energy, and the eighth-largest consumer of energy.[5] In brief, the oil and gas sector is very important to the Canadian economy—and, given the presence of Irving Oil in the province, to the New Brunswick economy. The sector can remain a key component of both economies provided it meets the challenges ahead.

CLIMATE CHANGE

PATRICK POUYANNÉ, CHIEF EXECUTIVE OFFICER OF FRANCE-based oil and gas giant Total, told a Paris conference that, "sometimes in all these discussions you have the impression that all fossil fuels are the bad guys" when it comes to climate change.[6] The issue, however, is much more complex. The European Commission, for example, identifies five main causes of rising

emissions of greenhouses gases: burning coal, oil, and gas; deforestation; increasing livestock farming; fertilizers containing nitro-
gen; and fluorinated gases.[7]

Still, the public perception is that the oil and gas sector has a
lot to answer for when it comes to climate change. It is also easier
for governments, notably politicians, to point the finger at large oil
and gas firms, rather than at consumers or voters, as the culprits.
No matter, climate change is real, and unless we address it, it will
wreak havoc on all facets of society—the economy is certainly no
exception. Succinctly put, a cleaner planet is in everyone's interest. I note that the United Nations has declared: "Climate Change
is the defining issue of our time and we are at a defining moment."
It adds: "There is alarming evidence that important tipping points,
leading to irreversible changes in major ecosystems and the plan-
etary climate system, may already have been reached or passed."[8]

Climate change deniers are fast losing ground in the face of
mounting scientific evidence. If nothing is done to deal with climate change, we have as much of a chance at stopping climate
change as King Canute had in telling the incoming tide to stop and
not get his feet and robe wet.[9]

A number of governments worldwide, including Canada's,
have decided to take action. In 1997, representatives from most
countries signed a protocol in Kyoto designed to "stabilize green-
house-gas concentrations at a level that would prevent danger-
ous anthropogenic interference with the climate system." The
Kyoto Protocol to the United Nations Framework Convention
on Climate Change came into force in 2005.[10] In 2015, representatives from 196 countries came together again to sign the Paris
Agreement Under the United Nations Framework Convention
on Climate Change; the Paris Agreement took effect in late 2016,
and 185 countries have become a party to it.[11] The objective is to

put in place measures to limit the increase in the global average temperature to below 2°c above pre-industrial levels. I note, however, that President Donald Trump announced in June 2017 that the United States would withdraw from the agreement, and subsequently began the formal process of withdrawing on November 4, 2019.[12] But that has not stopped many other countries from unveiling plans to meet Paris-established targets.[13] Some countries such as the Netherlands have gone further and enacted legislation to exceed them.

Canada played an important role in developing and promoting the Paris Agreement. It will be recalled that, in November 2015, that the federal government pledged $2.65 billion in climate finance over five years.[14] Still, Canada is having a difficult time reaching its Paris Agreement targets, and some observers are blaming, among others, the oil and gas sector.[15]

I asked Arthur Irving for his views on climate change. He was to the point: "Climate change is for real and we want to be a part of the solution." Irving Oil can also make the case that it has outperformed the competition in embracing measures to protect the environment. For one thing, the Irving refinery was the first in Canada to produce low-sulphur gasoline and the first to produce high-octane gasoline without the use of lead additives. For another, in 2002, Irving Oil was also the first oil company to be awarded the US Environmental Protection Agency's Clean Air Excellence Award.[16]

The important question is not whether climate change is changing the world's ecosystem. It is. We are already living with a warmer atmosphere, which entails changes to many natural habitats and increasing sea levels. Rather, the question is how best to respond to climate change. The challenge extends far beyond the oil and gas sector. We need, for example, to make changes in land

use, stop burning tropical forests, and modify agricultural practices aimed at reducing methane emissions.[17]

For their part, Irving Oil executives can make the point that they
are taking climate change seriously and doing something about
it. They told a committee of the New Brunswick legislature that
the company has done a lot to protect the environment—a great
deal more than others in their sector. The executives explained:
"The challenge that we do have, if you're already one of the best,
how much more room is there to improve? That will be our fundamental challenge." They added that the Irving Oil refinery has
a "strong record on reducing our emissions. Our facility [in Saint
John] is one of the best in the OECD (Organisation for Economic
Co-operation and Development)."[18]

Still, the challenge at hand for the oil and gas sector is not about
to go away. The shift away from an almost total reliance on oil
and gas to transport people and goods is fast underway and gaining steam. Consider the following: the German auto manufacturer
BMW will no longer sell gas-only vehicles by 2025. All Volvo models will shortly have only hybrid, plug-in, or pure battery-electric
drivetrains. Volkswagen AG announced it will offer at least one
battery-based drivetrain option for all its models. GM declared
in 2017 that it is working toward abandoning the internal combustion engine completely, although it did not say when it would
attain that goal.[19] Toyota also plans to do away completely with
gasoline-only vehicles by 2050, if not earlier.[20]

Tesla is credited with having changed the landscape. Although
the car manufacturer is dealing with its own difficult production
issues, its innovative technology has had ripple effects, forcing the
hand of automakers to look at producing electric or hybrid autos.
Elon Musk, Tesla's CEO, explains why the world is shifting to electric or hybrid cars: "If somebody said you're gonna pour the liquid

remains of dinosaurs into your vehicle and burn them in order to move from one place to another, releasing toxic fumes—and by the way, you better not have your car on in a closed room cause you're gonna die—you'd say, 'Why are we doing that?'"[21]

The shift away from the internal combustion engine is starting to take root, but there are still rocks in the way. Electricity is not always clean energy—some 30 percent of the electricity in the United States and nearly 9 percent in Canada still comes from coal.[22] Electric vehicles (EVS), in turn, are generating demands for lithium, cobalt, and other rare earth minerals, each of which entails its own environmental and economic challenges.[23] EVS do not emit climate-damaging greenhouse gases, but they are not without problems for the environment. It takes more than twice the amount of energy to produce an electric car as it does a conventional one.[24] Internal combustion engines are far more efficient and less damaging to the environment than they once were— today's automobiles only emit 1 percent of the pollution vehicles emitted in the 1960s.[25] Mining in search of rare metals in places such as China and the Democratic Republic of Congo is increasingly aggressive, causing its own ecological challenges—notably, contaminated soil, polluted rivers, and deforestation.[26] This is not to suggest that EVS or hybrid cars should be abandoned. The point is that there is no easy solution to dealing with climate change.

Canadians have been slow to embrace EVS, which account for only 1 percent of auto sales. Automotive analyst Dennis DesRosiers maintains it will take at least a decade before EVS hold even 10 percent of the market. The numbers, he points out, "are abysmally low," and he identifies a lack of "consumer acceptance" as the reason. He adds that consumers are thinking, "is there a real threat [to climate change] and why do I have to solve this on my own?"[27]

Another factor in the reluctance about electric cars is their struggle to operate in cold weather, since lithium-ion batteries are temperature-sensitive.[28] Atlantic Canada and New England deal with harsh winter conditions and cover a lot of geography. It is one thing for Israel, for example—with a population of nearly 9 million and 22,000 square kilometres—to embrace battery-only automobiles. It is another for, say, Nova Scotia, with a population of less than 1 million and 55,000 square kilometres of territory. Winter is also a great deal more challenging in Nova Scotia than in Israel.

The Irving Oil refinery generates a significant number of finished products. It produces, among many others, heating fuel, jet fuel, marine fuel, propane, and asphalt. The market for both jet fuel and asphalt should remain strong, at least for the foreseeable future. Irving Oil has captured the bulk of the jet-fuel market in Atlantic Canada and about half of the market at Boston's Logan International Airport. It counts among its customers JetBlue, American Airlines, WestJet, Air Canada, United, and Southwest.[29]

Irving Oil has also expanded its share of the asphalt market in New England and the southeast United States. The company recently signed a ten-year agreement to have dedicated access to an asphalt terminal in Charleston, South Carolina. This enables Irving Oil to establish a sales team for the asphalt business in the southern United States, which is one of the fastest-growing markets for asphalt products in North America.[30]

Irving Oil, moreover, is not about to throw in the towel on its retail locations; they are about much more then gasoline sales. It operates about eleven hundred service stations in three national jurisdictions. Arthur Irving noted, "we don't only sell gasoline in the service stations. We are really in the convenience retailing business; plus, at our Big Stop locations, we also operate restaurants and a full line of services for the professional drivers."

Irving Oil has also signed an agreement with Tesla to lodge its "supercharger" stations in Atlantic Canada. This will require Irving Oil to look for larger lots in future to build its outlets. The outlets will require numerous Tesla charging stations in addition to gas tanks. Unlike filling up a gas tank, charging an electric vehicle requires time—time for drivers to spend money in a convenience store or restaurant. Jeff Matthews, an Irving Oil executive, explains: "We hope that green-minded motorists will have a bite to eat while their car batteries top up with power."[31]

I note that in early 2020 Irving Oil opened its first "The Irving" convenience store, in Pembroke, Massachusetts, near Boston. It is a pilot project, but one can assume that Irving convenience stores tied to charging stations, gas tanks, and in-house restaurants speak to Irving Oil's future. Sarah Irving describes the initiative as going "beyond a traditional convenience store." The new approach looks to front-line employees to be "a part of the Irving Oil team" and "responsible for management of the site's day-to-day operations." The central purpose is to secure better and quicker customer feedback.[32] This suggests that looking to customers for guidance and evolving with the times will continue to be a cornerstone of how the company operates.

That has been the Irving Oil approach to meeting challenges in the past. The approach has worked well thus far, and has enabled the company to outperform the competition on many fronts, including in promoting a cleaner environment. The task remains a work-in-progress, however, and will only grow in importance in the years ahead. To be sure, there is much more work to be done.

ATTRACTING TALENT

FUTURE BUSINESS SUCCESS BELONGS TO FIRMS THAT ARE ABLE to attract top talent. McKinsey & Company, a leading business executive and management consulting group, has outlined the ten most important issues facing business executives. The issue leading the pack: "attracting and retaining talent."[33] We know that employers in North America and Europe will require between sixteen and eighteen million more college-educated workers over the next few years.[34] The report sums things up nicely: "The single biggest constraint on the success of my organization is the ability to get and hang on to enough of the right people."[35] McKinsey & Company's next nine most important issues flow from its number one: developing the talent you have; managing performance; creating leadership teams; making decisions; reorganizing to capture value quickly; reducing overhead costs for the long term; making culture a competitive advantage leading transformational change; and transitioning to new leadership roles.

The oil and gas sector faces its own distinct challenges in recruiting top talent. The sector is not only highly competitive, it also has to deal with many extraneous factors. One keen observer of the sector argues that it "might need a Tesla" to attract top talent. He explains: "The car industry has benefited immensely from excitement that a company like Tesla has brought into it...but also definitely attracted, and is attracting, a lot of talented people."[36] Different analyses of young professionals speak to the challenge. A recent survey of STEM (Science, Technology, Engineering, and Mathematics) millennials and Generation Zs reveals that 77 percent are interested in pursuing a career in the technology sector, 58 percent in life sciences and pharmaceuticals, and only 44 percent are looking to the oil and gas sector.[37]

Another more in-depth survey suggests that the oil and gas sector will be experiencing strong competition in attracting young STEM talent. The survey also reveals that interest in employment in the oil and gas sector is higher in emerging economies. One bright spot for the sector: the more the oil and gas industry looks to new technologies, the more it becomes appealing for young STEM talent to pursue a career in the sector. In addition, many still believe that oil and gas is a blue-collar industry, but the more the sector is able to project itself as a white-collar industry, the higher will be the interest in it.[38]

The Conference Board of Canada points to still more human resource challenges for the country's petroleum-refining sector. It makes the point that the sector is largely made up of "older and better-educated Canadian-born males." It adds that it is "missing an opportunity to increase recruitment among newcomers to Canada and among women." Women are rare in the industry, to the point that the "industry's scarcity of women is acute even by the standards of the broader manufacturing industry."

The Conference Board of Canada points to yet another human resource challenge for the sector. On this issue, it is worth quoting the report at length:

The relatively advanced age of the workforce suggests experience is abundant, but also hints at a looming demographic challenge as retirements accelerate. While this situation is hardly unique to the refining industry, resulting skill shortages could emerge earlier here. Workers over 45 make up 47 per cent of the industry's labour force, compared with 42 per cent manufacturing-wide. Moreover, the largest cluster of the industry's workers is the 45–54 age group. Calculations based on the current retirement age suggest that up to a quarter of those workers will retire within the next decade.[39]

Irving Oil has yet another difficulty in attracting top talent, a challenge that is not unique to the firm. Smaller cities like Saint John have to compete with the growing ability of large urban centres to attract talent. Large cities—Toronto, Montreal, Calgary, Vancouver—have a natural draw: job opportunities are many, varied, and strong; they have many ethnic networks; they provide sought-after facilities, including theatres, museums, top-flight universities, and fine dining; and they offer career opportunities for two-career families.

Saint John also has a branding issue. Halifax is widely seen as the region's growth centre and Moncton as an entrepreneurial community, while Saint John is perceived as a slow-moving community with a history of labour-management problems. The municipality is also dealing with a very difficult fiscal situation, which has been widely reported in the media. Branding and perceptions, whether founded or not, matter in efforts to attract ambitious, bright millennials.

Loyalty to community or region is not as strong as it once was. I see it in students at my university, many of whom are anxious to move to a big city as soon as they complete their education. They look to Ottawa, Montreal, Quebec City, and, regionally, Halifax to pursue career opportunities. Few, or not enough, are willing to return to their home communities to carve out a career after completing their university educations.

We are also witnessing a shift in attitude that favours the individual over the community. I have often been asked why I have spent the bulk of my career at the Université de Moncton, which admittedly does not rank among top universities. I have been told that, had I moved to a large, research-intensive university, I would not only have been better paid, but also better able to work with bright PhD students who could have helped with my research. But my Acadian roots became my touchstone, and my heartfelt commitment to the

Maritime provinces and to Atlantic Canada became a call to action, and I have never seriously considered leaving my alma mater. Things are different today, however, and not just for Acadians.

K.C. Irving told BP officials that he wanted to build the refinery in Saint John "because I live there." Arthur Irving has the same deeply felt commitment to his roots and to his community. I have also had many discussions with Irving Oil's current CEO Ian Whitcomb, and he, too, has a deep attachment to his community. Before joining Irving Oil, he had a successful career that saw him occupy senior positions outside the region, including in Toronto, only for him to return to Saint John. But things are changing with the coming generation of leaders.

The young generation is far more footloose than were K.C. or Arthur Irving and others of my generation. The challenge for Irving Oil and other Maritime businesses is one of attracting the next generation of leaders to communities that do not offer the kind of amenities, institutions, and varied employment opportunities found in large urban centres. These businesses can no longer take for granted that bright and ambitious university graduates from the Maritimes will want to stay in the region.

Irving Oil, however, has a number of advantages to attract younger people. It was named one of Canada's top employers in 2019 for the fourth year.[40] Its "Good Energy in Action" program provides employees with one paid day off a year to do some volunteering and matches employee donations up to $100. The company also offers generous benefits, including, in Canada, topping up parental leave payments for employees who are new mothers and fathers to 100 percent of their salary for up to seventeen weeks. In addition, Irving Oil offers scholarships to children of employees to pursue post-secondary studies, and the firm provides very generous health and dental care programs.

Irving Oil has other advantages that could help the firm pull against gravity or against large urban centres in attracting top talent. Sarah Irving is increasingly playing a key and highly visible role at Irving Oil, and she is widely seen doing so both inside and outside the firm. She is breaking the mould that the petroleum-refining sector is the preserve of older white men, which holds an important message for millennials, especially women.

The Irving Oil head office also offers amenities unlike few offices anywhere. I was deeply impressed by what I saw when I toured the new headquarters. There was a top-of-the-line onsite fitness facility, a first-class health-and-wellness centre, and nice, open offices housed in, arguably, the most employee-focused and modern office building in Atlantic Canada.

All of the above is to make the point that Irving Oil's ability to attract top talent is critical to its future success, as it is for all firms. *Forbes* magazine has put it well: "Your company is only as extraordinary as your people....There is nothing more powerful than employees' passion and initiative to make customers happy to spark long-lasting word of mouth about your brand."[41] The business management literature ranks attracting top talent as the key challenge, employing such terms as "the war for talent," suggesting that "the war for talent will only intensify," and advising comapnies to "go on the offensive to win the war for talent."[42] In their book *Leading Organizations*, Scott Keller and Mary Meaney underline the importance of attracting top talent, making the case that high performers are 400 percent more productive than average workers.[43] They also argue that top talent is scarce and highly mobile.

To sum up, Irving Oil has a strong focus on people, and features the region's most attractive and employee-focused head-office building, generous employee benefits, and employment opportunities that should enable the firm to attract top talent. It will not, however, go at it alone—there will be very strong competition, in part from firms located in large urban centres with all the advantages of such places. Irving Oil, like its competitors in the oil and gas sector, is facing a daunting challenge in attracting top talent and the next generation of leaders. Its continued success depends on meeting that challenge.

IT'S ABOUT COMPETITIVENESS

THE CONFERENCE BOARD OF CANADA, TAKING STOCK OF Canada's petroleum-refining sector, has good news for Atlantic Canada, but less for other regions. It concludes:

> Regional refining industries hold relatively different levels of importance across Canada. Moreover, in all regions except Atlantic Canada, the industry's importance has dwindled over time. This phenomenon has been most pronounced in the Western provinces, excluding Alberta. For example, the refining industry today accounts for just 0.1 per cent of real GDP in British Columbia and Saskatchewan, about one-third the level in 1982.[44]

The report is quick to add, however, that "Atlantic Canada is the country's largest exporter" of gasoline and related products.

This, in turn, speaks to Irving Oil's success. There is more. The Conference Board of Canada reports that labour productivity in the refinery industry has been poor. It points the finger at Ontario's refinery industry, insisting that it has the "lowest labour productivity among all regions of the country." It then notes: "In terms of absolute productivity, Atlantic Canada outpaces the national average by a wide margin. In 2009, each refinery worker in Atlantic

Canada produced 91,000 barrels of refined products, more than double the national average, and was 120 per cent more efficient than they were in 1991.[45] This, too, speaks to Irving Oil's success.

Luck does not explain this. Strong management and reinvesting profits to strengthen the firm's competitiveness do. Irving Oil's success has a great deal to do with the decision by both K.C. and Arthur Irving to reinvest profits in the company, to focus heavily on safety and reliability, to pre-invest in environmental standards, and to expand operations at the right moment. Other businesses in the petroleum-refining sector have not always been as forward-thinking and, as a result, they have shut down some of their refineries, as Imperial Oil recently did with its Dartmouth refinery.

But Irving Oil's success and its productivity are not solely dependent on its approach and work. Like other firms, Irving Oil does not operate in a vacuum. Broad economic conditions, monetary policy, political stability in the Middle East, and public policy at home—including the need to obtain a social licence to proceed with certain projects—also have an important say in the firm's success. Stability in the world's hot spots is beyond the control of Canadian governments, and certainly beyond Irving Oil's. But domestic government policies also matter a great deal to Irving Oil. Ottawa would have done Alberta, Saskatchewan, New Brunswick, and Irving Oil a great service had it said yes to Energy East, or had it at least not piled new conditions onto the approval process.

Government policy, when struck in isolation from business requirements, can undermine the ability of a business to compete. New Brunswick is its home, but Irving Oil competes throughout Atlantic Canada and in the United States and Ireland. If, for example, governments in Canada impose conditions on Irving Oil that are not found in the United States, the company's ability to compete in that market could be compromised. Irving Oil, like all businesses, needs to compete on a level playing field in order to prosper. Put differently, if government conditions on the petroleum-refining sector are applied uniformly in Canada, there is every reason to believe that Irving Oil will continue to outperform the competition. Things change, however, if Irving Oil has to deal with a government policy that adds, say, $4 to a refined barrel of crude oil in Canada while a refinery south of the border or elsewhere has no such requirement.

Tax policy also matters a great deal—more than it is generally believed. It can affect when and where firms choose to locate their head offices. Chief executive officers, chief financial officers, and vice-presidents of operations know how to add. If they have to decide between a jurisdiction that imposes, say, a 52 percent tax rate on personal income on top earners versus one with a 42 percent rate, they will opt for the jurisdiction with the lower tax rate, all other things being equal. This is not to take away from one of the most important challenges confronting policy makers in the Western world: rising income inequality and how best to address it.

THE NEW BRUNSWICK CHALLENGE

THE IRVINGS REMAIN FIRMLY COMMITTED TO NEW BRUNSWICK—indeed, they are tied at the hip—but running a global business in a have-less province is not without its challenges. Few New Brunswickers, however, are indifferent to the Irving family. As I noted in the introduction, I suspect that Frank McKenna spoke for many in the province's private sector when he said that "the great majority of New Brunswickers have a high opinion and respect for what the Irvings have done and continue to do." Both New Brunswick and the Irvings have lived through a fairly prosperous time since the end of the Second World War, as has much of the

Western world. Consequently, this has been conducive to a fairly productive relationship between governments and the private sector, and between governments and citizens.

The economic prosperity of the postwar period has been fuelled by the coming of age of the baby boomers, by strong demand for Canada's natural resources, by the birth of universities in all Canadian regions and the development of a more educated workforce, by relatively easy access to capital, and by federal governments flush with cash, looking to sign cost-shared agreements with the provinces in virtually every sector.

New Brunswick has been on the receiving end of generous federal spending for the past seven decades. By the 1970s, it had reached the point where every sector and every department in the provincial government had its own agreement with Ottawa.[46] There were federal-provincial agreements to build highways and to promote tourism, rural development, urban development, the fishery, agriculture—the list goes on. At one point, nearly 50 percent of the revenues flowing into the coffers of the New Brunswick government came from Ottawa. Today, the share is down to about one-third.[47]

But that does not tell the whole story. The federal government has also put in place transfer payments to individuals. This, too, has fuelled New Brunswick's consumer economy. In the early 1970s, Bryce Mackasey, the federal minister responsible for employment insurance, made the program more generous and made it easier for workers to qualify for benefits.[48] Since then, the federal government has tried, from time to time and with varying degrees of success, to scale back the program.[49] Other programs have also changed in recent years and will very likely continue to do so in the years ahead. The federal government has slowly but surely been pulling back on most policy fronts. It no longer signs agreements with provincial governments to promote economic development in economic sectors such as forestry and the fishery or to help develop rural or urban areas. In short, the federal government is slowly turning off the spending tap in New Brunswick when it comes to promoting economic development, and this will have wide economic implications for the province.

Ottawa has also reduced its contributions to other important federal-provincial programs. I am thinking, for example, of Canada's medicare program. When Ottawa first sought to sell medicare to the provinces, it committed to pay about half the cost; today, it pays only about a quarter. It seems that, whenever Ottawa has to cut back on its expenditure budget, it looks to federal-provincial agreements, as it did with the Chrétien and Harper program-review exercises.[50] It is, of course, easier for Ottawa to cut back on federal-provincial agreements and offload the tough decisions onto provincial governments. The provinces, not the federal government, are on the front line of delivering medical care services to Canadians. If health care has to be scaled back or medical facilities or staff cut, it falls on provincial governments to get the job done, but it makes little sense when it comes to establishing sound public policy.

The federal government's slowly reducing its participation in health care comes at a difficult time for New Brunswick. The province's population is aging quickly, with wide implications for its finances. Consider the following: by 2038, 31 percent of New Brunswick's population will be seniors, compared with 24 percent of Canada's as a whole.[51] As is widely recognized, providing health care to an aging population is far more expensive. Crunch time is around the corner, and the fact that New Brunswick continues to deal with a serious fiscal challenge hardly helps matters. I and others have been ringing the alarm bell about that fiscal challenge for the past fifteen years.[52]

There is a perfect storm in the making for New Brunswick—again with important implications for the private sector. New Brunswickers have become comfortable with top-quality health care, numerous government services, and provincial, local, and community institutions partly funded by the federal government. As all politicians know, challenging the status quo in government policies and programs is only for the brave. Brave or not, the dilemma is clear: either Ottawa comes up with new financial resources for health care in New Brunswick, given its fast-aging population, or substantial spending cuts will have to be made to the province's health-care facilities and programs.

Given that Ottawa in recent years has reduced transfer payments to the provinces for health care and shifted to a per capita basis to calculate its transfer payments, I do not hold much hope that it will soon open its spending tap for smaller, have-less provinces. It thus will fall on the New Brunswick government to deal with a situation it is ill-equipped to handle, especially without help from the federal government.

New Brunswick, as noted earlier, is arguably Canada's most difficult jurisdiction to govern. In recent years, we have seen three successive governments fall after only one mandate, and for the first time in nearly one hundred years New Brunswickers have elected a minority government. The province has a sharp linguistic divide, which some politicians do not hesitate to exploit for partisan purposes. It also has a sharp urban-rural divide. Politicians and the provincial government bureaucracy have to manage twenty-four hospitals and over three hundred schools with a dwindling student population, and support a municipal structure of more than 350 cities, towns, villages, and local service districts.[53] And all of this for a population of barely more than three-quarters of a million, with limited resources and a debt burden amounting to

$13.9 billion.[54] The provincial auditor general recently warned that, because of "[c]onsecutive deficits, the pace of growth of our net debt is not sustainable for the long term."[55] The City of Saint John also continues to deal with a very difficult fiscal situation.

Failure to meet the challenge would only fuel linguistic, ethnic, and urban-rural tensions, economic envy, and discontent with the role of government in society. It would also clear the path for politicians to peddle easy solutions to complex public policy issues and to point the finger of blame at anyone. This might hold partisan political merit for some, but it could play havoc with everything else, including economic stability. Irving Oil and other large successful New Brunswick businesses could become easy targets. More to the point, the call to tax big businesses and the rich could well become tempting as the provincial government is forced to make tough decisions. The fact remains that New Brunswick is already a jurisdiction with one of the highest levels of taxation in Canada, if not in North America.[56]

This will be a delicate situation for Irving Oil to navigate. Arthur Irving, Irving Oil, and other Irving businesses have shied away from publicity in the past. Because it is privately held, Irving Oil has been able to operate out of the limelight. To be sure, there are distinct advantages for privately held companies, as I have noted time and again in this book. It has, however, sheltered Irving Oil from having to engage in public policy debates outside issues dealing with the oil and gas sector.

K.C., Arthur, and Irving Oil have always avoided blowing their own horns. They assumed that New Brunswickers knew or likely had heard about their contributions to the New Brunswick economy. Although it is not in its DNA, Irving Oil, in concert with other New Brunswick businesses, might well need to engage in a public policy debate about its contributions to the economy, the number of jobs it has created and maintained, and the quantity of local purchases it makes every day of the week. It should also not shy away from a debate about New Brunswick's taxation level and the importance of keeping it in line with those in neighbouring juris-dictions. In short, there might well be a price for Irving Oil to pay if it avoids engaging in public debates about the state of the econ-omy and the positive role it has played and continues to play in emerging economic circumstances. Given its history, it might be difficult for Irving Oil to make the transition and engage both the government of New Brunswick and New Brunswickers in public policy debates. But on this issue, history might not be a good guide to deal with how the future will unfold.

LOOKING BACK

K.C., Arthur Irving, and Irving Oil have had a steady hand in meeting difficult challenges posed by the competition, by economic downturns, and by government action or inaction. The challenges on the horizon, however, are a combination of several forces that will be particularly difficult to navigate.

To be sure, climate change is one. Irving Oil has been ahead of the competition in adjusting its operations to attenuate the impact of its products on the environment. But this still remains a work-in-progress for both the oil and gas sector and Irving Oil. More will be needed from this sector as it adjusts to hybrid and battery-powered automobiles. These developments will continue to put Irving Oil and others in the sector to the test.

The search for top talent is another challenge that will test Irving Oil. It will have to search for top talent against the lure of the enticing employment opportunities found in large urban centres. The oil and gas sector also needs to update its brand to appeal to young workers, to professionals, to minorities, and to new Canadians.

Perhaps the most daunting challenge for Irving Oil will be the need to navigate the public policy environment in the jurisdiction that houses its head office. New Brunswick is confronting far-reaching political and economic challenges because of its fast-aging population—the distinct advantages the baby boomers brought to the New Brunswick economy are about to be turned on their head.

The time will be ripe for politicians and others to peddle easy solutions that bring few long-term solutions to complex problems. Irving Oil and other successful New Brunswick firms might well need to become more active participants in public policy debates. K.C., Arthur, and Irving Oil have been, at best, hesitant participants in public policy debates in the past on issues outside their sector, but the cost of remaining on the sidelines could prove too high for the business community. Arthur Irving had it right when he said that Ducks Unlimited needed to wave its own flag because no one else will. The same logic applies to Irving Oil and other businesses with their head offices in New Brunswick as the province enters a very demanding public policy environment.

Notes

1 Russell Hunt and Robert Campbell, *K.C. Irving: The Art of the Industrialist* (Toronto: McClelland and Stewart, 1973), 122.
2   L.M. Cumming, R.F. Miller, and D.N. Buhay, "Abraham Gesner," *Canadian Encyclopedia*, February 7, 2013, online at thecanadianencyclopedia.ca/en/article/abraham-gesner.
3 Allison Mitcham, *The Prophet of the Wilderness: Abraham Gesner* (Hantsport, NS: Lancelot Press, 1995).
4 These are figures for 2018. See Canada, Natural Resources Canada, "Energy and the Economy," n.d., online at nrcan.gc.ca/science-data/data-analysis/energy-data-analysis/energy-facts/energy-and-economy/20062.
5 Ibid.
6 Ron Bousso and Bate Felix, "Oil bosses fight 'bad guy' image ahead of climate talks," *Reuters*, October 16, 2015, online at reuters.com/article/oil-climatechange/oil-bosses-fight-bad-guy-image-ahead-of-climate-talks-idINKCN0S92ZV20151016.
7 European Commission, "Causes of Climate Change," n.d., online at ec.europa.eu/clima/change/causes_en.
8 United Nations, "Climate Change," n.d., online at un.org/en/sections/issues-depth/climate-change/.
9 I recognize that there are two versions of this event. Another version suggests that King Canute sought to show his followers that he did not possess supernatural powers—the real story!
10 See, among others, "What is the Kyoto protocol and has it made any difference?" *Guardian*, March 11, 2011, online at theguardian.com/environment/2011/mar/11/kyoto-protocol.
11 "Paris Agreement," *Encyclopaedia Britannica*, October 28, 2019, online at britannica.com/topic/Paris-Agreement-2015.
12 John F. Kerry and Chuck Hagel, "Trump has formally pulled the U.S. out of the Paris agreement. This is a dark time for America," *Washington Post*, November 4, 2019, online at washingtonpost.com/opinions/2019/11/04/trump-just-formally-pulled-us-out-paris-agreement-this-is-dark-day-america/.
13 See, among many others, Vesselin Popovski, ed., *The Implementation of the Paris Agreement on Climate Change* (London: Routledge, 2018).

14 Canada, "Canada's Approach for Implementing the Paris Agreement," n.d., online at canada.ca/en/environment-climate-change/services/sustainable-development/strategic-environmental-assessment/public-statements/canada-approach-paris-agreement.html.

15 See, for example, Barry Saxifrage, "Canada on pace to meet Paris climate target...two centuries late," *Canada's National Observer*, April 25, 2019, online at nationalobserver.com/2019/04/25/analysis/canada-pace-meet-paris-climate-target-two-centuries-late.

16 See Irving Oil, "Refining," Atlantica Centre for Energy, n.d., online at atlanticaenergy.org/refining, accessed August 18, 2019; and United States, Environmental Protection Agency, "Clean Air Excellence Awards Recipients, Year 2002," online at epa.gov/sites/production/files/2015-06/documents/clean_air_excellence_award_recipients_year_2002.pdf

17 See, for example, Rebecca M. Henderson et al., "Climate Change in 2018: Implications for Business," (Cambridge, MA: Harvard Business School Publishing, January 30, 2018).

18 Quoted in Shane Fowler, "Irving Oil claims it's on top of climate change but could do better," CBC *News*, September 2, 2016, online at cbc.ca/news/canada/new-brunswick/irving-oil-climate-change-1.3746864.

19 See, for example, "GM is going all electric, will ditch gas- and diesel-powered cars," NBC *News*, October 2, 2017, online at nbcnews.com/business/autos/gm-going-all-electric-will-ditch-gas-diesel-powered-cars-n806806.

20 David Kiley "Toyota predicts end of internal combustion engine by 2050," *Forbes*, August 7, 2018, online at forbes.com/sites/davidkiley5/2017/11/14/toyota-predicts-end-of-internal-combustion-engine-by-2050/#1d55ec9b211e.

21 Quoted in Evannex, "Tesla's market entry is akin to the world shift away from gas lamp lighting," *Teslarati*, February 25, 2018, online at teslarati.com/tesla-market-entry-shift-gas-lamp-electricity/.

22 Canada, Natural Resources Canada, "Electricity Facts," n.d., online at nrcan.gc.ca/science-data/data-analysis/energy-data-analysis/energy-facts/electricity-facts/20068; and John Muyskens, Dan Keating, and Samuel Granados, "Mapping how the United States generates its electricity," *Washington Post*, March 28, 2017, online at washingtonpost.com/graphics/national/power-plants/?utm_term=.9dc9be2e2d76.

23 "Will electric vehicles really create a cleaner planet?" *Thomson Reuters*, n.d., online at thomsonreuters.com/en/reports/electric-vehicles.html, accessed August 18, 2019.

24 Hilke Fischer and Dave Keating, "How eco-friendly are electric cars?" DW, April 8, 2017, online at dw.com/en/how-eco-friendly-are-electric-cars/a-19441437.

25 Jonathan Lesser, "Are electric cars worse for the environment?" *Politico*, May 15, 2018, online at politico.com/agenda/story/2018/05/15/are-electric-cars-worse-for-the-environment-000660.

26 Marine Ernoult, "Métaux rares: un véhicule électrique génère presque autant de carbone qu'un diesel," *Libération*, February 1, 2018, online at liberation.fr/planete/2018/02/01/metaux-rares-un-vehicule-electrique-genere-presque-autant-de-carbone-qu-un-diesel_1625375.

27 Dave Waddle, "Canadians still slow to embrace electric vehicles," *Windsor Star*, April 24, 2019, online at windsorstar.com/news/local-news/canadians-still-slow-to-embrace-electric-vehicles.

28 Jack Stewart, "Why electric cars struggle in the cold—and how to help them," *Wired*, January 30, 2019, online at wired.com/story/electric-cars-cold-weather-tips/.

29 Irving Oil, "Reaching new heights in the U.S. jet fuel market," *People Matters* (May 2019).

30 Irving Oil, "New South Carolina terminal deal expands opportunities for our asphalt business," *People Matters* 4, no. 2 (2019): 8.

31 Consultations with Jeff Matthews. See also Brett Bundale, "Tesla to install Atlantic Canada 'supercharger' stations for its vehicles," CBC *News*, January 22, 2018, online at cbc.ca/news/canada/nova-scotia/tesla-supercharger-stations-atlantic-canada-1.4497981.

32 Irving Oil, "New retail model pilot set to launch in Pembroke, MA," *People Matters* 4, no. 2 (2019): 12.

33 Scott Keller and Mary Meaney, "Attracting and retaining the Right Talent," McKinsey & Company (November 2017), online at mckinsey.com/business-functions/organization/our-insights/attracting-and-retaining-the-right-talent.

34 Ibid.

35 Quoted in ibid.

36 John Elkann, quoted in Andreas Exarheas, "Oil, gas might need a Tesla to attract best talent," *Rigzone*, January 30, 2018, online at rigzone.com/news/oil_gas_might_need_a_tesla_to_attract_best_talent-30-jan-2018-153321-article/.

37 Martin Menachery, "Workforce of the future survey by ADNOC: Half of young STEM talent interested in oil and gas career," *Refining & Petrochemicals*, March 14, 2019, online at refiningand petrochemicalsme.com/people/25086-workforce-of-the-future-survey-by-adnoc-half-of-young-stem-talent-interested-in-oil-and-gas-career.

38 Abu Dhabi National Oil Company, "Oil and Gas 4.0: Attracting the Workforce of the Future," n.d., online at bit.ly/2YobGCB.

39 Conference Board of Canada, *Canada's Petroleum Refining Sector: An Important Contributor Facing Global Challenges* (Ottawa: Conference Board of Canada, 2011), 26, online at conferenceboard.ca/temp/3c49c9of-9b81-44b3-b4d6-f1b00f5eda03/12-051_CanadaPetroleum RefiningSector_WEB.pdf.

40 "Irving Oil one of Canada's Top Employers for the third straight year," *Huddle*, January 8, 2019, online at huddle.today/irving-oil-one-of-canadas-top-employers-for-third-straight-year/.

41 Ekaterina Walter, "Your company is only as extraordinary as your people," *Forbes*, December 11, 2013, online at forbes.com/sites/ekaterinawalter/2013/12/11/your-company-is-only-as-extraordinary-as-your-people/#4cfae8a455d5.

42 See, among others, Elizabeth G. Chambers et al., "The War for Talent," *McKinsey Quarterly*, no. 3 (1998). More recent articles are Jacob Morgan, "The war for talent; it's real and here's why it's happening," *Inc.*, December 22, 2017, online at inc.com/jacob-morgan/the-war-for-talent-its-real-heres-why-its-happening.html; "5 talent trends to watch in 2019," *HR Drive*, January 7, 2019, online at hrdive.com/news/5-talent-trends-to-watch-in-2019/545053/; and Ira Wolfe, "Go on the offensive to win the war for talent," *TLNT*, January 25, 2019, online at tlnt.com/go-on-the-offensive-to-win-the-war-for-talent/.

43 Scott Keller and Mary Meaney, *Leading Organizations: Ten Timeless Truths* (New York: Bloomsbury, 2017).

44 Conference Board of Canada, *Canada's Petroleum Refining Sector*, 19.

45 Ibid., 25–6.

46 See, among others, Donald J. Savoie, *Federal-Provincial Collaboration: The Canada-New Brunswick General Development Agreement* (Montreal; Kingston, ON: McGill-Queen's University Press, 1981).

47 New Brunswick, *2019-2020 Main Estimates* (Fredericton: Government of New Brunswick, March 19, 2019), 171.

48 Andrew F. Johnson, "A Minister as an Agent of Policy Change: The Case of Unemployment Insurance in the Seventies," *Canadian Public Administration* 24, no. 4 (1981): 612–33.

49 See, for example, Meagan Fitzpatrick, "Workers' EI history to affect claim under new rules," *CBC News*, May 24, 2012, online at cbc.ca/news/politics/workers-ei-history-to-affect-claim-under-new-rules-1.1130174.

50 See, among others, Robert P. Shepherd, "Expenditure Reviews and the Federal Experience: Program Evaluation and Its Contribution to Assurance Provision," *Canadian Journal of Program Evaluation* 32, no. 3 (2018): 347–70.

51 New Brunswick, *We Are All in This Together: An Aging Strategy for New Brunswick* (Fredericton: Government of New Brunswick, January 2017), 5.

52 See, among others, Richard Saillant, *Over the Cliff? Acting Now to Avoid New Brunswick's Bankruptcy* (Moncton: Canadian Institute for Research on Public Policy and Public Administration, 2014).

53 Donald J. Savoie, "New Brunswick is Canada's most difficult jurisdiction to govern," *Globe and Mail*, November 4, 2018, online at theglobeandmail.com/opinion/article-new-brunswick-is-canadas-most-difficult-jurisdiction-to-govern/.

54 Elizabeth Fraser, "'Living beyond our means': Auditor general troubled by debt growth," *CBC News*, January 16, 2019, online at cbc.ca/news/canada/new-brunswick/auditor-general-report-kim-macpherson-1.4980002.

55 Ibid.

56 See, for example, Canada, "Income Tax," n.d., online at canada.ca/en/services/taxes/income-tax.html; and "Corporation Tax Rates," n.d., online at canada.ca/en/revenue-agency/services/tax/businesses/topics/corporations/corporation-tax-rates.html.

CHAPTER 11

ASSESSING THE CONTRIBUTIONS

HAVE, IN THE COURSE OF MY CAREER, MET OR SHARED A MEAL with a few Canadian prime ministers, several premiers from Canada's three main political parties, many leading academics, including a Nobel laureate in economics, prominent business people, and senior government bureaucrats. I have also interviewed many others. Some have a thick skin, many do not.

Business people, particularly the successful ones, always give me the impression that they have more important things to attend to than deal with criticism, whether valid or not. They either have a tough hide or they are too busy to pay much attention to criticism directed their way. Arthur Irving belongs to this group. He simply does not take to heart criticism directed at him or the Irvings.

I am not at all certain that Arthur even reads books and articles written about the Irvings—positive or negative. He has never raised any in our discussions. I do not even know if he will read this book! He always has a laser focus on his business, on his region, and on his efforts to support universities, hospitals, and community groups. His days are full of activities, and my sense is that he does not have the time, or perhaps does not allow, for negative views to divert his attention from things that truly matter to him. Arthur also took to heart the advice of his father's employees, who worked for K.C.'s Ford dealership. I noted that an Irving employee responded to a negative ad bought by a competitor by purchasing his own ad that read: "And the dogs barked but the caravan rolled on." Arthur has learned to pay no attention to barking dogs as he goes about his day.

In this concluding chapter, I want to assess the contributions Irving Oil has made and continues to make to my region, as well as Arthur's own contributions to numerous community and philanthropic endeavours. That Arthur Irving has a very thick skin or that he has learned, over the years, to be fairly immune to criticism is not the most important point. I am firmly of the view that we Maritimers need to celebrate success, particularly economic success, applaud the work of entrepreneurs, and encourage aspiring entrepreneurs. Sitting on the sidelines barking at economic success as the caravan rolls on accomplishes nothing for our region. More to the point, unless we are able to grow our private sector, I see a bleak future for our region.

THE REGION'S ECONOMIC STRUCTURE

I HAVE BEEN TOLD ON SEVERAL OCCASIONS THAT THE PRESENCE of the Irvings has stifled entrepreneurship in my province. I could never follow the logic behind this view or see evidence to support it. It is much like trying to make the case that, in the absence of Ottawa's family allowance program, many children would not have been born in Canada. What possible mathematical formula could come up with that answer? I am making the case that Saint John, New Brunswick, and the Maritime provinces would be worse off economically if George Irving had not landed in New Brunswick in 1822 and if K.C. Irving and his three sons had gone down the road to create or operate businesses elsewhere, rather than start and continue to grow their businesses from New Brunswick.

I have already noted many times in this book and in some of my other publications that national policies and the inherent bias found in our national political institutions have inhibited economic development in the Maritime region. National policies have long favoured certain regions, notably vote-rich Ontario and Quebec, for wealth creation. Leaving aside natural resources that have to be exploited where they are, the federal government has never agreed to shape its policies to accommodate regional circumstances in order to change where wealth is being created. It has, however, been willing to see benefits from the creation of wealth shared nationally. It has done this by embracing transfer payments to have-less regions, although this solution entails its own challenges that can make self-sustaining economic development more difficult.

It is widely accepted that the private sector is the engine that fuels economic growth, that it identifies opportunities for economic development, and that it then generates efforts that turn opportunities into revenues, dividends or surpluses, and employment. The private sector, however, is not homogenous. It is made up of a few large global firms, many national and mid-size firms, and numerous small and micro-businesses. It also encompasses three distinct sectors: the primary sector, which exploits raw materials; the secondary sector, which manufactures goods; and the tertiary sector, which provides services, including restaurants and retail stores. The public sector also plays an important role by producing goods that benefit everyone in society—political stability, law and order, and the infrastructure required to facilitate economic development.

Our province—indeed, our region—has a structural problem. We have moved away from a goods-producing and trading economy to become a consumer economy. Statistics Canada reports that, of the 353,800 New Brunswickers who held jobs in 2018, 73,100 were employed in the goods-producing sector and 280,700 in the service sector. By contrast, in the same year, of the 570,000 Saskatchewanians who had jobs, 145,200 engaged in the goods-producing sector and 424,800 in the service sector.[1] The point is that the New Brunswick economy is overly dependent on the service and public sectors. I note that today, parts of the service economy are highly valued—notably, firms that export services to other regions or countries. The province also relies on federal transfer payments to fuel a good part of the consumer economy, a point on which I elaborate below.

But that does not tell the whole story. Atlantic Canada leans heavily on the public sector for employment: Nova Scotia for 24.8 percent of total employment, New Brunswick for 25 percent, Prince Edward Island for 26.1 percent, and Newfoundland and Labrador for 28.6 percent. At the national level, in contrast, only 20.3 percent of the workforce is employed in the public sector.[2] The 2016 census reported that 29.3 percent of New Brunswickers were employed in the education, health care, and social services sector, compared with 25.3 percent at the national level. To be sure, the public sector provides many of the best employment opportunities available to New Brunswickers. Salaries are high, job security is strong, and pension and other benefits are offered that are rarely, if ever, available in the private sector, at least in New Brunswick.

It is also important to underline the point that the region is fast losing its capacity as a goods-producing and trading economy. It is not too much of an exaggeration to suggest that the public sector is fuelling our consumer economy, which, in turn, is fuelling economic development abroad, not at home. Items we purchase at Costco, Walmart, and Starbucks are produced elsewhere—in China or the United States—but rarely in Atlantic Canada.

Herb Emery has underlined the importance of the goods-producing sector for New Brunswick, and warns that the province lags behind the rest of Canada with respect to investment and productivity growth. He asks what is lacking in New Brunswick's manufacturing sector to drive a "transformation of the sector." He concludes: "Improving the business climate may be the first order of business to start investment in manufacturing to raise GDP [gross domestic product], employment and to modernize more of the sector. And the collateral benefit may be a larger and more profitable service sector."[3]

Irving Oil is in the wealth-creating and goods-producing business, the kind that all economies want. It imports raw material from other Canadian regions, the Middle East, the United States, Africa, and other parts of the world, and transforms it into a multitude of finished products, the bulk of which are then exported to the eastern seaboard of the United States. Irving Oil also has a complex operation in Ireland, where it runs a refinery and retail outlets. All of this is managed from its head office in Saint John, New Brunswick. It is worth repeating that one can count on the fingers of one hand the number of global goods-producing firms that have located their head offices in New Brunswick: JDI, Cooke Aquaculture, Imperial Manufacturing Group, and McCain Foods come to mind.

Once again, I cannot possibly overstate the importance of a head office to a regional economy. In 2019, the efforts of the Justin

Trudeau government to help SNC-Lavalin spare a criminal charge shook Canada's political landscape. Trudeau's argument was that he intervened in order to save jobs. The jobs he set out to save were head-office jobs in Montreal.[4] I note that they were jobs in the service sector, which is fast gaining importance in all economies. The point, as we saw earlier, is that it is possible to export services from one region to another and from one country to another. The premier of Quebec said that he would not oppose the sale of Air Transat to Air Canada because "the good news is that Air Canada has its headquarters in Montreal, so I'm happy to see the headquarters [of Air Transat] will stay in Montreal."[5] The Quebec premier, as do all premiers, easily sees the importance of head offices to a region's economy, for reasons I have already outlined.

But there is more. Irving Oil is in the goods-producing sector. If the economy has a pecking order, goods-producing and manufacturing sit on top. Policy makers favour this sector over others. As will be recalled, Donald Trump made bringing back manufacturing jobs to the United States a central theme of his 2016 election campaign. The economic development literature also favours the goods-producing sector. But there has been a change in the vocabulary of late—it is now labelled the "tradeable sector." This refers to goods and services that are consumed outside the community or region where they are produced. The change also speaks to the growing importance of some firms that are able to export "services" to other communities, regions, or countries. I note that some businesses fall between the tradeable and non-tradeable sectors.

The regional economic development literature underlines the importance of local multipliers in job creation. Clearly, not all regions are the same or have the same economic structure. Some regions are much more self-sustaining than others. Ontario, for example, is home to the country's financial and automobile sectors, is endowed with rich agricultural land, and has a vibrant service sector. It is also home to the senior federal public service, and the bulk of national firms have located their head offices in the province. New Brunswick has a small, open economy that is far from having the self-sustaining capacity of Ontario or, for that matter, of most other provinces. The important point here is that the goods-producing or tradeable sector should have a more positive impact on the New Brunswick economy than on economies in other regions, given its slow growth and dependence on the public sector.[6]

One could go further and establish a difference between the impact of high-skilled, high-salary workers and low-skilled, low-paid workers. Higher-paying jobs have a much higher multiplier effect on a regional economy. Irving Oil is home to many high-paying private-sector jobs. I accept that these jobs might pose a problem for small businesses and aspiring entrepreneurs in Saint John. The literature speaks of the "Intrusive Rentier Syndrome," whereby the large employer that drives the local economy often undermines the ability of local businesses to hire staff and to grow. Even if the large employer is aware of this problem, it is often impossible to do much about it because of the need to attract skilled workers, who are often mobile.[7] The problem is hardly limited to Irving Oil. I noted earlier the effect that federal government employment has on Atlantic Canada's private sector: high federal government salaries and generous benefits make it difficult for local firms to attract talent.

THE MULTIPLIER FACTOR

THE REGIONAL ECONOMIC DEVELOPMENT LITERATURE ALSO explores how to calculate the multiplier factor when new jobs are created, when assessing the impact of existing jobs, or when looking at the role of head offices versus regional offices in local econo-mies.[8] There is some debate around the size or scope of the multi-pliers, but I am on safe ground in suggesting a multiplier of 2.5 for Irving Oil. Indeed, one economist who has undertaken a number of studies in this area tells me that, if anything, I have likely under-estimated its importance.[9] Irving Oil directly employs about 3,000 people, while an approximately equal number come to work every day at Irving Oil operations. These 6,000 jobs at Irving Oil (and not including those in Ireland), multiplied by 2.5, translate into 15,000 other jobs, mostly in Saint John. To put this in perspective, the Saint John Census Metropolitan Area (CMA) in 2017 had a working-age population of 105,500. The size of its labour force was 69,700, with 65,500 employed individuals. The labour force participation rate in the Saint John CMA was 66.1 percent that year—a healthy rate, at least by New Brunswick standards.[10] Two trends are emerging, however, that should be of concern to all New Brunswickers.

The first is the growing dependency ratio. This ratio is based on the notion that children under the age of fifteen are likely to be dependent, as are adults over sixty-five who are likely to be retired. The New Brunswick government is well aware of the dependency ratio and its importance. It explains: "Children (through edu-cational spending) and seniors (through retirement and health related services) tend to require a larger proportion of tax payer dollars than the 15 to 64 year old group." It adds: "In 2015, more than 50% of government healthcare expenditures in the province were spent on those ages 65 and older, despite this group only accounting for approximately 20% of the population."[11]

In 1977, only 9 percent of New Brunswick's population was sixty-five or older. By 2017, the share had grown to 20 percent, and it is expected to grow to 30 percent by 2032. More to the point, today New Brunswick has the highest cohort of seniors in its history, a fast-shrinking typical working-age population (people ages fifteen to sixty-four), and an under-fifteen population that has shrunk by 40 percent over the past forty years.[12] The problem is not limited to New Brunswick, but New Brunswick has, by national standards, one of the fastest-aging populations in the country.[13]

The implications are clear for everyone to see. New Brunswick's institutions, notably health-care facilities, will be taxed for services as never before. This will require financial resources, and New Brunswick has essentially three sources: its own tax base, federal government transfers, and borrowing. The federal government, however, has always been very careful not to favour one province over another when it comes to health-care transfers. New Brunswick's capacity to raise taxes will be limited as its working-age population continues to shrink. The province's debt has climbed sharply in recent years, as has the cost of servicing it ($675 million in 2018).

The second trend that raises concerns for New Brunswick policy makers has to do with the province's economic structure. New Brunswick's goods-producing manufacturing sector is losing ground to other sectors. Employment in the service-producing sector went up by a few percentage points in terms of total employment between 2007 and 2017, while employment in the goods-producing sector fell by some 10 percent over the same period. In 2017, the sales and service category employed 92,000 New Brunswickers, or 26.1 percent of total employment—by far the largest share of occupational categories—while at the national level it accounted for only 24.3 percent of total employment. The greatest employment growth in the province between 2007 and 2017 was in occupations in health (20.7 percent) and in education, law, and social, community, and government services (9.8 percent).[14] These categories employed 43,700 New Brunswickers in 2017.

All of the above is to make the point that employment at Irving Oil is particularly important to New Brunswick. Jobs at Irving Oil do not constitute a drain on the public purse; rather, they generate revenues that, in turn, help sustain government services. They are private-sector, self-sustaining jobs that have an important multiplier effect because of the sector in which Irving Oil operates. Irving Oil can produce impressive numbers to show its importance to both the regional and Canadian economies. The firm exports over 50 percent of Canada's refined petroleum products that go to the United States, and 52 percent of all trade value in New Brunswick is from refined products. The Irving Oil refinery accounts for over 2 percent of New Brunswick's GDP and produces about a thousand products at its blending and packaging facility, many of which are destined for the export market.[15] In addition, the company accounts for about 90 percent of the total tonnage moving through the Port of Saint John.

ENTREPRENEURIAL COMMUNITIES

IS IRVING OIL STIFLING ENTREPRENEURIAL ACTIVITIES IN THE region, as I have heard on a number of occasions? I have seen no empirical evidence that this might be the case. Yet Green Party MP Jenica Atwin declared, shortly after being elected in 2019, that New Brunswick needs to "get out from underneath" the "thumb" of the Irvings because "it would provide so many more opportunities for entrepreneurship." She simply tossed this out to the media without explaining how she arrived at that conclusion or showing any evidence to support her view. In the same interview, she said that Saint John has "a really high child-poverty rate...and I want them (the Irvings) to be champions of that."[16]

I note that the Canadian Federation of Independent Business (CFIB) regularly takes stock of Canada's cities and how well they perform as entrepreneurial communities. It makes the point that no single factor makes a community more entrepreneurial. In 2018, it identified Whitehorse (Yukon Territory), Winkler (Manitoba), Victoriaville (Quebec), and Rimouski (Quebec) among the top-performing entrepreneurial communities, with Pembroke (Ontario), Cornwall (Ontario), Courtenay (British Columbia), and Bathurst (New Brunswick) as the lowest-performing ones. The CFIB assesses a number of factors, including where business owners are the most buoyant or have a very positive perspective about their economic future. Several Quebec and Ontario communities score high on this front, as does Moncton, which comes out at number four among major cities.

The CFIB produces a 125-city entrepreneurial index based on thirteen entrepreneurship indicators grouped under "presence," "perspective," and "policy" categories. Several Atlantic Canadian communities have consistently made the list, among them Grand Falls-Windsor, Newfoundland and Labrador (39), Summerside, Prince Edward Island (46), Moncton (62), Charlottetown (70), Saint John, New Brunswick (88), Truro, Nova Scotia (97), Halifax (98), Cape Breton Regional Municipality (117), and Bathurst (122). Although Saint John does not rank high, it does outperform thirty-seven other Canadian cities.[17]

What makes a community entrepreneur-friendly? The business community will point to tax policy, regulations, access to skilled workers, and the level of municipal government services as important factors. Proximity to a large urban centre also matters, as does the low cost of doing business.[18] The presence of Irving Oil and other Irving businesses in Saint John is hardly a negative force when it comes to these issues. Indeed, I argue that their presence makes a substantial contribution to Saint John's economic prosperity.

AN ENTREPRENEURIAL ECOSYSTEM

RECENT ECONOMIC DEVELOPMENT LITERATURE STRESSES THE importance of an "entrepreneurial ecosystem" as a way for communities to promote business start-ups. An entrepreneurial ecosystem has a number of components. One is the phenomenon of "clustering"—an example of this is the high-tech sector found along Route 128 outside Boston. Another is entrepreneurial recycling: entrepreneurs who have built successful firms, sold their businesses, and reinvested some of their new-found wealth in other businesses in their communities.[19] Put differently, they become serial entrepreneurs in communities that encourage new business start-ups. I am thinking here, for example, of Jon Manship, a Moncton businessman who sold his Spielo Gaming International company and subsequently decided to invest in local start-ups in the technology sector.

The economic development literature also underlines the importance of having at least one "large established business" with important head-office management functions and research and development activities. The consensus in the literature is that such large established businesses play a significant role in an entrepreneurial ecosystem. This takes on an added importance in peripheral regions. Daniel Isenberg writes: "You simply cannot have a flourishing entrepreneurship ecosystem without large companies to cultivate it, intentionally or otherwise."[20] Irving Oil is one such large business anchored in Saint John.

Universities can also play an important role in an entrepreneurial ecosystem, as can service providers, including lawyers, accountants, and business consultants. Additionally, immigrants are an important source of entrepreneurs, and they strengthen any and all entrepreneurial ecosystems. Other factors also matter, such as access to sources of funding and to mentors or seasoned entrepreneurs who can advise aspiring entrepreneurs at critical moments.[21]

Large companies, then, play a vital role, intentionally or not, in promoting an entrepreneurial ecosystem in a community. Saint John has a handful of large companies, including Irving Oil. The key is to look to these firms as important sources of self-sustaining economic growth.

To a small business struggling to compete, or in many cases simply to survive, the Irving businesses must appear like giants dominating the New Brunswick economy. But to Irving Oil, the business world looks different. Irving Oil does not compare with giants in the field such as ExxonMobil, Royal Dutch Shell, or Chevron in terms of size, scope, and revenues. Its executives are convinced that Irving Oil's presence in the New Brunswick economy is a positive force for the local business community and for the broader New Brunswick society. They see a number of reasons the firm is a positive economic force in Saint John, and no reason it would inhibit economic growth in the community. They are right.

PULLING AGAINST GRAVITY

ONE THING THAT COMES THROUGH WHEN RESEARCHING THE work of both K.C. and Arthur Irving and discussing their contributions with their friends and work colleagues is the extent of their deep and enduring commitment to their region. As one of my colleagues told me, "Well, the Irvings are as much Maritime nationalists as you are." Yes, they are. It all started with K.C. Irving, who saw first-hand how federal government policies never gave the Maritime region a level playing field with Ontario and Quebec in growing the economy—the Chignecto Canal being a case in point.

Here are some quotes by K.C. Irving that speak to the way he saw the challenge:

- "In New Brunswick, we have known this feeling of despair as long as we can remember. It is associated with our inability to rise to national levels."
- "We do not stay at this level because we like to live several steps below the national economy."
- "The choice—the decision—has not been ours."
- "Over the years the federal government—regardless of party—has been responsible for policies which have resulted in New Brunswick being a forgotten section of Canada."
- "When these national—or federal—policies are changed, then the economy of the province of New Brunswick will change."
- "But the economic facts of life cannot be changed by words of labor leaders or the words of management."
- "Words alone do not create jobs."
- "Words alone do not give experience to unqualified and untrained workers."
- "Words alone do not keep a business successful."
- "Words alone do not meet a weekly payroll."[22]

These sum up nicely K.C. and Arthur Irving's views on the matter.

What does this mean for the Maritime provinces? The above quotes are ingrained in Arthur Irving's DNA. One only has to look at the recently built head-office building in Saint John to see his deep commitment to the region. But when searching for new business opportunities, Arthur Irving and Irving Oil seem to be venturing outside Canada for growth. They are increasingly looking to New England and Ireland, rather than to Quebec or Ontario, to fuel future growth. In short, notwithstanding looking outside Canada for future growth, Arthur Irving and Irving Oil remain firmly anchored in Saint John, New Brunswick.

The federal government's policies and economic development initiatives have not been, on the whole, favourable to Irving Oil. The Chignecto Canal and Energy East come to mind, but they are not the only examples. There is evidence to suggest that Irving Oil has grown tired of pulling against gravity, and that it has decided to look to other jurisdictions to fuel future growth. Canadian and New Brunswick policy makers should take note.

GIVING TO OUR INSTITUTIONS

ARTHUR AND SANDRA IRVING, THE ARTHUR L. IRVING FAMILY Foundation, and Irving Oil have made substantial contributions to our health and educational institutions and to other organizations in other areas, but with an Atlantic bias—recall, for example, the C. David Naylor University Fellowships. The question is, in their absence, who would have stepped in to make the same contributions? I see no evidence that anyone would have.

All too often, Arthur and Sandra, the Family Foundation, and Irving Oil have not given a full public hearing of their contributions. As we saw earlier, Harvey Gilmour underlined this issue when he said that one of his most frustrating experiences as director of development at Acadia was that he was not allowed to talk about Arthur Irving's contributions to the university. Going back to K.C. Irving, Arthur Irving and Irving Oil prefer to keep things close to their chest. It is an approach that goes beyond their business and commercial interests. It is part of their DNA. Both saw "no need to brag," as Arthur Irving once told me.

But there is a price to pay. Their contributions often fly under the radar and remain unknown and unappreciated. In the course of my working on this book, friends and business associates of Arthur Irving told me that, over the years, he has made many contributions and donations that very few outside his immediate circle know about. Appreciated or not, these contributions have made some institutions in our region much stronger.

ABOUT TAXES

I AM NOT A TAX EXPERT BY ANY STANDARD. LIKE MOST OTHER Canadians, I pay taxes as required and on time. To be sure, I do not have the knowledge to assess if Irving Oil is paying what it ought to pay in taxes. I do know, however, that the question of whether or not they pay their fair share of taxation has dogged the Irvings since the 1960s. The arrival of social media, where claims are made without evidence or facts, has also given the matter new life in recent years. What I can do is report on the issues that have been debated about the Irvings and taxes in New Brunswick for half a century and try to put things in perspective.

The first observation is that it is important for New Brunswickers to apply the same standards to Irving Oil that they apply to other large multinational firms. All large firms will, as best they can within the parameters of the law, look for ways to reduce their tax bill. A senior Irving Oil executive told me that Irving Oil's philosophy when it comes to taxes is always to manage its affairs to be compliant with the law and to pay what is required.

A survey of over two thousand members of the Audit, Financial and Scientific Group at the Canada Revenue Agency (CRA) carried out in 2019 is revealing. The survey reports that nine out of ten CRA tax professionals maintain that it is much easier for rich corporations to avoid tax responsibilities than it is for average Canadians. The head of the Professional Institute of the Public Service of Canada, which administered the survey, explained: "There are a number of loopholes and grey areas in the existing laws. It's not illegal for companies or wealthy individuals to take advantage of those loopholes." A survey of Canadians also reveals that a sizable majority—79 percent of respondents—believes the tax system benefits the rich.[23] They have a point: Amazon made $11.2 billion in profits in 2018, but paid no federal income tax for the second year in a row; what is all the more remarkable is that the company actually received $129 million in a tax rebate the same year.[24] This is hardly an isolated case.[25]

Arthur Irving and Irving Oil are not about to sit idle on the sidelines leaving others, notably the competition, to explore the best possible arrangements to lower their costs. Irving Oil knows full well that getting the best possible advice to deal with taxes has become an important part of the business-planning process.

We saw earlier that Irving Oil established a non-Canadian subsidiary, Bomag (later known as Irvcal), to purchase crude at a price established in the Persian Gulf plus transportation costs, thereby delivering crude at the market price to the Irving Oil refinery. The 1971 deal enabled profits at Irving Oil to grow at a much stronger pace. I note that Irving Oil secured this deal with Standard Oil of California to ensure it would remain competitive, a point that Standard Oil executives accepted. I also note that John DeMont writes that, until the deal with Standard Oil was struck, Irving Oil was losing money.[26] Being unable to keep up with the competition and losing money is not a way to remain in business or to be of any help to the region.

There were other factors to consider. The Bomag-Irvcal arrangement was not unique to Irving Oil. It would have been absurd if Irving Oil had not employed a legal strategy that the competition did. I also remind the reader that the matter went before the courts and that the Federal Court ruled in favour of Irving Oil in a unanimous 3–0 decision. In any case, both Irvcal and this tax advantage no longer exist.

"NEW BRUNSWICK IS NOT
A LOW-COST JURISDICTION"

SO SAID ANDREW CARSON, AN IRVING OIL EXECUTIVE, WHEN he appeared before the New Brunswick legislature's law amendments committee.[27] He has a point, although I readily accept that it is difficult for many New Brunswickers to be concerned about whether Irving Oil pays too much in taxes.

New Brunswick has one of the highest personal income tax rates in Canada.[28] Including the federal income tax rate, New Brunswickers with taxable income over $154,382 pay as much as 20.3 percent. In contrast, Ontario's rate is 13.16 percent on amounts over $220,000 and Alberta's is 15 percent on amounts over $307,547.[29] All Irving Oil employees, without exception, pay income tax. Tax on personal income matters, particularly when Irving Oil seeks to attract top executives.

New Brunswick's corporate income tax is also high compared with several other jurisdictions in Canada, including Ontario, Manitoba, and British Columbia. Alberta and Quebec do not have corporation tax collection agreements with the CRA,[30] but Alberta's corporate tax rate is two percentage points lower and Quebec's is 2.4 percentage points lower than New Brunswick's.[31]

Andrew Carson explains: "We pay fairly high corporate income taxes, we have high personal income taxes, we have fairly high WorkSafe New Brunswick rates and we now have a fairly high carbon tax." He adds that Irving Oil has "the highest tax bill of any refinery outside Alberta."[32] He could have added that New Brunswick's consumption tax, at 15 percent, is higher than that of Ontario (13 percent), Alberta (5 percent), and British Columbia, Manitoba, and Saskatchewan (all at 12 percent). Carson's presentation to the New Brunswick Legislative Assembly also noted that the Saint John Irving Oil refinery pays more property tax than do the Shell, Suncor, and Imperial refineries in Sarnia "combined." Saint John is also the only Canadian city that is home to both a refinery and the firm's head office.[33]

The Organisation for Economic Co-operation and Development (OECD) has looked at various factors that shape a region or a country's ability to compete, including market size, technological innovation, higher education and training, labour market efficiency—the list goes on. To be sure, there is not one single dominating factor, but tax levels are also important. The OECD explains that cross-border investors and businesses are increasingly looking to maximize their post-tax returns, not their pre-tax ones. It adds that, in a world with high levels of capital mobility, countries (here, one can add regions) cannot ignore the potential effects on investment of how their tax rates compare with those of other jurisdictions.[34]

GETTING IT RIGHT

IT IS DIFFICULT FOR ARTHUR IRVING AND IRVING OIL TO SET the record straight on taxation, and it is only getting more difficult with the arrival of social media and "alternate facts." One only has to go to Facebook, make a claim, however baseless, and explain that he or she "heard it somewhere" to identify the source. The claim, true or not, is often widely shared.

The traditional media, with editorial control and fact checkers, are fast losing ground to social media. But Irving Oil has an added problem with the traditional media. An Irving business owns all the English-language daily newspapers in New Brunswick, and the perception is that whatever they might publish when it comes to the Irvings—and to Irving Oil—is suspicious. This, even though Arthur Irving and Irving Oil do not hold any shares in any of the province's English-language dailies and have no say in how they are run. As I noted earlier, when it comes to the Irvings and taxes, perception becomes reality to many New Brunswickers.

Someone claims on social media that Irving Oil does not pay property taxes on its storage tanks. The reality is that the tax exemption applies only to 10 percent of the tanks and was granted forty years ago. Irving Oil also pays a substantial amount in property tax not only on its refinery, but also on all its buildings, including its new head office. I note, however, that Irving Oil was able to secure a tax break from the City of Saint John in 2005 when it unveiled plans to build a liquefied natural gas (LNG) terminal at Canaport. By one estimate, the tax break was costing the city some $75 million in lost taxes over a ten-year period, with some pointing to an even higher figure.[35] However, this tax advantage was repealed in 2016, and Irving Oil now pays taxes in full on the LNG terminal.

Whether such tax breaks have merit is a legitimate public policy debate. In the past, I have debated this issue in my published work and in the media, and my take is straightforward: I would readily accept our communities, our provincial government, and Atlantic Canada doing away with such tax breaks if other jurisdictions did the same. If we did and they did not, we would stand to lose important economic opportunities.

Private firms—and, to be sure, Irving Oil is no exception—will push every button and pull every lever possible to secure cash grants and tax breaks before committing to invest large sums of money to establish a plant. Alabama, for example, became a centre for the auto industry through tax incentives.[36] The governments of Canada and Ontario rushed in with massive funding in the immediate aftermath of the severe economic downturn in 2008 to save the auto industry with a $9.1 billion aid package and ended up losing

$3.5 billion of taxpayers' money in the process.[37] Foxconn was able to negotiate a $4.5 billion aid package, including extremely generous tax breaks, to locate a plant in Wisconsin. It is now highly unlikely that Foxconn will create anywhere near the thirteen thousand jobs it promised.[38]

My point is that debating the merits of tax incentives or cash grants as tools for economic development is not only legitimate but long overdue. In launching the debate, however, New Brunswickers must take into account what other jurisdictions are doing. In addition, we should not hold Irving Oil to a different standard than we hold other large firms.

WHY I WROTE THIS BOOK

I WROTE THIS BOOK FOR TWO REASONS. FIRST, AS A BOUCTOUCHE native, I have always been fascinated with K.C. Irving's accomplishments. My father and brother, both successful entrepreneurs, liked what they saw, as I did, in K.C.'s business tenacity and his ability to grow a multitude of successful businesses, starting with a modest service station in a small, isolated community.

Second, I want to see more Maritimers celebrate homegrown business success. All too often, I have seen firms from away come to our region and talk our governments into giving them tax concessions and cash grants, then exploit our resources, and, once satisfied that there is little more to gain, run away faster than they came. Our home-grown entrepreneurs do not run away. They stay, they create jobs, they contribute to their communities and local institutions, and they pay taxes. Irving Oil and JDI combined have created some twenty thousand private-sector jobs, the bulk of them in the goods-producing sector. Both have their head offices in New Brunswick and both have created business opportunities for other entrepreneurs and aspiring entrepreneurs.

Some readers might have looked in this book for material on Irving family tensions or how much taxes the Irvings pay. I have no interest, however, in reporting on family relationships. I did not do so in my book on Harrison McCain and McCain Foods, and I do not do so here with regard to the Irvings. On taxes, as I have just argued, Irving Oil's approach is to be respectful of the law while recognizing they are a cost to be managed, like others. That is what all major firms do—nothing new here.

Much has been said and written about K.C. Irving's moving to Bermuda to avoid paying succession taxes. I urge readers to go back to the early 1970s, when both the federal and the New Brunswick governments were looking at new taxes that would have forced K.C.'s sons to sell nearly half their businesses to pay them. Let's assume that they would have sold Irving Oil in order to keep the forestry business intact, if only because forestry was K.C. Irving's passion. The Irving refinery could still have been in Saint John, although that is hardly certain given that Imperial Oil closed its Halifax refinery a few years ago. It is highly unlikely, however, that the refinery would have been expanded to the extent that it has, or that expensive environmental and regulatory initiatives would have been carried out. There would be no Irving Oil head office in Saint John—but likely in Texas or California. Ottawa would have quickly spent the revenues the taxes would have generated. Some of it would have come back to the Maritimes in the form of transfer payments and some would have fuelled new spending on national economic policy—and with history as a guide, most of the benefits would have gone to Ontario and Quebec. From experience, K.C. Irving understood this.

The above leaves us with the question: how important has the work of K.C. Irving and Arthur Irving been to New Brunswick's economic development? I put the question to Jim Casey, a former government official in the economic development field in New Brunswick and subsequently the owner of a highly successful family business, Paderno, the well-known Prince Edward Island manufacturer of cookware and cookware accessories. His answer, with no hesitation: "The Irvings are the best thing that ever happened to New Brunswick." He explained: "The Irvings know how to run a business, they know when to expand when the time comes, when to get out of a business when the time comes and how to adapt new technologies to make their businesses run more efficiently. And they know how to compete."

I have had a number of discussions with New Brunswickers in recent years, particularly since I have been working on this book. When asked, "What are you working on?" I answered that I was "working on a book about K.C., Arthur Irving, and Irving Oil." It always prompted a response. Though it hardly constitutes a scientific survey, my sense is that many who worked or work in the private sector applaud the work of the Irvings and their business acumen. However, many who worked or work in government or the public sector, broadly defined, have a greater tendency to be critical of the Irvings. As we saw earlier, *toute proportion gardée* (all things being equal), New Brunswick has more public sector employees than other jurisdictions in Canada.

To be sure, the "tall poppy syndrome" is no less visible in our region than in other parts of Canada, perhaps even more so because of our have-less status. The fact that both K.C. and Arthur prefer to hide their light under a bushel, even when it comes to their substantial donations to numerous initiatives, has not helped matters.

I asked Narrative Research in the fall of 2019 to assess the perception New Brunswickers have of the Irving businesses and their impact on the New Brunswick economy.[39] The firm asked four hundred New Brunswickers ages eighteen or older—a cross-section from all regions and income and education levels—how they view the impact of the Irving businesses on the provincial economy. The first thing to note is that only a very small portion (3 percent) of the province's population is not familiar with the Irving family businesses—97 percent of those surveyed were well aware of the Irving businesses and had an opinion on their impact on New Brunswick's economy.

Respondents' views of the Irving businesses on the New Brunswick economy were scored on a scale of 1 to 10, with 1 to 3 equalling a highly negative and 8 to 10 a highly positive view. The survey revealed that one in three respondents thought the Irving family businesses have a highly positive impact, some 15 percent had a highly negative opinion of the impact of the Irving businesses, while 48 percent had a somewhat neutral view. Overall, however, the survey reported a score of 6.1, indicating that the New Brunswickers surveyed generally had a positive view of the contributions of the Irving businesses to the province's economy. The survey also revealed little difference in opinion by sex or level of education. Those in southern New Brunswick had a slightly more positive view of the Irving businesses than respondents in northern New Brunswick (I remind the reader that all of the Irving head offices are located in southern New Brunswick). The survey also recorded a modest difference when it comes to income levels, with a moderate score more likely among those with mid-to-high income levels and a higher score more likely among those with a lower income.

The survey helps to put things in perspective. It makes the case that New Brunswickers are not indifferent to the Irving businesses. This, even though all the Irving businesses, starting with K.C.

Irving, see no merit in showing their cards before they are played, or even after. This is also true when it comes to their contributions to community projects and to educational and health-care institutions. We saw that Arthur Irving and his Family Foundation prefer to keep the size of their contributions hidden from public view and that, in some instances, they decided to contribute anonymously. We also saw that Arthur, like his father, sees "no need to brag."

My sense is that many New Brunswickers increasingly appreciate the difference between home-grown businesses with their head offices in the province and businesses from away that have only a passing economic interest in the province. New Brunswickers know that, when Bell Canada purchased NBTel outright, it left a big hole in the province's economic development infrastructure.

I leave the last word to Arthur Irving: "My dad would always say, remember Arthur, tell our customers and our employees that we could not do it without them and always thank them for the business."

Notes

1 Statistics Canada, "Labour Force Characteristics by Industry, Annual (x 1000)," table 14:10-0023-101.
2 Statistics Canada, "Employment by Class of Worker, Monthly, Seasonally Adjusted and Unadjusted, Last 5 Months," table 14-10-0288-01.
3 Herb Emery, "What's unique about N.B. manufacturing?" *Telegraph-Journal* (Saint John), September 11, 2019.
4 Bruce Campion-Smith et al., "Justin Trudeau takes 'full responsibility' after ethics commissioner says he broke rules on SNC-Lavalin," *Toronto Star*, August 14, 2019, online at thestar.com/politics/federal/2019/08/14/prime-minister-justin-trudeau-broke-ethics-rules-in-snc-lavalin-controversy-ethics-commissioner-rules.html.
5 Philip Authier, "Quebec premier emotional over possible sale of Air Transat to Air Canada," *Montreal Gazette*, May 16, 2019, online at montrealgazette.com/business/local-business/aerospace/quebec-premier-emotional-over-possible-sale-of-air-transat-to-air-canada.
6 See, among others, Jasper Jacob van Dijk, "Local Employment Multipliers in U.S. Cities," *Journal of Economic Geography* 17, no. 2 (2017): 466–7.
7 Mario Polèse et al., *The Periphery in the Knowledge Economy: The Spatial Dynamics of the Canadian Economy and the Future of Non-Metropolitan Regions in Quebec and the Atlantic Provinces* (Montreal: INRS-Urbanisation, 2002), 140.
8 Walter Isard et al., *Methods of Regional Analysis: An Introduction to Regional Science* (Cambridge, MA: MIT Press, 1960).
9 Author's consultations with Pierre-Marcel Desjardins, September 6, 2019.
10 New Brunswick, *Profile of the New Brunswick Labour Force* (Fredericton: Government of New Brunswick, Post-Secondary Education, Training and Labour, September 2018), 8.
11 Ibid., 3.
12 Ibid., 2.
13 In 2017, New Brunswick's median age was 45.3 years, well above the Canadian median age of 40.6 years.
14 New Brunswick, *Profile of the New Brunswick Labour Force*, 10–12.
15 Irving Oil, "Creating Value at Home" (Saint John, NB: Irving Oil, n.d.).

16 Jenica Atwin, quoted in Carl Meyer, "Green Party's Jenica Atwin wants to liberate New Brunswick from the Irvings," *Canada's National Observer*, November 2, 2019, online at nationalobserver.com/2019/11/02/news/green-partys-jenica-atwin-wants-liberate-new-brunswick-irvings.

17 Ted Mallett and Andreea Bourgeois, "Entrepreneurial Communities: Canada's Top Places to Start and Grow Businesses in 2018" (n.p.: Canadian Federation of Independent Business, April 2019), online at cfib-fcei.ca/sites/default/files/2019-04/Entrepreneurial-Communities-2018.pdf.

18 Edward Glaeser, *Triumph of the City: How Our Greatest Invention Makes Us Richer, Smarter, Greener, Healthier, and Happier* (New York: Penguin, 2011).

19 See, for example, Colin M. Mason and Richard T. Harrison, "After the Exit: Acquisitions, Entrepreneurial Recycling and Regional Economic Development," *Regional Studies* 40, no. 1 (2006): 55–73.

20 Daniel Isenberg, *Worthless, Impossible and Stupid: How Contrarian Entrepreneurs Create and Capture Extraordinary Value* (Cambridge, MA: Harvard Business Review Press, 2013).

21 Per Davidsson, "Culture, Structure and Regional Levels of Entrepreneurship," *Entrepreneurship and Regional Development* 1, no. 7 (1995): 41–62.

22 Ralph Allen, "The Unknown Giant K.C. Irving," *Maclean's*, April 18, 1964, online at archive.macleans.ca/article/1964/4/18/the-unknown-giant-k-c-irving.

23 Jessica Vomiero, "CRA insiders say Canada's tax system helps rich avoid paying taxes: study," *Global News*, August 17, 2018, online at globalnews.ca/news/4394612/cra-insiders-canada-tax-system-rich-avoid-paying/.

24 Joel Shannon, "Amazon pays no federal income tax for 2018, despite soaring profits, report says," *USA Today*, February 16, 2019, online at usatoday.com/story/money/2019/02/15/amazon-pays-no-2018-federal-income-tax-report-says/2886639002/.

25 See, for example, Jim Tankersley, Peter Eavis, and Ben Casselman, "How FedEx cut its tax bill to $0," *New York Times*, November 17, 2019, online at nytimes.com/2019/11/17/business/how-fedex-cut-its-tax-bill-to-0.html.

26 John DeMont, *Citizens Irving: K.C. Irving and His Legacy* (Toronto: McClelland and Stewart, 1992), 123–4.

27 Jacques Poitras, "Irving Oil claims it's a myth company gets off easy paying taxes," *CBC News*, September 5, 2019, online at cbc.ca/news/canada/new-brunswick/nb-property-tax-proposal-hearing-1.5271916.

28 Canada, "Provincial and Territorial Tax and Credits for Individuals—Rates for 2018," n.d., online at canada.ca/en/revenue-agency/services/tax/individuals/topics/about-your-tax-return/tax-return/completing-a-tax-return/provincial-territorial-tax-credits-individuals.html.

29 Ibid.

30 Canada, "Corporation Tax Rates," n.d., online at canada.ca/en/revenue-agency/services/tax/businesses/topics/corporations/corporation-tax-rates.html.

31 Raymond Chabot Grant Thornton, *Taxation in Quebec: Favourable Measures to Foster Investment* (Montreal, 2019), 9.

32 Poitras, "Irving Oil claims it's a myth company gets off easy paying taxes."

33 Irving Oil, "Irving Oil and Property Taxes" (presentation to the Law Amendments Committee, September 5, 2019).

34 Organisation for Economic Co-operation and Development, "What Is a Competitive Tax System?" (Paris: OECD, June 30, 2011), 7, online at oecd.org/ctp/48193714.pdf.

35 Robert Jones, "Irving made millions off deal to slash taxes on LNG property," *CBC News*, June 12, 2015, online at cbc.ca/news/canada/new-brunswick/irving-made-millions-off-deal-to-slash-taxes-on-lng-property-1.3111816.

36 See, for example, John Irwin, "How Canada could compete for new auto investment," *Automotive News Canada*, June 25, 2018, online at canada.autonews.com/article/20180625/CANADA/180629875/how-canada-could-compete-for-new-auto-investment.

37 See, among others, Greg Keenan, "Canadian taxpayers lose $3.5 billion on 2009 bailout of auto firms," *Globe and Mail*, April 7, 2015, online at theglobeandmail.com/report-on-business/canadian-taxpayers-lose-35-billion-on-2009-bailout-of-auto-firms/article23828543/.

38 Austin Carr, "Inside Wisconsin's disastrous $4.5 billion deal with Foxconn," *Bloomberg Businessweek*, February 5, 2019, online at bloomberg.com/news/features/2019-02-06/inside-wisconsin-s-disastrous-4-5-billion-deal-with-foxconn.

39 *Atlantic Quarterly: Autumn 2019—Commissioned Question* (Halifax: Narrative Research, November 2019). This was a telephone survey carried out between October 31 and November 19, 2019. The overall results of the survey are accurate to within plus or minus 4.9 percentage points nineteen times out of twenty.

APPENDIX

INTERVIEWS

Albert, Elide, architect, June 30, 2019

Auffrey, Vincent, C. David Naylor Fellow, University of Toronto, September 5, 2019

Bates, Pat, former senior Irving Oil executive, August 16, 2019

Bragg, John, businessman, August 26, 2019

Buggie, Glen, Irving Oil employee, various dates

Cail, Leslie, friend of Arthur Irving, July 25, 2019

Cail, Linda, friend of Arthur Irving, July 25, 2019

Cantwell, Michael, Irving Oil employee, various dates

Casey, Jim, former government official and business owner, November 4, 2019

Chevarie, Claude, Irving Oil employee, various dates

Cormier, Pierre, Chair, Kent County Museum, various dates

Cunningham, Norbert, journalist, September 5, 2019

Desjardins, Pierre-Marcel, economist, August 26, 2019

Doyle, Art, former editor, *Telegraph-Journal*, September 3, 2019

Fournier, Roger, Moncton businessman, August 17, 2019

Gallant, Frank, Irving Oil dealer in Moncton, July 30, 2019

Gaudreault, Ross, former senior Irving Oil executive, September 24, 2019

Gillis, Darren, senior Irving Oil executive, August 15, 2019

Gilmour, Harvey, former director of development, Acadia University, September 3, 2019

Grant, Barry, pilot, various dates
Grant, Charles, former student, Dartmouth College, September 7, 2019
Harding, Geoffrey, Ducks Unlimited, August 1, 2019
Harvey, Robin, Irving Oil executive, September 10, 2019
Hutter, Dr. Adolph M., Cardiologist, September 5, 2019
Irving, Arthur, various dates
Irving, Sandra, various dates
Irving, Sarah, various dates
Irving Campbell, Isabel, July 23, 2019
Ivany, Ray, former president, Acadia University, August 1, 2019
Johnson, Billy, C. David Naylor Fellow, University of Toronto,
    September 3, 2019
Lasher, Bob, senior vice-president, Dartmouth College, October 8, 2019
Maillet, Gérard, former Kent Home employee, various dates
Matthews, Jeff, Irving Oil executive, September 10, 2019
McGuire, Francis, senior government official and former private-sector
    executive, November 5, 2019
McKenna, Frank, former premier of New Brunswick, August 15, 2019
McLaughlin, Steve, Irving Oil executive, September 10, 2019
Mockler, Percy, senator, September 19, 2019
Novell, Alex, architect, October 8, 2019
Ogilvie, Kelvin, former president of Acadia University, August 27, 2019
Pinet, Jacques, businessman and former senior government official, August
    29, 2019
Richard, Guy, retired judge, December 8, 2019
Smith, David, retired judge, August 11, 2019
Sweetapple, Talbot, architect, August 11, 2019
Whitcomb, Ian, Irving Oil executive, September 10, 2019

Seven currently serving government officials who asked to remain
    anonymous, various dates

INDEX

Operation Falcon and, 170

Johnson, Billy, 253

Jones, H. Royden, Jr., 252

Jones, Jeffrey, 121

Juniper, 156

K

K.C. Irving Environmental Science Centre, 224, 242–44, 246–48, 249, 256

K.C.: The Biography of K.C. Irving (How; Costello), 1

Keenan, Lisa, 40

Keller, Scott, *Leading Organizations*, 274

Kent Homes, 5, 47

Ketchum, H.G.C., 110

Khomeini, Ayatollah, 98

Killam, Izaak, 14

Kinder Morgan, 142

pipeline, 124

King, William Lyon Mackenzie, 111

Kraemer, Dr., 70–71

Ku Klux Klan, 46

Kuhn, Clarence "Skeet," 56

Kuhn, Gordon "Doggie," 56

Kyoto Protocol, 264

L

Lac-Mégantic rail disaster, 124

Lahey, James, 148

Lahey Hospital & Medical Center, H. Royden Jones, Jr., MD Chair in Neuroscience, 252

Laurier, Sir Wilfrid, 32

Lawson, Mike, 56, 60

Leading Organizations (Keller/Meaney), 274

LEED (Leadership in Energy and Environmental Design), 225

Leman, Kevin, Birth Order Book, 132

Levesque, Joel, 193

Liberal Party, 32–33

J.D. and, 59, 105

K.C. and, 59, 105

liquefied natural gas (LNG) terminal/regasification plant, 170–71, 308

Looking for Bootstraps: Economic Development in the Maritimes (Savoie), 14

lumber business, 62

M

Macdonald, Sir John A., 108–9

Mackasey, Bryce, 278

Mackenzie, Alexander, 109

MacQuarrie, A.J., 52–53

Magdalen Islands, 57

Maillet, Gérard, 47

managers

Arthur and, 191, 192

and entrepreneurial edge, 203

front-line, 197

at Irving Oil, 196, 197–98, 203

Irving School of Business and, 196–97

K.C. and, 81

Saturday morning meetings, 193–94

in vertical integration, 65

See also executives; Irving School of Business

Manning, Fred, 67–68

Manship, Jon, 300

Maritime Freight Rates Act, 111

Maritime provinces. See Atlantic Canada/Maritimes provinces

Maritime Rights Movement, 111

Maritimes & North East Pipeline, 171

Mason, Gary, 122

Massachusetts General Hospital

Arthur, Sandra, and Sarah Irving Fund in Gastrointestinal Immuno-Oncology, 252

David P. Ryan, MD Endowment Chair in Cancer Research, 252

Hutter Family Professorship in Medicine, 251–52